Wicked Curve

ALSO BY JOHN C. SKIPPER
AND FROM MCFARLAND

*The Cubs Win the Pennant!
Charlie Grimm, the Billy Goat Curse, and
the 1945 World Series Run* (2004)

*A Biographical Dictionary of Major
League Baseball Managers* (2003)

*A Biographical Dictionary of the
Baseball Hall of Fame* (2000)

*Take Me Out to the Cubs Game: 35 Former
Ballplayers Speak of Losing at Wrigley* (2000)

*Umpires: Classic Baseball Stories from
the Men Who Made the Calls* (1997)

*Inside Pitch: A Closer Look at
Classic Baseball Moments* (1996)

Wicked Curve

The Life and Troubled Times of Grover Cleveland Alexander

John C. Skipper

McFarland & Company, Inc., Publishers
Jefferson, North Carolina, and London

LIBRARY OF CONGRESS CATALOGUING-IN-PUBLICATION DATA

Skipper, John C., 1945–
    Wicked curve : the life and troubled times of Grover Cleveland Alexander / John C. Skipper.
       p.   cm.
    Includes bibliographical references and index.

    ISBN 0-7864-2412-5 (softcover : 50# alkaline paper) ∞

    1. Alexander, Grover Cleveland, 1887–1950. 2. Baseball players—United States—Biography. I. Title.
GV865.A33S45   2006
796.357092—dc22   2006012641
[B]

British Library cataloguing data are available

©2006 John C. Skipper. All rights reserved

No part of this book may be reproduced or transmitted in any form or by any means, electronic or mechanical, including photocopying or recording, or by any information storage and retrieval system, without permission in writing from the publisher.

Cover photograph: Alexander sits alone next to the water cooler late in his career *(Baseball Hall of Fame Library)*

Manufactured in the United States of America

McFarland & Company, Inc., Publishers
  Box 611, Jefferson, North Carolina 28640
    www.mcfarlandpub.com

Contents

Preface		1
I •	Alone in a Crowd	3
II •	A Stone's Throw Away	9
III •	A Big League Pitcher	21
IV •	A Pennant Flies in Philadelphia	40
V •	Nobody Does It Better	56
VI •	The Changing of the Uniforms	63
VII •	The Cub Years	78
VIII •	Managerial Merry-Go-Round and McCarthy	98
IX •	A Strikeout for the Ages	110
X •	Forty Years Old and Counting	124
XI •	The End of the Road	136
XII •	When the Cheering Stopped	145
XIII •	The Long Road Downhill	152
XIV •	Brother Can You Spare Me a Dime?	166
XV •	The Last Hurrah	176
XVI •	Coming Home	186
XVII •	Bottom of the Ninth	198
Appendix: Lifetime Statistics		211
Notes		213
Bibliography		223
Index		231

Preface

Grover Cleveland Alexander's story spreads across several landscapes of the human experience. His is the "small town boy makes good" story, a boy who grew up in St. Paul, Nebraska, husking corn and throwing stones across the farmyard at trees, fence posts and an occasional chicken with startling accuracy. It is the story of a young man who almost got passed up in his first try for the big leagues and then set a National League record for wins by a rookie (28) that still stands, nearly a century later.

It is the story of a man who left his career behind for one year so that he could serve his country in "the war to end all wars," only to come back with illnesses and demons that plagued him for the rest of his life. And finally, it is a love story between Grover and his beloved Aimee, who married and divorced him twice because she discovered that while she was better off if she quit living with him, she could not bring herself to quit loving him. And he expressed his love for her through the day he died, literally.

In this work, the author's intention is to capture the essence of a man whose passion and talent helped him rise to become one of the greatest pitchers of his or any other era and whose weaknesses brought him tumbling down. It is a story that is a matrix where inevitably the lines of triumph and tragedy meet. Every effort is made to inform with facts rather than to influence with speculation.

In that light, it is important to establish some points of clarification. The woman Alexander married (twice) was Amy Arrant. Early in her adult life, she began spelling her first name as "Aimee." For consistency, that is how her name is spelled throughout this book. When Alexander was growing up, his nickname was Dode. He was also called Alex and Alec. When he joined the Philadelphia Phillies in 1911, the ballclub had a player with the nickname of Dode, so that nickname for Alex didn't stick except with the folks back home. He is best known by the nickname "Ol' Pete," for which there are two possible reasons. It is said that when he was a young ballplayer, he went on a hunting trip in the off-season and fell off a buckboard into some peat moss. Those who were with him started calling him "Ol' Pete," or so the story goes. While that is said to have happened to him fairly early in his career, the author could find no newspaper references to "Ol' Pete" until 1921. This gives rise to another possible reason for the nickname. By 1921, Alex's penchant for drinking was well known. During Prohibition, bootlegged liquor was sometimes referred to as "sneaky Pete"—and there is plenty of documentation to assure that Alexander partook in his share of bootleg liquor. The author has chosen to use the nickname "Pete" or "Ol' Pete" in the text that deals with his life and career from 1921 and beyond.

Alexander suffered from alcoholism and epilepsy. Aimee Alexander said some of Alex's problems later in life were the result of epilepsy rather than alcoholism, but there is no way for the author to know for certain. He has relied on accounts of police and hospital reports published in newspapers as well as the published views of managers, teammates and Mrs. Alexander.

I am indebted to Ted Savas for cajoling me many years ago into writing a biography and thereby allowing me to prove to myself that I could do it. His confidence in me six years ago with an entirely different work is, in large part, the reason this book was even undertaken. Several other people assisted in the research, including Gabriel Schechter of the National Baseball Hall of Fame Library; MaryAnn Frederick of the Nebraska Historical Society Museum in St. Paul, Nebraska; Jeff Tecklenburg, editor of the *Muscatine* (Iowa) *Journal;* Bill Fuhr of the Muscatine Public Library; the staff at Richardson-Sloane Special Collections Center in Davenport, Iowa; baseball history buffs Bill Deane, Cliff Kachline and Steve Steinberg; the staff of the Society for American Baseball Research; and the staff at Retrosheet. A book like this would not be possible without people who may not understand the passion for the work but understand the importance of supporting the person with the passion. People like Jim Collison (who, as an accomplished writer himself, does understand); and Bob Link and Dick Johnson, reporters for the Mason City (Iowa) *Globe Gazette,* who have been hearing about this for two years, as has Michael Grandon, treasurer of Cerro Gordo County, Iowa.

Special thanks is due to Ed Nevrivy, an 84-year-old retired clothing salesman in St. Paul, Nebraska, one of the few people still alive who knew Grover Cleveland Alexander, who was kind enough to share some recollections with the author.

And finally, none of this would have been possible without my life partner, Sandi Skipper.

John C. Skipper
Mason City, Iowa
April 11, 2006

• CHAPTER I •

Alone in a Crowd

"There is nothing as empty as the echo of yesterday's cheers."
— New York Mayor Jimmy Walker

On October 6, 1950, 64,505 fans jammed Yankee Stadium for the third game of the World Series between the New York Yankees, on the brink of a dynasty, and "The Whiz Kids," the Philadelphia Phillies, who won the pennant by beating the Brooklyn Dodgers on the last day of the season. The Yankees were on their way to winning their second of five straight World Series titles. The Phillies wouldn't win another pennant for 30 years. They paid a steep price for this championship, using their pitching ace, Robin Roberts, in three of the last five games of the season. Roberts came up with the Phillies in 1948 and posted a 7–9 record. He improved to 15–15 in 1949 and then hit his stride in the 1950 championship season, winning 20, losing 11, the first of six consecutive 20-win seasons. But after the grueling last week of the 1950 season, the Phillies wanted to give Roberts an extra day of rest.

Manager Eddie Sawyer tried to pull a rabbit out of the hat. In an effort to rest Roberts and give the rest of the staff a break, too, Sawyer started big, bespectacled Jim Konstanty in the first game of the World Series at Philadelphia. Konstanty had failed to make much of an impression in brief stints with the Reds in 1944 and the Braves in 1946, but after developing a new pitch, a palm ball, he hooked on with the Phillies in 1948, winning one and losing none, and then in 1949, winning 9, losing 5. He enjoyed a tremendous season in 1950, winning 16 and losing only 7 while appearing in 74 games, a league record at the time. But of his 133 major league appearances, all but 13 had been in relief, and he hadn't started a game since 1946 with Boston. Konstanty's work in 1950 earned him the league's most valuable player award, the first ever given to a relief pitcher. But Sawyer took a chance and gave him his first start in five years in the first game of the World Series. He did his job admirably, working eight innings and giving up only one run on four hits, including a run-scoring single by Bobby Brown. Konstanty's mound opponent, Vic Raschi, gave up just two hits, and the Yankees won, 1–0. Game two was almost a repeat of the opener, with Roberts battling Allie Reynolds and the Yankees coming out on top, 2–1.

Now the series shifted to New York, where the crowds would be twice the size they were in Philadelphia and the Yankees were gunning for the first World Series sweep since they turned the trick on the Cincinnati Reds in 1939. It was standing-room-only as Eddie Lopat took the mound for the Yankees. Sawyer once again reached into his grab bag and started left-hander Ken Heintzelman, a 35-year-old journeyman who had his best year in the majors in 1949 at 17–10 but had managed only a 3–9 record during the 1950 season. The Phillies' pitching staff had suffered a major blow in September when their top left-hander, Curt Simmons, was drafted into the Army. He was 17–8 with 11 complete games when he left the team. Sawyer wanted a lefty to start in Yankee Stadium, with its 296-foot right field wall that was so inviting to New York's left-handed power hitters. So Heintzelman got the call in what was to be the biggest game in his career and a crucial game for his team.

High up in the mezzanine that day stood a man who looked old beyond his years, bracing himself on a metal railing as he watched the action on the field. He was just another face in the crowd, and not a pretty face. He had but one ear, the other having been lost to cancer several years before. The many lines on his face were embedded in his skin as if they had been chiseled, including crow's feet that started at his eyes and straggled down both cheeks. His head was covered with a tattered old tan fedora. His dark suit coat appeared to be hanging on him rather than being worn. His clothes, like his life, had seen better days. The man was the victim of neglect, self-neglect at the mercy of alcohol, and the victim of disease — epilepsy and cancer. Even in a crowd of thousands, he was alone. It wasn't so much that people didn't pay attention to him as that he just looked like the kind of guy that most people would try to avoid.

Billy Cunningham, a syndicated columnist sitting in the press box, noticed the fellow and pointed him out to Fred Lieb, the great sportswriter who was covering the series for *The Sporting News*. "Isn't that Grover Cleveland Alexander?" Cunningham asked Lieb. Indeed it was, said Lieb. Grover Cleveland Alexander, considered by many to be one of the greatest pitchers in National League history, was now a man struggling to keep his balance, standing behind the cheap seats in a ballpark that 24 years earlier had been the scene of his greatest triumph when, as a member of the St. Louis Cardinals, he won two World Series games against the New York Yankees and saved another with the help of a dramatic strikeout of Tony Lazzeri with the bases loaded in the seventh inning of the seventh game.

Lieb found him a seat in the pressbox and introduced himself. Alexander remembered him and mentioned that Lieb had written some nice things about him, something that hadn't happened often to Alexander in recent years. They chatted about the old days as they watched the game. Alexander retold the story that was part of his legend, striking out Tony Lazzeri with the bases loaded on that very diamond down below, in the 1926 World Series. Speaking in a voice just above a whisper, Alexander entertained his hosts with one story after another as they watched the ballgame — how he always had trouble getting Rogers Hornsby out and had an easier time with Babe Ruth.[1] Heintzelman took a 2–1 lead into the bottom of the eighth inning. Then, with two out and nobody on, he inexplicably lost his control, walking Jerry Coleman, Yogi Berra and Joe DiMaggio in succession. In the press box, Alexander shook his head. "I don't believe I ever walked three men in a row," he said.[2] Alexander was also disappointed in the Philadelphia offense. "They don't hit any better than they did in 1915 when we lost those four games to the Red Sox by one run," he said. While his stories about baseball were fascinating, Lieb was struck by something else, an uncomfortable feeling he had from observing and listening to Alexander, and it was hard to look at him without thinking about his life after baseball. He told the writers about being inducted into the Hall of Fame and receiving a plaque instead of money. "You can't eat a tablet," he said. Lieb's reaction to his encounter with Alexander that day was simple but poignant. "I was face to face with a human tragedy."[3]

Louis Effrat reported in the next day's *New York Times:* "There was a day in the life of Grover Cleveland Alexander when he had to hide from a crowd at the stadium.... But yesterday, the same Grover Cleveland Alexander, older, grayer and not the robust figure of yesteryear, was lost in a crowd."

Getting Alexander to the World Series was symbolic of what his life had been like since his glory days. A New York newspaper agreed to finance the trip until it learned Alexander needed a traveling companion because of partial deafness and other health issues. Alexander then sought the help of the *Omaha World-Herald,* Nebraska's largest newspaper, showing up in person to ask for help. While there, he suffered what was described at the time as a fainting spell and was hospitalized briefly until doctors determined there was nothing seriously wrong with him. Then two friends, Quentin Lynch, a St. Paul jeweler, and Bill Graumke, co-owner of a flying service in Grand Island, Nebraska, raised enough money to fly him to Chicago, where he appeared on Tommy Bartlett's "Welcome Travelers" radio program. The program's sponsors agreed to pay for his trip to the World Series in exchange for his appearing on the show before and after the series. On the way to New York, the plane experienced engine problems and landed in Cleveland for some quick repairs. While there, Alexander suffered yet another "spell" and was bedridden for a day. He made it to New York in time for the third game of the World Series, securing a pass that had been left for him at the gate. He wandered around until he found a place to roost at the back of the mezzanine, where he was when Cunningham and Lieb spotted him. Effrat wrote: "For the courtesy of a press box seat, Alexander repaid his benefactors with numerous anecdotes during the progress of the game. He relived the Lazzeri strikeout and other great experiences of his glorious past."[4]

Alexander's record in baseball reads like this: 373 career wins, tied for highest in the National League, tied for third highest in the major leagues; 90 shutouts, second only to Walter Johnson's 110; winner of 30 or more games in three consecutive seasons, 1915 through 1917; record for most wins by a rookie, 28, in 1911; record for most shutouts in a season, 16, in 1915; led National League in wins five times, in lowest earned run average five times, in strikeouts six times; 437 complete games, 73 percent of the 599 he started; six seasons with earned run average under 2.00; career earned run average of 2.56. In 1916, the year in which he threw 16 shutouts, he also had four games in which he allowed only one run, winning three of them by scores of 2–1 and the other by a 7–1 score. He also lost a game by a 2–0 score where both runs were unearned and was the starting pitcher in three other games in which the Phillies didn't score. So he came close to having 21 shutouts in one season. Much of this was accomplished in Baker Bowl, the Phils' old ballpark, which was a pitchers' nightmare because of its right field wall, 280 feet from home plate, and the right-center field "power alley," a little more than 300 feet away.

In baseball, Ol' Pete, as he was called, was the master of control, exemplified by his 1923 season when he walked only 30 batters in 305 innings. Out of baseball, his was a life out of control—arrests for drunkenness and disorderly conduct; numerous instances of begging for money to buy food and drink; hospitalizations that were often the result of a fall, either from alcoholism or an epileptic seizure; divorced twice from the same woman who loved him but couldn't live with him; and employed by anyone who would hire him, including a flea circus where he stood and told baseball stories to passers-by who had already seen the sword-swallower and the elephant woman.[5]

In the public's eye, he did not match up well with three men with whom comparisons were inevitable: Cy Young, winner of 511 games, who was ending his career in the season Alexander was starting his; Walter Johnson, a contemporary of Alexander's, who won 406 games for the Washington

Senators in the American League and went on to be a respected manager; and Christy Mathewson, the New York Giants star who is tied with Alexander for most wins in the National League, each having 373. Because they pitched in the same league, faced each other several times, and finished with the same number of wins, the comparison to Mathewson is the most natural one. Mathewson was a great ballplayer on the field and a model citizen off the field. He didn't drink, he didn't curse, he didn't carouse. Donald K. McKim writes, "Baseball's pure idyllic status was taken to a new level by the Christian moralist who so gracefully combined skill, intelligence, virtue and patriotism within himself."[6] Like Alexander, Mathewson fought adversity when his career was over. He contracted tuberculosis and died in October of 1925 when most of the nation's attention was focused on the World Series. McKim writes, "Even in the face of his tragic suffering, this role model of the American nation and the American sport heroically fought and maintained his dignity."[7]

Alexander, much through his own doing, was not afforded the same adulation. Many who idolized him in baseball mocked him, demeaned him and avoided him off the field and when his career was over. Cunningham, the Boston writer who recognized him in the press box in 1950, was author of a column nine years earlier alerting readers not only to Alexander's troubles but to who was to blame for most of them. The column was prompted by a well-meaning New York sportswriter who was trying to get a national campaign going to raise money for Alexander, whom the writer portrayed as being down on his luck.

Cunningham wrote, "I'd be the last to want to add to the woes of the former star, who's had 'em and still has 'em but the truth of the matter is he's been his own worst enemy and has mostly himself to blame for his thorny path." Cunningham said Alexander wouldn't be in the fix he was in "if he had played the all-important game of life as he played the less essential one of baseball."[8]

The old pitcher would not have disagreed. One of the players he saw in Yankee Stadium that day was Robin Roberts, the 24-year-old Phillie pitcher who was the loser in game two and who would pitch in relief in game four. About 10 years earlier, when Roberts was a youngster in Springfield, Illinois, and about the time Cunningham wrote the column about Alexander, Ol' Pete visited Roberts' school. Roberts remembered his message well. He could have told the boys to work hard and practice and they too could grow up to be ballplayers. He could have shown them how to throw a curveball. He could have told them the key to his success as a pitcher was always throwing the first pitch for a strike and always hitting the corners with the breaking stuff. Instead, he sadly alluded to a life that was out of control. He said, "Boys, I had my day and I made big money for the times. But I wasted the years and the money. Don't let it happen to you."[9]

In the ballgame that day, Konstanty came in to relieve Heintzelman, who was four outs from victory when he hit the streak of wildness and walked three batters in a row. As Alexander and about 65,000 spectators watched, Konstanty got Yankee pinch hitter Bobby Brown to hit an inning-ending ground ball to shortstop Granny Hamner. But Hamner booted it and the tying run scored. The Yankees pushed across a run in the ninth, with three singles after two were out, to win the game, and they won the following day, 5–2, behind rookie left-hander Whitey Ford, to sweep the series.

Alexander didn't hide his disappointment. "After seeing what the Phillies showed in those last two games, I'd like to see what the seven other clubs in the National League looked like this year. I wonder how those fellows won the pennant," he said.

Alexander, wearing a suit given to him and using money donated to him, went home to Nebraska, to the place of his birth and his early triumphs, a place where now no bar would serve him a drink. What happened to Heintzelman in Yankee Stadium that day had long ago happened to Alexander in life. He lost control. How does a man go from the top of his game to the humiliating game of trying to figure out where his next meal is coming from and which flophouse is he going to stay at tonight? How does a man go from being a pitcher in total control to a man whose life is out of control? The answer may lie in the experiences of one year in the life of Grover Cleveland Alexander, much like one bad inning in a ballgame. It was a year away from major league baseball, a year away from family and friends, a year in the trenches of Germany when mortar blasts rattled his eardrums and shocked his system. It was a year in which the demons that plagued him for the rest of his life started to take over.

The Phillies hadn't won a World Series game since 1915 when Grover Cleveland Alexander beat the Red Sox. It would be 1980 before Philadelphia won another World Series game. In 1952, Roberts would win 28 games for the Philadelphia, the first Phillie pitcher to win that many since Alexander's three successive 30-plus win seasons in 1915, 1916 and 1917.

When Alexander left Yankee Stadium and headed back home, he had seen his last ball game. A month after the 1950 series, he was found face down on a floor, as he had been so many times in the past 20 years. This time it was not drunkenness or epilepsy but apparently a heart attack that knocked him down in the second floor apartment of a rooming house in St. Paul, Nebraska, the hometown that at one time loved him and most recently shunned him. Death came at the age of 63 and took him in a circumstance to which he had become accustomed. He was alone.[10]

• CHAPTER II •

A Stone's Throw Away

"Oh, I can play with these farmers around here, but that's about as far as I can go."
— Grover Cleveland Alexander

Young Grover Cleveland Alexander walked around the green and yellow farmland of Elba, Nebraska, picking up rocks and idly throwing them at trees and other targets across the way. There's nothing new about the notion of a kid and a rock. When a youngster sees one, he picks it up and either throws it at something or keeps it for the collection he has just decided to start. Grover, or "Dode," as he was called by friends and family in his youth, liked to throw the stones he found with kind of a side-arm motion, and he was pretty good at hitting his targets.

When the freckle-faced kid grew up to be one of the greatest pitchers in major league baseball history, his stone-throwing became part of his legend, and as the legend grew, the story might have grown a little, too, not unlike George Washington cutting down the cherry tree or Abraham Lincoln walking five miles barefoot to a library.

His mother, Margaret "Martha" Cootey Alexander, told of him throwing stones with such accuracy that he knocked clothespins off of clotheslines.[1] His niece, Elma O'Neill, did not detract from the legend when she talked of how when Grover's mother wanted to have a chicken dinner, she would tell Grover and he would go out with a rock or a ball and, with pinpoint accuracy, fire it at an unsuspecting chicken and "brain" it.[2] Twenty years later, that same control would allow him to have the best strikeout-to-walk ratio in the National League.

Elma O'Neill said that when Dode was a youngster, he was once summarily banned from participating in a carnival game at the county fair in which the object was to knock down all the wooden milk bottles stacked one on top of the other. Grover did it several times, continually winning a Kewpie doll or some other prize, until the manager of the game sent him on his way.[3]

His little brother Ray also talked about Grover's stone throwing. "He always had a good eye," said Ray. "He got so that he was almost a dead shot with a pebble. And I don't doubt that the experience he got in this way has always been worthwhile to him as a pitcher."

When Alexander talked of his days growing up on the Nebraska farm, he recalled his stone-throwing adventures without the theatrics that proud friends and relatives added to it. "Around the farm, I was always throwing things and usually throwing at something else," he said. "I was continually being scolded by my mother for coming home with holes in my pockets, worn by rocks. For whenever I found a nice stone, I put it in my pocket and carried it around until I found something to throw at."[4]

Grover Cleveland Alexander was born on February 26, 1887, in the back bedroom of the farmhouse of William and Margaret Alexander. He was one of 13 children — 12 boys and a girl. Five of the boys died in infancy. His sister, Mary, and brothers Charles, Nicholas, Alva, George, Warren and Raymond grew up with Grover on the farm. His birthplace was Elba, Nebraska, a little keyhole of a town in west central Nebraska, about 185 miles from Omaha, that had been settled just five years before his birth and got its name because it was situated on the elbow where the Union Pacific Railroad tracks veered. Elba was eight miles west of St. Paul, the county seat of Howard County, Nebraska, the "big city" of the region with 800 people and hotels, saloons and doctors. Because of those amenities, it was a supply stop for stagecoaches and wagon trains making their way west. When he was an adult, Grover had fond memories of the Alexander family hitching up the horse and buggy in the summer and heading on over to St. Paul to see the circus when it came to town. That was big entertainment in those days, and an entertaining ride for the Alexander children as the horse and buggy traversed the bumpy roads of western Nebraska.[5]

Grover was named for Grover Cleveland, who was elected as the nation's 22nd president in 1884. Cleveland lost a bid for a second term and then was elected again in 1892, the only president to serve non-consecutive terms. It is not clear why William and Margaret Alexander chose to name their son for the president. None of their 12 other children had historical namesakes. It is possible that after having named so many other boys, they had run out of "favorite" names and chose one that they believed had integrity woven into it.

The world was changing rapidly in 1887. The Civil War had been over for two decades, reconstruction was part of the nation's vocabulary, and the world was on the verge of an industrial and technological revolution. There were already some signs of it. On March 4, Gottlieb Daimler, a German inventor, displayed a new concept in transportation by attaching an engine to a buggy in an effort to speed up road transportation. In July, another German, Emile Berliner, got a patent on a thing called a gramophone, the first recording device, and Dorr Felt, a Chicago man, patented the comptometer, the world's first calculator.

William Alexander was a hardworking grain and livestock farmer who was not opposed to settling down with a little alcohol for his system at the end of a long day. He had lost five sons at birth or in infancy and, like most parents, wanted the best for his surviving children. His hope for young Grover was that he would grow up to be a lawyer, as President Cleveland had been. As his son achieved fame as a major league pitcher, William attributed Grover's physical strength and durability to the years he spent husking corn on the family farm. He bragged that Grover once averaged husking 100 bushels of corn a day for 13 days straight when most boys his age could husk that amount for only one or two days straight.[6]

His great arm and wrist strength were being noticed on the ballfields as Dode became a teenager and started playing with adults in local baseball games. On June 5, 1903, at the age of 16, he got a chance to play in a game that was part of the festivities of the local Danish community, who looked upon June 5 as their Independence Day, much as most Americans celebrate July 4. Alexander was playing second base that day, and his team was getting clobbered by a score of 12–3. When the outcome was no longer in doubt and there were several innings yet to play, the youngster with the good arm was called in to pitch. A fan in the stands reportedly accepted 16-to-1 odds and bet on Alexander's team to win. He also offered to pay the new pitcher $5 if he won the game. The 16-to-1 odds were a reference to statesman William Jennings Bryan's contention that the silver-to-gold value was 16-to-1.

"Then the future star, who had never pitched before, determined to get that $5. Realizing affairs could not be worse, he took his place on the slab and held the opposition hitless for the remainder of the game, while a batting rally behind him resulted in ultimate victory, 13–12. That ended Alexander's days as an infielder. Thereafter he was a pitcher or an outfielder when not working on the mound."[7]

He threw with the same motion that he used when he threw stones at clothespins a few years earlier or when he was striking out Tony Lazzeri in the World Series several years later — sidearm, mostly with the forearm, and seemingly effortlessly. Grover was a big kid, tall and gaunt, with sandy-red hair and freckles, and possessed with a quiet but good disposition which made it easy for him to fit in with players who were older and, as time would prove, less talented.

By 1908, he was earning $5 a game in local contests in Howard County but needed to start making a more permanent living. He got a job digging postholes for the Howard County Telephone Co., work that was made to order for a tall, strapping young man with good arm strength. He earned $1.75 a day and got a few extra bucks playing baseball on Sundays, first for the St. Paul team, then for nearby Central City. On June 30, 1908, Central City beat Aurora 17–2 behind the pitching of Alexander. The Central City newspaper was impressed enough to report that Alexander's pitches were a "mystery" for his opponents, but the newspaper mistakenly referred to Grover as "George." Before long, almost every fan in the area would know his name. Alexander was 21–4 for Central City and threw a no-hitter.

J.F. Webster, editor of the local paper, the *St. Paul Phonograph,* was also manager of the St. Paul town baseball team and was well aware of Dode Alexander's talents. The team had another good pitcher, a left-hander named Sevcik. Webster's team was to play another town team in the championship game at the Howard County Fair when the other team came up with a big problem. Their pitcher didn't show up. Since the game had already been scheduled, a crowd had gathered, and the show must go on, Webster offered the other team one of his pitchers. Sevcik declined. Alexander didn't mind. He just wanted to play ball. Nobody seems to remember who won or lost that county fair game but Alexander continued to be impressive.

In the summer of 1908, a team called the Oklahoma Indians came to Nebraska and Alexander pitched against them. The Oklahoma shortstop, Jap Wagner, liked what he saw and talked to Alec after the game.

Alexander recalled the conversation this way: "Have you ever thought of playing ball for a living?" he asked me.

"Oh, I can play with these farmers around here but that's about as far as I can go," I said.

"Well, I'm connected with the manager of the Galesburg club and I'm going to recommend you to him," Wagner said, according to Alexander's version of the story. Alex consulted with Webster, his friend, manager and, as it turned out, counselor. Alex said it just didn't seem like the right thing to do, to leave a good job to go play ball for a couple of months. He was concerned he wouldn't get his job back when he returned. Webster urged him to follow through on the baseball offer. A few months later, in January 1909, he signed his first professional contract with Galesburg.[8]

Young Dode Alexander soon proved he could play with the professionals. His first appearance was in an exhibition game against the hometown college, Knox College. Alexander came on in relief in a 6–4 win. Wagner was impressed enough to give him the starting assignment on opening day. Alexander performed well but lost 5–4 to Monmouth when his teammates made three errors behind him.

Galesburg	AB	R	H	Monmouth	AB	R	H
Batlett, lf	4	0	0	Fleming, lf	4	1	1
Wagner, 2b	2	2	0	Johnson, cf	3	1	0
Shields, 3b	4	1	1	Siner, 2b	4	0	2
Rodman, 2b	4	1	1	Carter, 1b	3	0	0
Kilpatrick, cf	1	0	1	Irmscher, 3b	4	0	0
Kiernan, ss	4	0	0	Turner, ss	3	1	0
Rowells, cf	3	0	0	Meixel, rf	4	1	2
Raines, c	2	0	0	Hart, c	3	0	1
Brunett (a)	1	0	0	Williams, p	3	1	1
Alexander, p	4	0	0				
Totals	29	4	3	Totals	31	5	7

(a) Brunett pinch hit and grounded out for Raines in ninth

```
Galesburg   2 0 0 0 0 1 1 0 0–4
Monmouth    0 0 0 0 0 1 4 0 x–5
```

Doubles — Siner, Kilpatrick. Double play — Siner and Turner.

	IP	H	R	BB	SO
Alexander	8	7	5	4	9
Williams	9	3	4	9	8

Hit by pitcher — Alexander (Johnson). Passed ball — Hart. Umpire — Rathun. Time: 2 hours

Alex continued to pitch well, throwing two shutouts against the Pekin ballclub, allowing just one hit in one of the games and striking out 16 batters in the other. The Galesburg newspaper called the young pitcher "a blonde of the ruddy type with the build of a switch engine. Manager Jap Wagner figures he can see the big strawberry slinger floating up puzzles to the opposing batsmen already and is much taken by his looks." His greatest fan base was still his hometown pals, including the sportswriters at the *St. Paul Phonograph* who informed their readers, "It is evident that Dode has won a home in Galesburg. May he continue to strike them out every game."

He was a pretty good hitter, too, and Wagner used him in the outfield when he wasn't pitching to take advantage of his live bat. By midseason, Alexander was 15–8, and all of his decisions were complete games. He was well on his way to climbing the ladder toward a successful baseball career.

His pitching was spectacular. On July 22, 1909, he threw a no-hitter against Canton, Illinois, striking out 10. The Galesburg newspaper did not hold back its enthusiasm for the young right-hander and hung a new nickname on him while at the same time informing readers of a tragedy at a local church:

"Emulating the example of Nero who fiddled while Rome was consumed by the flames, Alexander the Great fiddled with Canton while the Methodist religious edifice went up in smoke."

On July 25, he took the mound again and threw an 18-inning shutout against Macomb, Illinois, winning 1–0, striking out 19, and extending his scoreless inning streak to 42. It seemed that nothing could stop Alexander until suddenly something did. On July 28, Galesburg was playing in-state rival Pekin again. Alexander was playing right field and having a pretty good day at the plate. He had doubled in the second inning and then singled in the eighth. With Alexander on first, the next batter hit a ground ball to the second baseman, who flipped to the shortstop to start the double play. Somehow, some way, Alexander either didn't slide or slid high with his head up. The shortstop's throw to first hit him between the eyes and knocked him unconscious. He was taken to a nearby hospital, where he remained unconscious for 36 hours. When he awoke, he had a headache that eventually went away and double vision that didn't. William Alexander was notified and came to Illinois to be with his son. When Alexander was well enough to travel, he and his father went home to the farm with the young pitcher's future in doubt.

Recalling the circumstances years later, Alexander said, "I was unconscious for 36 hours. When I revived, I saw everything double. If you had put out your hand to shake with me, I would have seen two hands." Expressing the fear that his career might be over, Alexander said, "I didn't see how I was going to pitch to two hitters at the same time when there was only one at the plate." Neither did Galesburg. They sold his contract to Indianapolis of the American Association. The *St. Paul Phonograph* continued to express its unbridled loyalty. "We hope to be able to tell our readers, within a short time, of his complete recovery, and that he is back in the game once more doing his usual effective work."

When Alex reported to Indianapolis, he knew something the ballclub didn't know but soon found out. He couldn't see right. An eye specialist examined him and determined he had damaged two optic nerves and that only rest would help. Once again, the young pitcher went home to Nebraska. After several weeks, his vision improved, but it was too late in the year to go back to Indianapolis. So he stayed home, rested, practiced pitching a little and went hunting a lot. Hunting was one of the few things unaffected by the impaired eyesight because Alex shut one eye anyway in zeroing in on his prey. He tried pitching again in October, appearing in three games for the local St. Paul team and winning all three. He said his blurred vision had cleared up.

He reported to Indianapolis for its 1910 home opener. The ballclub did

II—A Stone's Throw Away

not summon him for spring training in order to save that expense. During batting practice, Alexander's usual pinpoint control abandoned him. He hadn't faced a hitter in several months, so it is unclear whether his sight was impaired or he was just wild. He hit several batters, including manager Charlie Carr, who suffered two broken ribs from the errant pitch. Carr was a businessman as well as a ballplayer, and he figured out a way he could unload his ailing young pitcher. He sent him to the Syracuse Stars in the New York State League. Instead of getting a player in return, he got the team's endorsement of the sporting goods company in which he was a part owner.

(Carr was a major league first baseman for Washington in the National League in 1898, and with Philadelphia, Detroit and Cleveland in the American League from 1901 through 1905. He hooked on with Cincinnati in the National League in 1906 before starting his minor league managing career. He resurfaced with Indianapolis in the Federal League in 1914. Many reference books pay more attention to his successful sporting good business than his ballplaying career, in which he hit under .200 in three of his seven seasons.)

Alexander went to Syracuse. It was there that the Indianapolis eye doctor was proved right in his prognosis. He had said Alex's vision would return in time, and it did. So did his pitching prowess. He won 29, lost 14 and had a string of 53 scoreless innings to end the season. Along the way, he threw 12 shutouts. On August 27, 1910, the *Syracuse Journal* reported that Alexander "had accomplished what no other player has even come close to doing and he has substantial cause to feel proud, although he isn't. Alexander is one of those unassuming chaps that takes things as they come, good, bad, or indifferent. He is the same quiet individual at all times."

When Dode Alexander returned home to St. Paul, he was greeted as if he were a war hero. Townspeople cheered as he got off the train. The locals had heard about his accomplishments and had read about them in the *Phonograph,* but they were anxious to see him pitch once again. Alexander didn't disappoint them. He pitched in a couple of town games, beating Ravenna and Ord.

By now, Alex had developed some habits that would stay with him the rest of his career. He wore his uniform loose, as if it were a little too big for him; his cap tight, as if it were too small for him, and he always wore it a little crooked. If he could, he'd wear the same pair of baseball shoes all season, wrapping tape around them if necessary to keep them from falling apart. Despite the brilliant season with Syracuse, the Stars declined to sign him for the 1911 season, and the reason might be another habit of Alexander's that was more prominent in later years. Baseball historian Fred Lieb speculated, "reports were no doubt already in circulation that Aleck was inordinately fond of a corn by-product of his native Nebraska, and if Aleck couldn't get corn, he wasn't particular. He'd drink anything. Yet only in infrequent occasions—and mostly toward the end of his career—did he permit his drinking to affect his pitching. And he lasted in the big leagues until he was 43."[9]

There is nothing in the public record or news accounts of the day to suggest that Lieb is correct in his assumption. Nor are there any accounts that epilepsy, a disease that drastically affected Alexander's behavior later, had surfaced. But the fact is that a 23-year-old pitcher who had just won 29 games was not re-signed. Instead, his name was placed in the draft, and any club had a shot at signing him.

It is difficult to determine why Alex wasn't courted by major league teams after the year he had with Syracuse. He won 29 games, threw 13 shutouts, ended the season with a string of 53 consecutive scoreless innings, had an early string of 33 straight scoreless innings and won 12 games in a row to end his season, including winning both ends of a doubleheader on one Sunday afternoon. From a statistical standpoint, Alexander had quite possibly been the best pitcher in the world in 1910. Yet Indianapolis, which had an option on him, failed to exercise it. Nobody else seemed interested except for the Phillies, who picked him up for pocket change and then very nearly left him behind in spring training. Indianapolis personnel may not have trusted his eyesight after their brief experience with him.

Lieb's conclusion that a possible reason for ballclubs passing on Alexander, despite his obvious pitching prowess, was his fondness for alcohol is reiterated by biographer Jack Kavanagh many years later: "Reports might already have been circulated that the prospect from the Cornhusker State was partial to raising a jug of corn 'likker' between games."[10]

Yet F.C. Lane, in his lengthy 1916 article on Alexander, writes, "It goes perhaps without saying that Alexander is free from the vice of drink, which has cursed many a ballplayer's career. His position at the head of his profession is perhaps a sufficient guarantee of that."[11]

The Philadelphia Phillies ballclub was in a state of transition. It had been owned by two political bosses, Israel Durham and Jim McNichol, and a banker, Clarence Wolf. Durham was the driving force of the three but became ill and died on June 28, 1909, at the age of 52. McNichol and Wolf had little interest in continuing their ownership. They finished out the season and then sold the ballclub to Horace Fogel, a fast-talking, cigar-smoking sportswriter with the reputation of a poker player who was always willing to bet the house on the next card. The sale price was $350,000, money everyone knew Fogel didn't have. It was later determined that he was financially backed by Charles P. Taft of the politically powerful Taft family in Cincinnati and that Mrs. Taft held title to the Philadelphia ballpark.

As a former sportswriter, Fogel knew the value of publicity and invented ways of getting it for his ballclub. Sportswriter Lieb described him as "an early version of the Larry MacPhail-Bill Veeck type of colorful, dynamic club president."

To build a little fan excitement, Fogel wanted to change the name of the team to the "Live Wires." The idea never got off the ground. But Fogel was intent on winning a pennant and was willing to listen to any and all ideas on how to get it done.[12]

Patsy O'Rourke, a scout for the Phillies, saw Alexander pitch for Syracuse and recommended the Phillies sign him. Fogel bought the contract for less than $1,000 — some reports say $750, others say $500. Whatever the price, it turned out to be one of the greatest steals in major league history. But it still took some maneuvering for Alexander to make the big club.

He reported for spring training at Wilmington, North Carolina, where some of the veteran players and coaches were a little put off by the confidence he seemed to show because of the casual way he went about his business, with the short windup and the sidearm delivery that looked effortless compared to the styles of some of the veterans. Red Dooin was the Phillies manager. He had the final say on who made the club and who didn't. He had jotted down Alexander's name as a player to be cut, but Pat Moran, one of his coaches, saw the list and pleaded on Alexander's behalf.

Author Lieb describes the conversation this way:

"What's that fellow Alexander's name doing on that list, Charlie?"

"Oh, you mean the big fellow we drafted from Syracuse?" replied Dooin. "Well, Pat, I can't carry them all. We've got to get from under the expense of carrying all of these youngsters. I've got to release some of them."

"But not this one, Charlie. Not Alexander," insisted Moran. "He's really got something. I could help him become a real pitcher."[13]

Dooin kept him. When the Phillies training camp broke up, the team was divided into two squads, the first going straight back to Philadelphia to play the Athletics in the city series, the second one barnstorming back, playing various teams along the way. Alexander was put on the barnstorming team, managed by Moran. By the time the barnstormers reached Philadelphia, Connie Mack's A's, the 1910 American League champions, had beaten the Phillies in three straight games. Possessed with the "$100,000 Infield" of Stuffy McGinnis, Eddie Collins, Jack Barry and "Home Run" Baker, the A's had won 102 games in 1910, lost only 48, and disposed of the mighty Chicago Cubs, four games to one, in the World Series. They were an intimidating bunch. Down three games to none in the city series, Dooin decided to give young Alexander a chance. He gave him the start in the final game of the series and designated Moran to be his catcher.

Dooin, a minstrel singer in the off-season, was a big-league catcher with the Phillies for 14 years and was player-manager of the club from 1910 to 1914. Moran was a backup catcher most of his career but took over for Dooin as manager of the Phillies in 1915 and guided them to their first National League pennant.

O'Rourke, who recommended the drafting of Alexander, was the manager of the Albany team in the New York State League, and also worked for the Phillies as a scout. He was a better judge of talent than he was a ballplayer. His major league career consisted of 53 games in 1908 with the St. Louis Cardinals when he hit .191. He urged Fogel to sign Alexander, but Fogel preferred George Chalmers, a pitcher for Scranton, who had a season record of 25–6 and had seen some major league action at the end of the 1910 season while Alexander still labored in the minors. In the end, Fogel got Chalmers for $3,000 and Alexander for less than $1,000. Chalmers lasted seven years in the majors, all with the Phillies, and retired with a record of 29–41.

Alexander took the mound against the A's on a Saturday afternoon, with the opening of the official baseball season just around the corner. For five innings, he mowed down the A's, one after the other, allowing

Charles "Red" Dooin was a catcher and Phillies manager who almost cut Grover Cleveland Alexander from the squad when the Philadelphia ballclub headed north from spring training in 1911. Alexander won 28 games, which is still the all-time record for wins by a rookie (National Baseball Hall of Fame Library, Cooperstown, N.Y.).

no runs on no hits, walking two, striking out one. The A's eventually won the game 2–1 in 12 innings but the young, sidearming farm boy from Nebraska had assured himself of a place on a major league roster.

Alexander could have been part of another major league roster, and baseball history would have been changed, had it not been for an ill-advised scouting report. Hugh Jennings, manager of the Detroit Tigers, said the Tigers got a tip that young Alex was a pretty good pitcher in the New York State League. They sent a scout to watch him pitch for Syracuse. On the day the scout arrived, Syracuse was playing Wilkes-Barre in a doubleheader. Alexander worked the first game and lost 1–0. He then pitched the second game and won 2–0. But the scout advised against signing him because he threw sidearmed. The scouting report said, "If he's going to get anywhere in the major leagues with the stuff he's got, he must pitch overhand and I don't think this fellow will ever learn to pitch overhand. He's one of those you can't change the style of."[14]

Grover Cleveland Alexander looks more like a hitter than a pitcher as he confers with Pat Moran on the steps of the dugout. Moran was a catcher and coach who convinced Red Dooin to keep Alexander on the 1911 roster and was his mentor during the early years of Alexander's career (National Baseball Hall of Fame Library, Cooperstown, N.Y.).

Fogel wasn't around too long to watch the young pitcher develop. In August of 1912, he accused National League umpires of favoring John McGraw's New York Giants and said that St. Louis Cardinal manager Roger Bresnahan, a former Giant player, took it easy on his old team. For his reckless and unfounded statements, Fogel was banned permanently from the National League, and the American League didn't want anything to do with him either.

Moran's place in baseball history would be secure for being the man who "discovered" Grover Cleveland Alexander — but his baseball life took an unusual twist a few years later. He was the manager of the 1919 Cincinnati Reds, winner of the World Series over the Chicago White Sox in the series in which eight Chicago players were subsequently banned from baseball for their parts in fixing the series. Moran went to his grave saying the Reds would have won the series anyway. He remained manager of the Reds until spring training of 1924, when he died while with his team in Florida. His death certificate listed the cause of death as Bright's Disease, but many who knew him said his lifestyle was a contributing factor, for Moran, the first mentor of young Grover Cleveland Alexander, was a heavy drinker.[15]

• CHAPTER III •

A Big League Pitcher

"Alexander was in a class by himself, a man who made pitching seem like an effortless chore."
— Frankie Frisch

In the early 1900s, the National League was dominated by three teams and their Hall of Fame managers: The Pittsburgh Pirates, managed by Fred Clarke, the New York Giants, managed by John McGraw, and the Chicago Cubs, managed by Frank Chance. In the first decade of the 20th century, the Pirates won the pennant the first three years, New York won it the next two years, and Chicago won it four out of the next five years with Pittsburgh winning it the year Chicago didn't in that five-year span. During that same period, Philadelphia finished second, seventh, seventh, eighth, fourth, fourth, third, fourth, fifth and fourth. As they headed for spring training in 1911, they were coming off a fourth place finish in 1910 in which they finished 25½ games behind the champion Cubs. Clearly they could not compete at the level of the Cubs, Giants and Pirates with the personnel they had.

In 1910, owner Fogel tried to light a fire under what he hoped would be his "Live Wires" by dismissing manager Billy Murray and replacing him with Charlie "Red" Dooin, who was a veteran catcher. He had caught for the Phillies for eight years and was known for his range in going after foul balls and for his ability to block the plate, preventing runners from scoring. Dooin always claimed he was the first catcher to wear shin guards, not Roger Bresnahan, as legend has it. Dooin said Bresnahan, who caught for and managed the St. Louis Cardinals, got the idea from him.[1]

Under Dooin, the club moved up in the standings, from fifth to fourth, and outfielder Sherry Magee won the batting title with a .331 average. Magee was the only bona fide star in the Phillie lineup. Two acquisitions in 1910 set the stage for better days ahead. Dooin injured his shoulder in midseason, so Fogel picked up a backup catcher from the Cubs — Pat Moran. The club also acquired a hard-hitting first baseman named Fred Luderus, who was under contract with the Cubs but had been playing for Milwaukee in the minor leagues.

The biggest deal occurred just before spring training when the Phillies unloaded third baseman Eddie Grant, center fielder Johnny Bates and pitchers George McQuillan and Lew Moren in a trade with Cincinnati. In return, Philadelphia got the Reds' third baseman, Hans Lobert, center fielder Dode Paskert and pitchers Jack Rowan and Fred Bebee. The deal was the biggest in Phillie history. The new players formed the nucleus of what would be the Phillies' only pennant winner in the first 50 years of the century. Many observers believe it also led to Clark Griffith's departure as manager of Cincinnati and his return to the American League, where he would eventually purchase the Washington Senators and be an American League kingpin for 50 years.

One of the things that occurred as a result of the trade was that Alexander would never be called Dode, his boyhood nickname, because George Henry "Dode" Paskert already had the moniker, and he was an established star. (The rookie pitcher would be known as Alec or Alex, Ol' Pete, and, before long, Alexander the Great.)

Paskert and Lobert were the key figures in the deal with Cincinnati. Paskert was a fleet-footed center fielder who had the reputation of being able to catch anything that stayed in the park. He was also a good hitter who liked to work opposing pitchers deep in the count. From 1911 to 1917 Paskert was either the Phillies' lead-off hitter or batting second in all but two years. It didn't take long for Paskert to show off his defensive abilities. In the second game of the 1911 season, the Phils were playing the Giants at the Polo Grounds. A Giant hitter smashed a line drive into deep left-center field. Paskert took off after it and made a desperation dive, his body parallel to the ground, catching the ball with his bare hand. Magee, playing left field, said years later it was the greatest catch he ever saw. So did sportswriters who witnessed it.[2]

Lobert was considered the fastest base runner of his era. He was once timed running around the bases in 13.8 seconds. He also beat Olympic gold medal winner Jim Thorpe in a race. On another occasion, as a promotional gimmick, he ran against a race horse and won that one, too. Lobert's speed and his ability to get on base gave the Phillies a pretty good tandem in Paskert and Lobert at the top of their lineup, ready for hitters like Luderus to drive them in.

Luderus (pronounced Lu-DARE-us) was a power-hitting first baseman who feasted on Baker Field's right field wall, just 272 feet from home plate. He couldn't run well, and his fielding was suspect — he was the National

League leader in errors in four different years — but he could hit with power, and he was always ready to play. In one stretch, he appeared in 533 consecutive games, a Phillie record at the time. Luderus broke in with the Cubs but never reached his full potential. In August of 1910, he was traded to the Phillies and hit .294 in limited action, playing in place of the regular first baseman, Kitty Bransfield, who was injured. At spring training in 1911, Bransfield didn't play well and Luderus did. He won the starting job at first base, hit 16 home runs and batted over .300. Before the year was out, Bransfield was released.

Sherwood "Sherry" Magee, the left fielder, was one of the best hitters of the Dead Ball Era — and one of the best fighters, too. Magee took on anyone who crossed him, including umpires. He was a great all-around ballplayer, but one of the most remarkable parts of his story is how he got to the big leagues in the first place. Phillie scout Jim Randall got off a train in Carlisle, Pennsylvania, and overheard some townspeople raving about the Magee kid and what a ballplayer he was. Randall went and saw him play and was impressed. He offered Magee a contract. Two days later he was in the starting lineup for Philadelphia.

His best year with the Phillies was 1910, with his .331 league-leading batting average to go along with 39 doubles, 17 triples, six home runs, 110 runs scored, 123 batted in and 49 stolen bases. Magee's main drawback was his temper and his disposition. Writers in his era compared him with Johnny Evers of the Cubs, who often went for long periods of time without speaking to teammates. Newspapers referred to him as both a "grouch" and a "hothead"— and a violent run-in with an umpire during the 1911 season had a hand in costing the Phillies their best chance in history at a National League championship. Baseball is full of ironies, and one of them regarding Magee is that when his playing days were over he became, of all things, an umpire. Alexander called Magee one of the best hitters of all time.

Rounding out the outfield, along with Paskert and Magee, was right fielder John Titus, who had one of the best arms — and best mustaches — in the National League. Titus was everything that Magee was not, quiet, unassuming and polite. He was never thrown out of a big league game for arguing with umpires. Teammate Kid Gleason said, "He doesn't even make any noise when he spits." Alexander called him "Silent John," a man who said hello in spring training, good-bye in the fall and did his job in between. He was rarely seen without a toothpick in his mouth. He was not overly concerned about money. At one point in 1912, the ballclub wrote to him and asked that he kindly cash his paychecks. He had carried several of them around in his pockets for months. Titus quietly endured a nickname teammates hung on him, a takeoff on his last name, and perhaps a reference to his spending habits: Tight Ass.[3]

Shortstop Mickey Doolan was a great fielder who had an unusual way of throwing. A childhood injury prevented him from being able to throw the ball overhand with any kind of distance or accuracy. So Doolan, whose real name was Michael Dolittle, learned how to snap the ball, using his wrist more than his arm, and he was good at it. In an eight-year stretch, he led the National League in putouts in four different years, in assists in five different years and in double plays in five different years. The highest he ever hit in nine years with the Phillies was .263, but his fielding and his leadership more than made up for his weak bat. When Grover Cleveland Alexander joined the Phillies, Doolan was team captain.

The second baseman was Otto Knabe, a veteran who threw a scare into rookie Alexander early in the season. The Phillies were playing the Giants and blew an early lead. Knabe, sitting on the bench, groused about Phillie pitchers not being able to win a game unless they had about a 12-run lead. Alexander said he looked over at Knabe and mockingly stuck out his tongue at him. Knabe exploded. "When we get to the clubhouse, I'll show you how to talk to a regular," he said. After the game, Alexander said he approached Knabe in the clubhouse in case he wanted to fight. "Oh, the game's over now," said Knabe. Alexander said he learned from that incident that ballplayers say things in the heat of battle that they don't really mean, and that most of them leave it on the field.[4]

Alexander had the highest respect for Knabe and for Doolan. "Knabe and Doolan were not the greatest second baseman and shortstop that ever lived, not by any means, but if there was ever a pair who hustled harder than they did, I'd like to see them. They gave you everything they had as long as the game was being played."[5]

Red Dooin did the catching and the managing, backed up by Moran. By midseason, the club had acquired Bill "Reindeer Bill" Killefer who would become Grover Cleveland Alexander's catcher for five seasons.

Ace of the pitching staff was Earl Moore, who won 22 games for the fourth place Phillies in 1910 and led the league in strikeouts. Eight years earlier, Moore, a side-arming right-hander, threw the first nine-inning no-hitter in the American League as a member of the Cleveland Indians against the Chicago White Sox. He lost the no-hitter and the game in the 10th inning. Rowan, the right-hander acquired from Cincinnati in the eight-player deal in February, was the number two starter. He had been 11–12 and 14–13 in his last two seasons with Cincinnati and was expected to be in double figures in wins again with a Philly team that was expected to provide much more support for him than the Reds had. Rounding out the starting pitching staff were the two rookies, Chalmers and Alexander.

On Wednesday, April 12, the Phils opened the season at the Polo

Grounds with a 2–0 win over McGraw's Giants with Moore throwing the shutout. The next day, Rowan made his debut with the Phillies and was matched up against the great Christy Mathewson. The starters toiled in a 1–1 tie for 17 innings before Philadelphia broke through with six runs in the 18th to win the game. This was the game in which Dode Paskert made the diving bare-handed catch in left-center field. The Phillies were 2–0, the Giants were 0–2 and no one would have guessed that Rowan would win only one more game all year. That night the grandstand and left field bleachers at the Polo Grounds burst into flames. The Giants played their home games at Hilltop Park, the home of the American League New York Highlanders until the Polo Grounds could be readied for use again.

The Phillies were off the next day and traveled by train to Boston to meet the Braves. When they arrived, they learned of a tragedy in the baseball world. Addie Joss, the brilliant young pitcher for the Cleveland Indians, had died from tubercular meningitis. His death came two days after his 31st birthday and after a nine-year career in which he won 160 games, lost 97 and had a career earned run average of 1.88.

As baseball imitates life in so many ways, so it was that the day after the passing of one of baseball's all-time greats, a future great made his major league debut. Grover Cleveland Alexander took the mound against the Braves on April 15. Though he was just 24, he had the cartoonish comportment usually associated with men much older. Throughout his career, Alex always seemed to have on a uniform that looked too big and a cap that looked too small and was always cocked at a bit of an angle. He stood a little over six feet tall and weighed about 180 pounds. His mound opponent that day was Cliff Curtis. Alexander pitched well and finished what he started. An unearned run in the ninth inning killed him as the Braves beat the Phillies 5–4.

Philadelphia	AB	R	H	*Boston*	AB	R	H
Titus, rf	4	0	1	Clarke, lf	4	1	0
Knabe, 2b	3	0	0	Goode, cf	5	2	2
Lobert, 3b	4	0	0	Herzog, ss	4	0	1
Magee, lf	3	1	1	Miller, rf	4	1	2
Paskert, cf	5	1	1	Ingerton, 3b	3	0	0
Luderus, 1b	5	0	0	Sweeney, 2b	3	1	0
Doolan, ss	4	1	1	Tenney, 1b	3	0	1
Dooin, c	5	1	3	Rariden, c	3	0	0
Alexander, p	4	0	1	Curtis, p	0	0	0
				Pfeffer, p	4	0	1
Totals	37	4	8	Totals	33	5	7

Philadelphia   0 0 0 1 0 2 1 0 0 0–4
Boston   0 1 0 0 0 1 0 2 0 1–5

Doubles—Goode 2, Tenney, Titus. Home run—Miller. Stolen bases—Paskert 2, Lobert, Doolan, Magee. Sacrifices—Rariden, Herzog, Ingerton, Knabe

	IP	H	R	BB	SO
Alexander	10	7	5	4	5
Curtis	1	1	0	0	1
Pfeffer	9	7	4	6	1

Wild pitch—Alexander. Umpires—Klem and Doyle Time—2 hours

Moore then beat the Braves 10–2 in his second start, and Rowan started again but did not finish and did not get the decision as the Phillies won their third straight, beating Boston 10–9. Dooin decided to give Fred Beebe a start. Beebe, the other pitcher besides Rowan who came over from Cincinnati in the winter deal, won 15 for St. Louis in 1909 and 12 for the Reds in 1910. When he beat the Braves 5–3 in the first game of a doubleheader on April 19, the Phillies had won three in a row. In the second game, Alexander made his first relief appearance of the season, but Ad Brennan got the win as the Phillies won their fourth straight game and were on top of the National League with a 6–1 record. Two more victories came at the hands of the Giants at Baker Bowl in Philadelphia with Moore and Rowan picking up the wins. On April 25, the six-game winning streak ended when Moore lost a 4–3 decision to Brooklyn.

On April 26, Alex made his second start of the season. It wasn't pretty, but he overcame six walks and had the benefit of some timely hitting as the Phillies beat the Dodgers, 10–3. Philadelphia finished April with an 11–3 record and was the surprise team of the league.

While the other Philadelphia starters hit a stretch in which they were winning just about as many as they were losing, Alexander, the sidearmer from Nebraska, started mowing down batters with the precision of a farm boy throwing rocks at clothespins. On May 11, he threw the first of his 90 big league shutouts as the Phillies downed Brooklyn 5–0 on Alex's three-hitter. On May 11, he won again as Philadelphia trounced the Pirates 19–10. On May 13, he made his second relief appearance of the season, coming on for George Chalmers in the ninth inning against Cincinnati and shutting out the Reds for the next eight innings as the Phillies won, 2–1. On May 17, Luderus homered in the 11th inning to give Alex a 4–3 win over Pittsburgh. The Phillies were 23–9 and hanging on to first place. But they dropped their next six in a row, including Ed Reulbach of the Cubs besting Alexander 6–2 on May 22 to fall from the top spot in the league. Alex had won six in a row after losing his first start and now, with the latest loss, had a record of 6–2. The next day, Philadelphia lost again and suffered another blow when right fielder Titus broke his leg sliding into Cardinal catcher Roger Bresnahan in a 12–4 loss to the Cards. On May 25, the Phils went back into first place temporarily as Alexander beat the Cardinals 4–3 to stop the losing streak. The next day proved to be a milestone day, because Alex and Christy Mathewson pitched against each other for the first time — both in relief. Mathewson got the win. The Phillies finished May on a high note with a doubleheader win over the Braves on May 30 with Moore and Alexander picking up the victories.

Alex had a great June, winning five in a row before dropping a 5–0 shutout to Brooklyn on the last day of the month. On June 5, in a game against the Pirates at Forbes Field, Alexander and the Phillies won 5–4 in a game in which Alex committed the only balk of his major league career, a career that totaled nearly 5,100 innings. On July 2, Alexander came on in relief of Bill Burns to help preserve a win in which the losing pitcher was Mathewson, the second time in a month that the two winningest pitchers in National League history had faced each other in a game. They had yet to start against one another, in great part because neither Red Dooin nor John McGraw wanted that match-up when they knew their aces could beat anyone else on the opposing staff. When Fred Luderus hit two home runs to help the Phillies beat the Giants 7–5 on July 4, the Phillies found themselves in first place in the National League standings, just as their counterparts, Connie Mack's A's, were on top in the American League.

Two incidents in July pretty well killed the Phillies' pennant hopes. On July 10, Alex beat the Cardinals 4–2 but fiery outfielder Sherry Magee went berserk after being called out on strikes by umpire Bill Finneran. In the course of the argument, Magee punched Finneran and rendered him unconscious. National League president Tom Lynch suspended Magee for the rest of the season. That, coupled with Titus's broken leg, meant the Phillies were without two-thirds of their outfield. Then on July 26, in the Phillies' next series with the Cardinals, manager and starting catcher Red Dooin broke his leg when Rebel Oakes slid into him hard but cleanly on a play at the plate. Moran, the man who had "discovered" Alexander, tried to fill in, but he was old and his arm was weak. The Phillies tried four other youngsters, all of whom were ineffective at the plate and inexperienced at handling pitchers. The fourth of the bunch was Bill Killefer, who hit .188 in six games in 1911 but would win fame in years to come as Alexander's battery mate. The desperate Phillies appealed to Lynch to lift Magee's suspension in light of all the other injuries, and finally, Lynch gave in, allowing Magee back on August 16 with the Phillies in fourth place, 6½ games out of first. They finished the season with a seven game losing streak, ending with a 79–73 record, in their customary fourth place.

The brightest light for the Phillies continued to be Alexander. He lost several games as his team struggled to score runs and while opposing teams were running wild on the young Philadelphia catchers. Another factor made it difficult for Alex: Opponents, now trying to win the pennant, were throwing their best pitchers against him. He was matched up against Mathewson (in relief), Rube Marquard, Mordecai "Three Fingers" Brown, Ed Reulbach and other stars. On September 7, he was up against Cy Young, the winningest pitcher in baseball history (and still is), who was 20 years older than Alex and was on his way out. But he had one more good game left in him. Pitching for the Boston Braves, Young gave up just a lone run, but Alexander gave up just a single hit. The youngster beat the old master 1–0 in the first one-hitter of Alexander's career. Legend has it that it was Young's last game, but it was not, though his career did end when the season ended three weeks after his classic match-up with Alexander.

As writers all around began taking a closer look at the Nebraska farm boy, some interesting speculation developed. The *Washington Post* published a piece in which it examined the importance of catchers to the success of pitchers and named several battery mates as examples: Walter Johnson and Gabby Street, Cy Young and Lou Criger, Ed Walsh and Billy Sullivan, Christy Mathewson and Roger Bresnahan, and Alexander and Red Dooin.

According to the *Post:*

> Whenever a sensational pitcher breaks into major league company, it will always be found that the tried catcher is his mate. The shining example this year is Grover Cleveland Alexander, the wonder acquired by the Phillies.
>
> It took the old crafty hand and master mind of Charlie Dooin to place Alexander on the pedestal he now enjoys. Could Alexander have been half so successful if an untried receiver had been working with him? Dooin is acquainted with the failings of every player in the National League while Alexander probably does not yet know the kind of a ball a certain player does not care for. Now that Dooin is out of the game, it will be interesting to see how Alexander does with Pat Moran catching him.[6]

That didn't concern Alexander because, as he said many times, he had great respect for the old catcher, coach and future manager. "I think Pat Moran was more responsible for making a big league pitcher out of me than any other man," said Alexander."[7]

After shutting out Boston and Young on September 7, he shut out the Dodgers 2–0 on September 13, then beat Cincinnati 6–0 on September 17.

Alex beat his old nemesis, Reulbach and the Cubs 4–0 on September 21 for his fourth straight shutout. He ran his consecutive scoreless inning streak to 41 before the Cardinals scored on him in the sixth inning, but Alex still won the game, 8–2. With his record now at 27–12, Alexander had a shot at winning 30 games, but he needed to win his three remaining starts. On September 29, he won number 28, a 7–4 decision over Pittsburgh. Four days later, McGraw's Giants were too much, and Alex was on the low end of a 12–3 drubbing. With just a few days remaining in the season and his chances for 30 wins gone, Dooin chose not to start him in any more games.

His was the greatest rookie season of all time: 28 wins and 13 losses; 31 complete games (out of 37 starts); 367 innings pitched; seven shutouts; 227 strikeouts to 129 walks; and an earned run average of 2.57. The Phillies finished at 79–73, so Alex had 35 percent of his team's wins. The next year, he would reduce his number of walks from 129 to 105. For the next 18 years after that, he never walked more than 76 batters in a season. His sidearm delivery and his uncanny ability to hit the corners of the plate were his trademarks. Also, Alex didn't waste much time between pitches. He knew what he wanted to do with the hitters. He didn't want to give them time to think about what he was going to do. Most of his complete games were finished in an hour and a half or less. Frank Frisch, who faced him many times later in his career, said, "Alexander was in a class by himself, a man who made pitching seem like an effortless chore. He had amazing control, but strangely enough, he was one of the most difficult pitchers to handle behind the plate. He had a keen eye and a quick brain. If he saw a batter make a move, shift his stance or give a cue as to what he was going to do or how he was guessing, Old Pete would change his pitching plans in the middle of his motion and trust that the catcher would be able to handle the situation."[8]

Teammate Lobert said Alexander was an amazing pitcher who didn't do the usual running between starts or other conditioning routines usually associated with pitchers. He would sometimes play third base during batting practice and scoop up ground balls and catch pop-ups. It was this kind of apparent nonchalance that alienated him from some teammates, and particularly to other pitchers, when he first came up. It became much more tolerable when associated with a 28-game winner. Lobert said Alexander was a big man but had little fingers and threw a "heavy ball." He said later in his career, when he was playing for the Giants, that Alexander hit him in the chest with a pitch, and it felt like a piece of lead boring into him. Mathewson, by contrast, threw a "light ball," said Lobert.[9]

Luderus came through as expected, hitting .301 with 16 home runs and 99 RBIs. Moore, the veteran pitcher who won 22 games in 1910, lost 19 in

1911 and had a 15–19 record. Chalmers, the pitcher the Phillies selected ahead of Alexander, finished at 13–10. Magee hit .288 with 15 homers and 94 RBI, but his suspension, coupled with the injuries to Titus and Dooin, proved to be the downfall of the Phillies, who were in first place on July 4 before most of the trouble hit. Despite all the excitement they created and the hopes they raised among the Phillie faithful, the result did not defy preseason predictions or past performance. Philadelphia was once again a distant fourth in the National League.

Despite the disappointing finish in 1911, Philadelphia management thought they had the nucleus of a contending ballclub going into the 1912 season. They added some pop to the lineup with the addition of Clifford "Gavy" Cravath, an outfielder, and two pitchers, left-hander Eppa Rixey and right-hander Tom Seaton, who, like Alexander, was a Nebraska farm boy with a live arm. In addition, Reindeer Bill Killefer, though young, thin, and seemingly brittle, was emerging as the catcher of the future, the heir apparent to Dooin and Moran behind the plate who would become the regular catcher for Grover Cleveland Alexander.

Cravath was one of the dominant sluggers of the Deadball Era and set an organized-baseball record in 1911 when he hit 29 home runs for the Minneapolis Millers to go along with a .363 batting average. The Phillies purchased his contract for $9,000. Cravath was a man of few words who once said he had only one piece of advice for young hitters: "Hammer the ball." He was the top slugger in major league baseball for a few years until the Deadball Era ended and Babe Ruth, who began his career as a promising pitcher, became the greatest home run hitter in baseball a decade later.

Rixey also had a promising career ahead of him. He would become the winningest left-hander in the National League with 266 lifetime wins — tops until Warren Spahn surpassed him in 1959 — but in 1912 he was an erratic kid with a lot of potential. At 6 foot, 5 inches, he was one of the tallest players in the majors. Seaton didn't last as long as Rixey, but at one point he replaced Alexander as the Phillies stopper.

Alexander had been a holdout, ever so briefly, after the 1911 season, wanting more money than owner Fogel was willing to dish out. At the end of the season, Fogel wanted to not only sign his star pitcher but get him to agree to a three-year contract. The shrewd owner probably wanted to get Alex to commit to a salary that couldn't be raised no matter how many games he would win for the Phillies in the next three years. It was reported that Fogel wanted to pay Alexander $5,200 a year and that Alex wanted $6,000. It also became known that some Phillie boosters had talked Alex into asking for more money, convincing him to put a scare into his boss. When word got out that he had gotten some outside advice, Alexander notified the club that he wanted more money but that he had every intention of signing. Newspapers reported the stalemate on October 5. By January 1912, Fogel was getting more than a little nervous. He had not signed Alexander, Luderus or Paskert, so he set out on a "road trip" to get the signatures of all three. Alexander had a key ally on his side—manager Red Dooin. Because of the controversy caused when Alexander balked at the contract in October, he sought and received Dooin's counsel on how to handle the contract and at the same time mend fences with the owner. Dooin's solution: Alexander would get a $1,000 raise plus the promise of a bonus if the Phillies won the pennant and Alex won one-third of their games. Alexander signed the contract at his Nebraska home and sent it back with an optimistic note: "You just count one-third of the pennant won already. I won 28 last year. I'm going to be better this year. If the other pitchers win the other two-thirds, we can't lose the flag."

As it turned out, one of the big differences between 1911 and 1912 for Philadelphia was that injuries crippled the ballclub early in the season. Magee, still the team's premier hitter and sparkplug, missed the first month of the season after breaking his wrist in a spring training game. Lobert went down with a broken rib. Magee came back and then was hurt again in an outfield collision with Paskert. Lobert returned to the lineup only to crack a kneecap on May 4 and be out for the rest of the season. Pitchers Moore and Chalmers, who won 15 and 13 respectively in 1911, both suffered injury-riddled seasons. Moore slipped to 9–14, and Chalmers was only 3–4 in limited service.

Ad Brennan, another pitcher, came down with diphtheria, which created an unusual dilemma for manager Dooin. He worried because Brennan was a notorious spitballer, and Dooin feared there might be an epidemic that would spread throughout the league. In fact, Dooin saw a risk from the possibilities of all spitballers spreading illnesses and asked the National League office to order baseballs sprayed with disinfectant in games in which spitballers were scheduled to pitch. The league scoffed at the request.

Dooin and Moran, the aging catchers, were hurt more often than they were healthy. The Phillies tried several youngsters behind the plate before settling on Killefer. The results of their experiments were sometimes pathetic, sometimes amusing. Alexander said one of the problems was that opposing teams knew they could run on the Phillie catchers. Years later, he recalled a game in which Philadelphia was playing McGraw's Giants and Ed "Tubby" Spencer was Alex's battery mate. When Giant base runners got on first, they were stealing at will as the young catcher consistently threw the ball high, often all the way into center field. Alex said Spencer gritted his teeth and promised his pitcher he would get the throws down. The next time a Giant base runner attempted to steal, Spencer fired the ball toward second — and hit Alexander in the ankle.

Alexander's season was baffling. Sportswriter Lieb reported that "early in the season, young Alexander was out of condition," but he did not elaborate.[10] Biographer Kavanagh doesn't mention Alexander's being out of condition at the start of the year but hastens a guess as to why he was so mediocre in the first half of the season. "In light of later understanding of his off-the-field interests, it might be that the farm boy from Nebraska had made too many new friends among the city folk from the east," he wrote.[11] Throughout his career, Alex never worked at staying in shape during the off-season or bearing down in spring training drills. His off-season exercise was going back to Nebraska to hunt and fish with his brothers.

He lost on opening day, April 11, 7–4 to the Braves, then won the Phillies' home opener on April 19 by beating Boston by a 9–5 score. In between those two starts, Tom Seaton, the other pitcher from Nebraska, made his major league debut with the Phillies and shut down the Braves by a 14–2 score. Alex struggled and lost five of his next nine decisions and was just 5–5 in mid–June and was only 8–7 on July 4. One of those wins was an 8–6 decision over the Giants on May 3 in which the losing pitcher was Mathewson. It was one of the few times in their respective careers when Alexander and Mathewson each got a decision in the same game. In this game, Mathewson was the losing pitcher in relief. The next day, second baseman Lobert broke his kneecap chasing a foul ball into the stands, one of the turning points in what turned out to be a long season for the Phillies.

While McGraw avoided the Mathewson-Alexander match-up, he frequently went with his star left-hander, Rube Marquard, and he and Alex had some classic games. On June 25, Marquard was the victor in a 2–1 decision over Alexander — Marquard's 17th consecutive win.

Alex rebounded in the second half of the season. On July 8, the Phillies beat the Pirates, 5–1, with Alexander picking up the win and Howie Camnitz absorbing the loss, ending a seven-game win streak for Camnitz. On July 12, Alex beat the Reds 6–4 and beat them again on July 16 with a 5–0 shutout. On July 20, he coasted to a 14–2 trouncing of the Cubs in a game in which Sherry Magee set a major league record by stealing home twice. Alex ended his month with another win over Camnitz and the Pirates 4–1 on July 29. The Phillies had won three in a row but were buried in fourth place, 19½ games behind McGraw's Giants.

Alex won again on August 1 in a 4–3 decision over the Cardinals but lost a 5–3 decision to Reulbach and the Cubs on August 5. Then came a 10–2 victory over Cincinnati on August 10 in which Alexander contributed a home run. He lost a 2–1 decision to the Pirates at Forbes Field on August 14 when he gave up an unearned run in the 10th inning. It was his first loss to the Pirates. He lost a 6–1 decision to the Cubs on August 20, a 4–1 decision to the Cardinals on August 26 and a 4–2 decision to the Dodgers on September 2. At the end of the season, when Alexander finished with 19 wins, he could look back on his four starts between August 14 and September 2 in which his teammates supplied him with only five runs, a big factor in preventing him from having a 20-win season. That, and catchers who threw the ball all over the ballpark.

Alexander was 19–17 as the Phillies finished in fifth place. Not only had the Giants, Cubs and Pirates finished ahead of them, but Cincinnati sneaked into fourth place. A *Washington Post* columnist, tongue in cheek, summed up Alex's season and, at the same time, displayed a bit of racial insensitivity that was not considered inappropriate in that era:

"G.C.A. in 1911 looked like the spiciest, juiciest young bet in the world to cop all the change and drag down all the bets. Had a record that shone like the whites of a negro's eyes. Proved beyond doubt and caval that he was the g-o-o-d-s. Was expected to have a superb year this season. But Grover Cleveland only won 19, losing 17, a showing that was pretty strong for a pitcher with a team that finished in the second division but not exceptionally kippy for a twirler who was expected to be the loud explosion in the majors this season."[12]

Philadelphia's problems in 1912 were not confined to the playing field. Owner Horace Fogel, a man who made his living spouting his opinions on sports pages before he purchased the Phillies, made little effort to restrain himself from expressing his views, even with his new job and status. As the Phillies' hopes for a championship disintegrated with each broken bone of key players, the man who wanted to

Horace Fogel was a fast-talking gambling man, a former sportswriter who bought the Philadelphia ballclub and wanted to change its name to the "Live Wires." He signed Grover Cleveland Alexander to his first contract. Eventually, Fogel's talking would result in his being banned from major league baseball (National Baseball Hall of Fame Library, Cooperstown, N.Y.).

name his team the "Live Wires" was livid because McGraw's Giants were once again rising to the top. To Fogel's way of thinking, if the Phillies couldn't win it, he hoped the Cubs, owned by his pal Charlie Murphy, would be the champions. When that possibility started to fade, Fogel offered his own explanations. Fueled by liquor that was part of his daily staple and an imagination that could dream up scenarios that made sense to him, Fogel declared that the 1912 National League pennant race was fixed, that National League umpires favored the Giants and that Cardinal manager Roger Bresnahan purposely fielded a weak lineup against the Giants late in the season to help them retain first place. Bresnahan was a former Giant player. Fogel believed he still had allegiance to McGraw.

Fogel had been frustrated with umpires ever since Magee had the run-in with Bill Finneran and was suspended for several weeks. He was upset with Bresnahan and the Cardinals because most of the Phillies' key injuries came in games against the Cardinals. But Fogel found himself in deep trouble. It was one thing to blow off steam with your buddies in a barroom somewhere and quite another to do it in the sports pages of America as owner of a rival ballclub.

Tom Lynch, president of the National League, met with the seven other club owners and voted to hold hearings in which Fogel was called on to substantiate his allegations. In a meeting on October 16, 1912, Lynch said:

> If he can prove that the National League race was crooked this year and that the umpires or the president of the league were party to it, then the umpires should be discharged and blacklisted from ever taking part in organized baseball and the president of the league should step down and out of his position in disgrace.
> On the other hand, if these charges cannot be proved, then it is up to the National League to pass legislation preventing this man from representing a National League club in any capacity.[13]

After hearing two days of witnesses, a total of 12 hours of testimony, the other National League owners voted unanimously that Fogel be "forever excluded from further participation in the councils of this league as the representative of the Philadelphia ballclub or any other club."[14]

The fun and games were over for Fogel. William H. Locke, who was an officer of the Pittsburgh Pirates, scraped up enough cash to become the majority stockholder in the Phillies. William F. Baker, a former New York police commissioner, had the second-highest investment and was Locke's right hand man. The significance of all of this to Alexander and his teammates is that Locke was a hardworking baseball man. He was not flamboyant and controversial as his predecessor had been. It was felt the Phillies finally had someone who could lead them to the promised land. They were stunned when on July 15, 1913, just three months into the baseball season, Will Locke dropped dead of a heart attack. The team was taken over by Baker, and in time, the Phillies' venerable old ballpark, known as both Huntingdon Street Grounds and National League Park, became known as Baker Bowl, the site of some of Alexander's most memorable pitching performances.

Observers at the time and historians later on all agreed that Alex's accomplishments with the Phillies were all the more phenomenal because he achieved them while pitching in that ballpark. Built mostly of wood, it opened in 1887 and burned to the ground eight years later. It was rebuilt on the same site, using mostly steel and concrete, and was best known for its unusual dimensions. It was 341 feet down the left field line, 408 feet to straight-away center field and just 278 feet to right field. The right field wall was 40 feet high and had a 20-foot screen about it. The scoreboard was on the wall, and so was an advertisement for Lifebuoy soap that informed patrons, "Health Soap Stops B.O." It was such a short distance to the right field wall that left-handed batters, even in the Deadball Era, easily increased their home run totals just by hitting high pop flies that carried into the stands. Right-handed pitchers such as Alexander were particularly vulnerable.

Baker Bowl was the home of the Phillies until 1938. One of its quirks was a short right field wall that was about 272 feet from home plate. Casey Stengel said one of the measures of Grover Cleveland Alexander's greatness is that he won so many games while playing about half of them in that ballpark during his early career.

Alex returned to his rookie form in 1913, winning 22 games, but his season had some strange twists and turns. Though his numbers were good, they could have been better had it not been for some lengthy and unexplained absences, one at the start of the season and one at the end. The season started on April 9. Alex didn't pitch until April 25. There is no documentation for the reason for the delay. Did he report once again out of condition as he did in 1912? Was there a health problem that went unreported by the club and undetected by the press? Whatever the reason, one consequence was his place in the rotation. Just as quickly as Alex had gained the status as the Phillies' number one pitcher in 1911, he lost it in 1913 to fellow Nebraskan Seaton, a 16-game winner in his rookie season in 1912. Seaton went on to win 27 games in 1913.

Alexander, despite the late start, pitched well once he got in the rotation. He won his first 10 decisions and later on had an eight-game winning streak. Then, without explanation, he did not pitch from September 12 to September 22. Combined with his absence from the rotation at the start of the season, Alex missed nearly a month of the season. The Phillies finished second, 12½ games behind the Giants.

Just as the Philadelphia 1912 and 1913 seasons had been disrupted in part by the shenanigans of Horace Fogel, another disruption emerged in 1914 with the formation of the Federal League. It was a competitor to major league baseball not only for fan support but, more important, for talent. The Feds came in with big pocketbooks and whisked away major league players. They placed teams in Baltimore, Brooklyn, Buffalo, Chicago, Indianapolis, Kansas City, Pittsburgh and St. Louis, and some of the top stars of the American and National leagues took the bait, players such as Mordecai "Three Fingers" Brown and Joe Tinker from the Cubs and Eddie Plank and Chief Bender from Connie Mack's A's. Alexander stayed put, as did Ty Cobb, Tris Speaker and Walter Johnson, although Washington owner Clark Griffith had a close call with Johnson. Chicago of the Federal League offered "The Big Train" $16,000 plus a $10,000 signing bonus. When Johnson asked Griffith to match Chicago's offer, Griffith responded in a letter telling Johnson he didn't deserve that kind of raise since his win total had shrunk to 28 in 1914, four below what he had won in 1913. When it appeared that Johnson was going to make the move to the Federal League, Griffith quickly matched Chicago's offer — with one catch. He convinced White Sox owner Charles Comiskey that it would be bad business for the White Sox to have Johnson pitching for a competing team in Chicago. Therefore, according to Griffith, it made sense for Comiskey to come up with the $10,000 to cover the signing bonus. It was a case of one tightwad helping another, but it worked and Johnson stayed with the Senators.

The Phillies lost shortstop Mickey Doolan, second baseman Otto Knabe, pitchers Tom Seaton and Ad Brennan and utility man Runt Walsh. Seaton and Brennan had combined for 41 wins in 1913, and Doolan and Knabe had been the Phillies double play combination and steadying force up the middle for several years. Philadelphia had no way of recuperating quickly from that big a loss of manpower and plummeted to sixth place. Losing breeds tension and finger-pointing, and the Phillies had plenty of both. Clubhouse fights were common. Sherry Magee liked to pick fights even when times were good. Early in the season, he chided Milt Reed, a young infielder whose fuse was as short as Magee's. Reed responded by pinning Magee in such a way that the veteran's body was "draped over" the clubhouse pool table, according to one account. Another time, Magee stood on the sixth floor fire escape of a hotel and dropped a paper bag full of water on the head of Eppa Rixey, standing on the street below him. Rixey, a southerner, was often the victim of practical jokes that he did not find funny and may have contributed to his 2–11 record.

Why was Alexander not part of the exodus to the new league? It is reasonable to assume that he was approached and he might even have been tempted, but there was one thing for sure that held him back. At the end of the 1911 season, when Alex staged his brief holdout, Fogel may have exercised the best judgment of his short career as the club's owner. He gave his star rookie pitcher a raise and signed him to a three-year contract. So as the 1914 season approached and Seaton, Brennan, Doolan and Knabe departed, Alex honored his contract and stayed. It was a difficult year for him both professionally and personally. He won 27 and lost only 15, but on some days when he wasn't pitching, he was asked to play center field so that Magee could play shortstop as manager Dooin tried to fill the void of Doolan's departure as best he could. In May, Alex left the team for several days to attend the funeral of his only sister, Mary, with whom he was extremely close.

Pitching for a team that struggled to break even and grieving the loss of his sister, Alexander was just 5–5 on Memorial Day after losing a 3–2 decision to the eighth-place Boston Braves. On June 13, Alex made a relief appearance, coming into the game in the sixth inning and pitching 8⅔ innings of scoreless ball as the Phillies beat the Reds, 5–4 in 15 innings. On June 30, he made another relief appearance, spelling Rixey in the 13th inning with a man on first. He gave up a triple but then struck out the next three batters. The Phillies rallied for two runs in their half of the 13th to beat the Braves. On August 7, three days after playing center field so Magee could play at shortstop, Alex was on the mound again, but his bat won the game for him. He had three singles and a double in a 2–0 shutout of the Reds at

Baker Bowl. Alexander, winner of 11 of his last 15 decisions, now had a season record of 16–9. After a so-so August of two wins and three losses, he reeled off 10 consecutive victories and was not stopped until September 30, when he lost a 2–1 decision to the Dodgers at Baker Bowl. By this time, the Phillies were in sixth place, 18½ games out of first. The championship team of 1914 represents one of baseball's great stories—the rise of the lowly Boston Braves from worst to first from July 4 to the end of the season.

When the season ended, Alexander was a 27-game winner. Now a bona fide star, he went back to Nebraska briefly, and then joined a group of other major leaguers on a barnstorming tour across the U.S. and to Hawaii. The tour was put together by a wily entrepreneur, Frank Bancroft, former manager of the Providence ballclub in the 1890s and business manager of the Cincinnati Reds. Surely one of the goals of the excursion was to make money, but another was to give baseball exposure to parts of the world that had only heard about it. Bancroft was credited with introducing the sport to Cuba in a previous tour. The National League All-Stars included Bill James, 26-game winner for the world champion Boston Braves, but Alex was clearly the drawing card. Bancroft had hoped to land Walter Johnson on the American League squad and to have match-ups between Johnson and Alexander on the tour. But Walter was a newlywed and chose to spend the off-season on his Kansas farm with his wife, Hazel. One writer who followed Alex's career wrote, "Given the footloose ways of Grover Cleveland Alexander, who turned to barnstorming when his big league career was over and wandered in search of any kind of job in his later years, the 1914 tour of Hawaii might have set a lifetime's agenda.[15] Alex had the reputation of being a good guy—a fellow who wouldn't hesitate to buy a round of drinks, according to one observer.

Alexander's second baseman during his first four years, Hans Lobert, made a startling revelation in his conversation with Lawrence Ritter 60 years later. Lobert said that to the best of his knowledge, Alexander didn't drink in those days, that his serious drinking problems started at about the time of Prohibition and afterwards.

But Lobert said Alexander's big problem with the Phillies was epileptic seizures in which he would froth at the mouth and have to be held down by teammates while someone poured some brandy down his throat to settle him down. There's no question that Alexander suffered from epilepsy, but Lobert's story, which he told for the first time when he was an old man, is the only recorded account of Alexander's having epileptic seizures that early in his life. Lobert said it never happened on the field but happened several times on the bench.[16]

Alexander the Great, with whatever demons were looming inside him, was about to embark on a three-year run that ensured his place as one of the greatest pitchers of all time, a run that has been unequaled by another pitcher since then. He was to accomplish it under the tutelage of a new manager, for Red Dooin did not survive the dismemberment of the club by the Federal League, the clubhouse rowdiness that he was unable to control, and finally and most significant, the sixth place finish of the ballclub. Named to replace him was Pat Moran, the old catcher who is credited with "discovering" Alexander and giving him his shot at big league success.

• CHAPTER IV •

A Pennant Flies in Philadelphia

"This is your bread and butter as well as mine."
— Pat Moran

Every once in a while in professional sports, a manager or a coach seems to make a difference, to be the missing link, to be the added ingredient that turns an ordinary supper into a gourmet meal. Vince Lombardi holds that legacy with the Green Bay Packers football franchise and, to a lesser degree, Mike Ditka with the Chicago Bears. Arnold "Red" Auerbach helped turn the Boston Celtics basketball team into a dynasty, as did Phil Jackson with the Chicago Bulls a generation later. For a brief but shining moment in baseball, Pat Moran was the man of that moment with the Philadelphia Phillies.

Patrick Joseph Moran was an Irishman from Massachusetts who was a major league catcher for 14 years. He began his career with the Boston Beaneaters in 1901 and was traded to the Chicago Cubs after the 1905 season. There he was the backup catcher to Johnny Kling but was the personal catcher for Chicago's great pitcher, Ed Reulbach. He played for Hall of Fame player/manager Frank Chance and participated in the World Series in 1906 and 1907 with the Cubs. In 1910, he was traded to the Phillies, where he remained a second-string catcher for the next five years. When his playing career was over, he had only a .235 lifetime batting average to show for it, but his biggest strength was his knack for identifying pitching talent in youngsters and helping to develop it. Were it not for Pat Moran, Grover Cleveland Alexander would have lingered longer in the minor leagues, creating opportunity for injury, discouragement or drunken foolishness, any of which would have short-circuited his brilliant career.

Moran had a nickname of "Whiskey Face," for he was not a man known to turn down a drink when it was put before him, nor did he mind if his players made their way to barrooms after games as long as they were in bed on time and ready to play at game time. Alexander said many changes occurred on the ballclub between 1914 and 1915, but none was more important than the elevation of Moran from player/coach to manager.

"Pat Moran never showed his feelings," said Alex. "He kept his thoughts to himself. But if there was anything Pat didn't know about baseball, I don't know what it could have been."

Looking back on the 1915 pennant year, Alexander compared Moran to Burt Shotton, who managed the club in Alex's final season, 1930. "I never saw anybody like him until I played for Burt Shotton. Moran had patience, as Shotton has, and, also like Shotton, knew the game well enough to realize that players make mistakes sometimes and so he didn't expect things that were not humanly possible."[1]

One of the things that occurred right away after Moran was named manager was the dismantling of a team that had been mired for years in the second division. A signal of the changes to come came in November 1914 when the Phillies unloaded their former manager, Charlie "Red" Dooin, trading him to Cincinnati for infielder Bert Niehoff, who seemed to be in the doghouse all the time with his manager, Buck Herzog. While Niehoff needed a change of scenery, the Phillies felt Dooin also needed a new home. The trade was a courtesy to him, for had he stayed, he would have gone from manager to backup catcher, a potentially humiliating demotion for a man who had been a loyal employee. Niehoff had been a third baseman for the Reds but would fill the void at second that Philadelphia experienced when Knabe jumped ship the year before.

The Phillies also purchased the contract of a minor league infielder, Dave Bancroft, from Portland in the Pacific Coast League. Bancroft was a slick-fielding, switch-hitting singles hitter who gave the ballclub stability at shortstop where Magee and others had been playing since Doolan skipped off to the Federal League.

The next moves were franchise shakers. On December 24, 1914, Philadelphia sent their best hitter, temperamental Sherry Magee, to Boston for cash. On February 10, 1915, Boston sent outfielder George "Possum" Whitted and infielder Oscar Dugey to Philadelphia for cash. On January 4, Lobert was traded to the Giants for infielder Milt Stock, pitcher Al Demaree and catcher Bert Adams. Demaree was also an accomplished cartoonist whose work appeared regularly in *The Sporting News*.[2]

What a facelift for ballclub in the space of a couple of months. Whitted joined the veterans Cravath and Paskert in the outfield. Bancroft and Niehoff became the new double play combination at short and second. Bobby Byrne, whom the Phillies acquired from Pittsburgh in 1913, started the season at third base, but newcomer Stock was playing there most of the time after midseason. Luderus anchored first base. Killefer was now the number one catcher and the "personal catcher" of Grover Cleveland Alexander.

Ol' Pete would continue to carry the biggest share of the load on the mound, but he had some help. Erskine Mayer won 21 games in 1914 and was the number two man on the staff. The addition of Demaree, along with Rixey, gave the club two left-handers. They still had Chalmers, the man the Phillies picked ahead of Alexander five years earlier, who was a .500 pitcher but provided some depth to the pitching corps.

Alexander sized up the team this way: "We had great pitching that year, with Chalmers, Humphries, Rixey, Brennan and Mayer to shoot at the other clubs. Day in and day out the scores were 3 to 2, 2 to 1 and 1 to 0. As I remember, the entire staff had an earned run percentage of very little more than one run. If we had lost games as teams lose today, 10 to 9 and such scores, we would have been wild. When a pitcher was batted for four or five runs in a few innings, he was considered ready for the minors.... Cravath furnished our batting punch that season. Whitted was a good player, a hustler, and Paskert was a sweet outfielder. Our infield worked well and Killefer did great work behind the bat."[3]

The Phillies held spring training in St. Petersburg, Florida, and had their practices and games at a place called Coffee Pot Park. The park itself was about as plain as its name, with one shower (that produced only cold water) and a wooden grandstand that held about 500 people — if 400 of them were thin. The park was on a bayou, and many of the players brought fishing poles to the ballpark and threw in a line to relax between practices. The ballplayers knew a new regime had taken over when Moran instituted two-a-day practices and required them to walk the two miles from their hotel to Coffee Pot Park every day, then walk back to the hotel after practice. The hotel provided lunches that were brought to the field and often consisted of fish sandwiches with the heads still on the fish. The meals at the hotel were no better. One of the great stories that came out of spring training 1915 occurred on the day the players sat down at their long table in what passed for a hotel dining room and were served a roast beef dinner. Alexander asked for a hammer to be brought to the table. He then took the piece of beef from his plate and nailed it to the bottom of his shoe to serve as a sole.

One of the amusing sights at spring training that year was St. Petersburg Mayor Al Lang. He was proud to have the Phillies in town, pleased with how they were helping stimulate the economy of his city and intent on making Phillies management happy so that they would be sure to return next year. So Lang was pretty much a permanent fixture at the spring training games, shagging foul balls like a teenager trying to impress a girlfriend so he could return them to the club and thereby save them some dough.

Moran liked a loose clubhouse and didn't much care what the players did when they left the ballpark. But he demanded discipline on the field. He wanted his players to be mentally prepared to enter a ballgame. It was as important as being physically fit. He required them to pay attention to the slightest details and to know how to react to various game situations. Under his system, even players on the bench had to concentrate, and he was a stickler for making sure everyone was with the program.

He drilled his squad on the fundamentals, practicing over and over again the little things on defense like hitting the cutoff man, backing up plays, throwing to third, second or first on bunts and picking runners off base. When they were at bat, the men worked endlessly on laying down bunts, running out ground balls and pop-ups, breaking up double plays and executing double steals. Moran wanted his troops to be so well prepared that they would react automatically when these situations came up in games during the regular season.

Also, the new skipper's background as a catcher came into play. He wanted his players, particularly those on the bench, to study the opposition intently and steal their signs. Conversely, he wanted his pitchers and catchers to have signs that no opposing team could steal. Moran is believed to be one of the first managers to do away with the traditional signals of one finger-fastball, two fingers-curve, thumb down-change up, and instead employ three sets of signs. Among them was a signal from the catcher to the pitcher as to which sign was the real one and which were the decoys.

Moran never lost his savvy for handling pitchers, the kind of rapport that allowed him to take a young Grover Cleveland Alexander under his wing in 1911 and to rap Eppa Rixey on the shoes with a fungo bat in the dugout in 1915 when he didn't think Rixey was paying enough attention to what was happening on the field. In batting practice, Moran liked to stand behind the pitcher, a catcher's mitt being his only protection against the line drives that whistled by him, at him and near him. He would holler game situations like "runners on first and third, two out" or "tie game, runner on third, one out" and then ask the pitcher, "What are you going to throw?" If the pitcher didn't come up with the right answer, Moran would either chew him out or stop and patiently explain why the next pitch had to be low and outside or a fastball right under the hitter's chin. If the Phillies flopped in 1915, it would not be for lack of preparation.

He was not a man for long speeches, because he knew how to get his point across. As the players went through all their mental and physical drills, walking four miles a day just to get to and from work, executing all the basic plays, learning new signs and how to steal opponents' signs, sweating profusely under the hot Florida sun and eating what could only be compared to army food — with all of this going on — their manager walked among them telling them over and over again, "This is not a sixth place team." His pre-game pep talk was, "This is your bread and butter as well as mine." And on days when he felt particularly inspired, he would expand his oratory to include, "Win this one today." The Phillies played the World Champion Boston Braves seven times toward the end of spring training, and won six of the seven.[4]

The players found various ways of relaxing after their long days on the ballfield. Some headed for the bars. Some found women in the bars. Some had romantic interludes with women they found in the bars. When two women complained to authorities that they had been taken advantage of by a couple of Phillie players, Lang, the publicity-conscious mayor, stepped in as a mediator so as not to disrupt the good thing he had going with the Phillies as a major tourist attraction every spring.

On an off day, Rixey, Stan Baumgartner, Joe Oeschger and Ben Tincup took a boat from St. Petersburg to Pass-a-Grille, a nearby island. Somehow, the boat got stuck on a sandbar. By the time the boat got unstuck and the players returned to the mainland, it was 8 o'clock the following morning. Another time, Alex and several other players went fishing in Tampa Bay and got caught up in a storm. There was concern for their safety getting back to shore, but the biggest problem turned out to be some bad cases of seasickness from being rocked back and forth in the stormy waters.

The Phillies opened the regular season at Boston on April 14 and whipped the Braves twice, allowing just one run in the two games. Alex handcuffed them in the season opener and won, 3–0. Then Erskine Mayer followed with a 7–1 victory. Two days later, Alexander went up against Mathewson at the Polo Grounds — the match-up McGraw usually tried to avoid. Cravath hit a homer and a double, and the Giants' ace lasted just four innings as Philadelphia cruised to another 7–1 victory. The Phillies had won three in a row, and Alex had won two of them. Al Demaree got the start on April 19, and he notched Philadelphia's second shutout of the season, besting the Giants 3–0. Mayer and Chalmers completed the four game sweep of McGraw's talented Giants with 5–2 and 6–1 victories. When the Phillies returned to Baker Bowl for their home opener, they were off to their best start in history, winners of six in a row, and outscoring their opposition, 31–5.

They almost lost the season opener at Baker Bowl, but a five-run eighth inning saved them and provided Alex with his third victory in eight days as the Phillies beat the Braves, 8–4. Eppa Rixey got the start the next day, and he too turned in a brilliant performance as Philadelphia marched to its eighth straight victory, 2–1, over Boston. The defending National League champions had gotten out of the gate with a 4–5 record — and all five losses were to the Phillies. Philadelphia's streak had to end some time, and it did the following day when Mayer got pounded by the Braves, who finally beat the Phillies. The score was 10–2. Alexander, pitching for the fourth time in 12 days, wasn't sharp, but he was good enough to get his fourth win as the Phillies increased their record to 9–1 with a 7–4 win over the Braves on April 26. The Dodgers were the next victims in Baker Bowl, losing 5–2 and 3–0 decisions to Chalmers and Mayer. When Brooklyn came back to win the next two games of the series, 7–4 and 2–1 over Demaree and Rixey, Philadelphia had its first losing streak of the season, two games, but finished April in first place with an 11–3 record. Cincinnati, who had not yet played the Phillies, was second with a 9–6 mark, 2½ games off the pace. They were followed by the Cubs, Braves, Cardinals, Dodgers and Pittsburgh, in that order, with the Giants in an unfamiliar role of being in last place, with a 3–9 record and already being seven games behind the league-leading Phillies.

Moran had instilled in his players a tough work ethic, but the boys still knew how to have fun. Luderus, the first baseman, was a good hitter and in fact had been the club's top slugger until Cravath came along. But Luderus was the "Dr. Strangeglove" of his day in the field, particularly with ground balls that found their way through his legs. Even his manager would kid him about it when times were good. The clubhouse was loose. Killefer would often be hunting down the culprit who put a dead bird in his catcher's mitt. Dode Paskert, the old veteran, liked to spit tobacco juice into an electric fan, spraying anyone who happened to be walking by. When things were not going well, they reacted accordingly. Rixey once ripped his shirt off, with buttons flying, after a particularly tough day on the mound, and Cravath, mired in a slump, threw his uncooperative bat out a clubhouse window. Alexander was unquestionably the star of the team, but he was not immune to mental lapses. Teammates hardly let him forget it the day he tried to steal third, forgetting that the bases were loaded.

Traveling in those days was by train, with the rookies, substitutes and pitchers who were not likely to work tomorrow getting the upper berths. Players found ways of entertaining themselves on the long rides. The 1915 Phillies were partial to crap games. One night, Alexander gave up his diamond ring in a crap game. The next day, Moran banned craps, and the players reverted to the old days and, for the rest of the season, played poker with a 10-cent ante.

The rookie manager was well ahead of his time in trying to think of ways to get the edge on an opponent. More than once, he talked with pitchers on teams who were headed for games with contenders after they played the Phillies. Moran promised to buy the opposing pitchers new suits if they beat their next opponent.

Alex was becoming legendary on many fronts. His sidearm delivery made his pitches seem as if they were coming out of a slingshot. For left-handed and right-handed batters alike, the ball always seemed to be coming at them at an angle. He had the same motion for his fastball and his curve, and the curveball broke late, giving batters little time to adjust. He was also a master at hitting the corners, much like Greg Maddux almost a century later. He wasted no time between pitches. He knew what he wanted to do with each batter, and he did not want to give the batter time to figure it out. It was unusual for one of his games to go more than 90 minutes unless there were extra innings. It is said that manager Moran, who had a cottage in New Jersey, planned trips there on days when Alex was pitching because he knew he could count on an early getaway. Alexander was not a fashion plate on the mound. Throughout his career, his cap looked too small, his uniform looked too big and his shoes were ragged because he never got rid of them. He started the season with a pair of spikes and continued to wear the same ones, regardless of their condition. It was not unusual to see him pitching with shoes that were held together with string and tape.

Alex kept the Phillie machine rolling on May 1 with a 4–2 decision over the Giants, facing Mathewson for the second time in a month. The loss pushed McGraw's crew further into the cellar, eight games behind league-leading Philadelphia. Chalmers lost a 3–2 decision on May 3, and when Alex lost a 4–2 decision two days later, the Phils had their second two-game losing streak of the year and Alexander had his first loss. Alex didn't lose again until May 20, but May was pretty much of a break-even month for the ballclub as a whole. The Phillies dropped into second place on May 29 when the Braves routed Al Demaree and won 9–4. When they beat Chalmers 2–1 the next day, the Phillies had their longest losing streak of the year — four games. As they began play in June, they were 20–15, 1½ games behind the Cubs. Alex couldn't stop the bleeding as Wheezer Dell and the Dodgers beat the Phillies, 5–4, on June 1. Rixey and Baumgartner were losers in a doubleheader with Brooklyn the following day, putting the Phillies at their lowest ebb of the season. They were just two games over .500 at 20–18. After starting the season with an 11–1 run, they had lost 17 of their next 26 games and were beginning to look and play like the second-division Phillies of old.

Alexander's next two starts looked at the time as if they could be the turning point in the season. It didn't turn out that way. On June 5, he came the closest he would ever come in his career to throwing a no-hitter. He held the Cardinals hitless for the first eight innings as the Phillies scrapped to a 3–0 lead. He then retired the first two batters in the ninth inning. The man who stood between Alexander and a piece of baseball history was Artie Butler, a scrappy outfielder with a .241 lifetime batting average who would get 119 hits that year for the Cardinals. One of them was a single that whistled past Alexander's ear on the way to center field to break up the no-hitter. Alex then struck out Bob Bescher to end the game. Four days later, Alexander took a no-hitter into the seventh inning against the Cubs in a game the Phillies eventually won 4–3 in 11 innings. More important, it put Philadelphia back in first place. Alex was 10–3, but the ballclub, except for Alexander, continued to play inconsistently. On June 22, Alexander pitched brilliantly against the Cubs, allowing two hits in the first two innings and then throwing 8⅔ innings of hitless baseball. The game was called because of darkness with the score tied 1–1. On June 26, Alex took a no-hitter into the eighth inning before Brooklyn's Zack Wheat broke it up with a base hit. The Phillies won 4–0. But beyond Alexander's dominance, not much else was happening. On June 28, the Phillies had slipped to fourth place with a mediocre 30–27 record, although they were only 3½ games behind the Cubs.

Alexander's third one-hitter of the season came on July 6 at the Polo Grounds, but there was no suspense since the hit came in the second inning, a double by Fred Merkle. Three days later, Alex threw a two-hitter against the Pirates, and four days after that, he shut out the Cardinals 8–0, vaulting the Phillies back into first place with his ninth consecutive win. The string was broken on July 17 when the Cardinals turned the tables and whitewashed the Phillies and Alexander by a 4–0 score. The Phillies stayed in first place for the remainder of the month, and, for that matter, for the remainder of the season. Their stunning march to the championship was not as dramatic as the Braves' uphill fight of the year before but was nonetheless remarkable for a team that was fighting to stay above .500 in late June.

Alex lost a heartbreaker on August 1 when Heinie Zimmerman of the Cubs hit a sinking line drive on which Possum Whitted tried for a shoestring catch and missed, resulting in an inside-the-park homerun and 2–1 victory for the Cubs. Four days later, Alexander lost 1–0 when Killefer made a wild throw in the bottom of the ninth inning, allowing Pittsburgh to score the only run of the game. On August 8, Gavvy Cravath finally provided some offense to help Alex and, as it turned out, he needed it. The Phillies beat the Reds 14–6 on the strength of four Cravath doubles and eight RBIs. Two of the doubles came with the bases loaded. Cravath, who had become the premier power hitter in baseball, hit 24 home runs for the

Phillies in 1915, more than many teams hit. He held the single-season home run record with the 24 and also held the record for lifetime home runs until Babe Ruth far surpassed both records about a decade later.

On Friday the 13th, Alexander won his 20th game with a 5–3 decision over Dick Rudolph of the Braves. He then was the victim of a Fred Toney shutout on August 17 as the Reds beat the Phillies 2–0 but then won a 7–5 decision against the Cubs on August 21, an 8–0 shutout of the Reds on August 25, and a 4–3 win over the Cardinals on August 30. Headed into the September stretch drive, the Phillies were in first place, three games ahead of Wilbert Robinson's Brooklyn Robins, three and a half ahead of defending champion Boston and eight ahead of Chicago.

The pennant race was still close enough for both Brooklyn and Boston to make a run at it, but it wasn't to be, as the Phillies had found their groove and stayed in it. They were 21–10 in September and 3–1 in October, not giving anyone a chance to overtake them. As hot as they were, their early season ups and downs resulted in a final record of 90–72, the worst record of any National League champion at that time. Alexander threw shutouts on September 2 against the Giants, on September 9 against the Giants again and on September 29 against the Braves. The September 2 shutout, a 2–0 triumph over New York, was against Mathewson, which made it special, and was Alex's 25th win, earning him a $1,000 bonus, which made it even more special. The September 29 shutout was his fourth one-hitter of the year and his 12th shutout of the season. Also, it was his 31st victory. Far more important, the 5–0 victory over Boston clinched the pennant for the Phillies—their first championship and their only one until 1950. Fittingly, Gavvy Cravath provided the offense with a three-run homer. He led the league in homers, walks, RBIs, runs scored and slugging percentage.

Wire services took note of the Phillies' feat with a dispatch published in newspapers throughout the country:

> PHILADELPHIA, September 29 — Old Pat Moran and his cast-off crew can sit back now and rest their wearied limbs in preparation for the world series. After repulsing assault after assault on the part of the fighting Boston and Brooklyn teams, which all season have been trying to drive him from his hard-won leadership, Moran today clinched the National League pennant with a 5–0 victory over the title-holding Braves. Manager Stallings picked his most reliable pitcher, the might little Dick Rudolph, in a valiant endeavor to stave off the inevitable, but the still more mighty Grover Alexander was in form, not to be denied, and from the opening instant of the game was the master of the situation. Alexander's remarkable show of form was a wonderful encouragement to the local fans, for it showed he is quite on edge for the crucial series with the Red Sox. From the start, his speed was dazzling and his control uncanny.[5]

IV—A Pennant Flies in Philadelphia

The wire service dispatch gave a glimpse of how hometown fans celebrated when their team at long last won a championship:

> Not only was the crowd in the grandstand tremendously enthusiastic, but a great wave of enthusiasm swept through the business district of this city today with the announcement flashed on many scoreboards that the Phillies had finally clinched a pennant and would be contenders for the world's baseball title. Old and middle-aged men who have been faithful rooters for the local club for thirty-two years hugged each other and even total strangers on City Hall Plaza, when the electric lights on the scoreboard, which had told the story of the game to a multitude of spectators, flashed Compton's final fruitless swing.[6]

The final National League standings were:

Philadelphia	90–62	.592	—
Boston	83–69	.546	7
Brooklyn	80–72	.526	10
Chicago	73–80	.477	17.5
Pittsburgh	73–81	.474	18
St. Louis	72–81	.470	18.5
Cincinnati	71–83	.461	20
New York	69–83	.453	21

Alex's 31 victories fulfilled a promise he had made four years earlier when Fogel re-signed him after his rookie year. He had won more than one-third of his team's games in a season in which they won the championship. Sportswriters and other baseball enthusiasts marveled at his statistics for the season. Of the 1,274 batters who faced him, only 250 hit safely—a batting average of .196. He gave up only two home runs—one to Honus Wagner in a victory over the Pirates and one to Cy Williams that was the difference in the game in a 2–1 loss to Chicago. He threw 12 shutouts, four one-hitters, three two-hitters, one three-hitter and one four-hitter. His 31–10 record gave him a league-leading winning percentage of .756, and he also led the league in earned run average (1.22), complete games (36), innings pitched 376⅓, and strikeouts (241). Of all the games and all the innings he pitched, it was a 6–3 loss to the Dodgers on September 6 that had some repercussions. Alex let a 3–1 lead slip away and felt some soreness in his pitching arm after the game, not an unusual ailment for a starting pitcher in September but unusual for Alex at any time of the year.

The World Series began Friday, October 8, in Philadelphia. The Red Sox, winners of 101 games in the regular season, were led by a trio of hitters, outfielders Tris Speaker, Harry Hooper and Duffy Lewis, and a pitching staff featuring two 19-game winners, Rube Foster and Ernie Shore; a burly, young left-hander by the name of George Herman "Babe" Ruth, who won 18 games; and Dutch Leonard and Joe Wood, both of whom won 15.

The previous year, when the Braves won the pennant, Red Sox management allowed them to use the Red Sox ballpark for the World Series while Braves field was being renovated. This year, the Braves returned the favor and Boston's home games in the World Series were played at modernized Braves Field.

Hugh Fullerton, a noted sportswriter who would gain prominence five years later with his revelations of the fixing of the 1919 World Series, offered his readers an interesting look at the 1915 series that was about to unfold:

> If you took the figures and discovered that the Boston Red Sox have five of the leading pitchers of the American League and four second-string men, any one of whom is above average in ability; if you discovered that among these five stars, four hit .279, .286, .308 and .320 and help with their games; if you discovered that three of these pitchers are great fielders and likely to help the infield, what would you think? Next, if you found that the opposing staff consisted of one great pitcher, an erratic, uncertain genius and four fair pitchers, you'd begin to feel sorry for that club. Then, if you remembered that the club with the strong pitchers has a stronger hitting team and a stronger fielding team to back them up, and that there is not much difference in the catching, you'd say, "Shucks, the Phillies haven't a chance. Right here is where the oddity of the American game and the uncertainty of a world series arises. A man with a sharp, strong ice pick can cut just as much ice as the fellow with the five strong, sharp ice picks unless his one pick wears out. If the Phillies and Red Sox were to play 22 games a season in the same league, the Red Sox would beat them in two-thirds or more of those games. But whether the Red Sox can beat them four out of seven games in the series is another matter.... For the purposes of this series, the Philadelphia pitching staff is better. There are two questions: Will Moran know how to use his one great ice pick, and will that ice pick break?[7]

The "great ice pick," of course, was Grover Cleveland Alexander.

The first game was nearly cancelled because of an all-night rain and was played on a soggy field with Shore pitching for Boston and Alexander taking the mound for the Phillies. The right field wall was even shorter than usual because Baker had installed 400 temporary bleacher seats in right-center field. The short fence didn't matter in this game. A soggy infield proved to be the difference. A great pitchers' duel emerged, as expected, and the teams battled to a 1–1 tie until the bottom of the eighth inning. The Phillies scraped together two runs without hitting the ball hard at any time in the inning. Milt Stock walked. Davy Bancroft hit a ground ball to short that should have been a double play. But when Boston's shortstop Everett Scott didn't cover second in time — one writer said he stood "transfixed"— Stock was safe and Scott's throw to first was too late to get the speedy Bancroft. When Paskert walked, the bases were loaded without the benefit of a ball being hit out of the infield. Gavvy Cravath grounded out, but the lead run scored. Then Luderus hit a ball to deep short and beat it out, driving in the second run of the inning. Shore allowed just three hits for the game, all in the rain-soaked infield, but the Phillies and Alexander escaped with a 3–1 victory. Ruth pinch-hit in the ninth inning and grounded out. It was his only appearance in the series. The Associated Press reported that Alexander was "plainly nervous" in the early innings of the game but by the end outpitched Shore. Overall, however, the AP wrote off the game as a "freak episode in World Series baseball."

Grover Cleveland Alexander matched up against Ernie Shore of the Red Sox in the 1915 World Series. The Red Sox won the series, four games to one. Alexander got the lone Phillie win. Philadelphia didn't win another World Series game until 1980 (National Baseball Hall of Fame Library, Cooperstown, N.Y.).

The next day, Foster of the Red Sox was matched up against Mayer, the Phillies' 21-game winner, and quite a match-up it was. President Woodrow Wilson threw out the first ball and then watched as Foster threw a three-hitter and drove in the winning run in the ninth inning as Boston won 2–1, evening the series at one game apiece. The Red Sox scored a run in the first inning, aided by an error on Eddie Burns, the Phillies reserve catcher who was playing because Killefer was injured. Luderus and Cravath, Philadelphia's two best power hitters, did what they got paid to do and hit back-to-back doubles in the fifth inning to tie the game. Foster singled home the go-ahead run in the top of the ninth and then retired the Phillies in order to preserve a 2–1 victory.

Game three shifted to Boston, after a mandatory off-day on Sunday because of "blue laws" in both cities. A World Series record crowd of 42,300 saw another classic battle of pitchers. Alex took the mound again for the Phillies, this time taking on Dutch Leonard. Again the two teams scratched to a 1–1 tie until Duffy Lewis singled home Harry Hooper in the bottom of the ninth inning, the second consecutive game in which Boston won, 2–1, in its final at-bat. Alex gave up just six hits, three of them to Lewis, but the day belonged to Leonard, who threw a three-hitter and retired the last 20 Phillie batters.

The Associated Press, sparing no hyperbole, described the game-winning hit this way. "Alexander, stout of heart, fighting as he never fought before, calling upon all the reserve cunning of his strong arm, put into his first pitch all the wile he could command and sent the sphere speeding on its way. Lewis met the ball with a smashing crack. It flashed over second base and Hooper raced across the plate with a historic run."[8]

Philadelphia was in a hole, down two games to one despite allowing just five runs in three games. In game four, Moran passed over Demaree, a 14-game winner, and Rixey, winner of 11 regular season games, and instead handed the ball to Chalmers, the once promising rookie who was just 8–9 during the regular season. His opponent was the mighty Shore, loser to Alexander in game one. Again the teams scratched for whatever they could get, and again the outcome was the same. Boston won 2–1. In this one, the Red Sox scored runs in the third and sixth innings. Shore lost his shutout when Cravath tripled home the Phils' only run in the eighth.

Philadelphia was now down three games to one, but their fortunes were even worse than those statistics showed — because Alexander, the warhorse, the man who constantly answered the call and carried the team on his back for much of the season, could not answer the call for the fifth game. His arm hurt too much. Alex said later the soreness he felt after the September 6 loss to the Dodgers was due to a wrenched shoulder. He hid the pain as long as he could. It caught up with him in the fifth game of the World Series. If a sixth or seventh game were necessary, he might be able to go. But the pain was too great on this day, and Moran turned to Mayer, his other ace. Playing once again in Baker Bowl, the Phillies gave their fans hope, scoring two runs in the first inning off Foster. Moran, the manager who had transformed the lowly Phillies into champions, left himself wide open for unabashed second-guessing after Philadelphia botched a chance to break the game open in the first inning. Having scored two runs already, Cravath, the home run champion of baseball, came to the plate with the bases loaded. Moran, apparently trying to catch the Red Sox napping, ordered a suicide squeeze bunt. Cravath bunted the ball in front of the plate and Boston turned it into an easy double play. The Red Sox chipped away, scoring single runs in the second and third innings to tie the game. Philadelphia got two more in the fourth off Foster on a Luderus home run, but that's all they would get. Boston scored two in the eighth and one in the ninth, all of them the result of owner Baker's decision to put temporary bleachers in. Lewis hit a two-run homer in the eighth when his line drive hit bounced into the bleachers. In those days, that constituted a home run. When Harry Hooper did the same thing in the ninth inning for a solo shot, the Red Sox had a 5–4 lead. Philadelphia went down meekly in the bottom of the ninth. Boston won the game 5–4 and the series four games to one. Four of the games had been decided by one run, and in three of them, the Red Sox pushed across the game winner in their final at bat.

The defeated Phillies availed themselves of the kegs of beer that had been brought into the locker room for them in anticipation of victory. They got drunk, trashed the clubhouse and went their separate ways. As the story goes, Killefer woke up somewhere near Altoona.

The Phillie fans, not known for their patience and understanding then or now, cast blame on manager Moran for not having Cravath swing away with the bases loaded in the final game, and on owner Baker for putting in the cheap seats that resulted in Boston's homers in the seventh game. The players were not upset with either. They had seen Moran pull off miracles too many times during the regular season to doubt him when the chips were down. And although the ploy worked against them on the field, Baker's efforts to increase attendance put a few more dollars in his players' pockets, even though they were losers' shares. They knew also that a healthy Alexander might have made a big difference in the outcome.

Alex made an impression on the Red Sox. Only Lewis really solved him, getting five hits in eight at bats off him. Lewis said afterwards, "I was lucky against Alexander. He was a great pitcher, one of the best. I was just lucky the ball was going through the slot."[9]

Ernie Shore knew a great pitcher when he saw one, but he was also impressed with Alex's easy-going style even under World Series pressure. "He seemed utterly delighted by the most foolish antics or the merest jokes, giving out an easy, unforced laughter like a boy at a circus," said Shore. "Great pitcher or not, he was still a country boy pure and fresh, and all our fellows thought he was tops, even though we knew he was going to stand us on our heads."[10]

Alexander was impressed not only by Boston's pitching and hitting, but by their defense as well. "They had the greatest defensive team I ever saw, I believe," said Alex. "In the outfield were Lewis, Speaker and Hooper, all great fielders. Why it seemed you just couldn't get a hit out there." Alex didn't make any excuses, acknowledging that the Phillies lost to a great ballclub. But he said he thought the loss of his catcher and his buddy, Killefer, made a difference.

In a magazine article in 1916, Alexander elaborated on how the injury on September 6 in Brooklyn came back to haunt him in the World Series. The Phillies were opening a three-game series with the Dodgers with a Labor Day doubleheader. Alexander worked the first game and entered the eighth inning with a two-run lead. He got the first batter out on one pitch. "But then something happened," he wrote.

> I have never been able to understand it but, in some way, I strained my shoulder and the muscles in my back. I had the bad habit of getting a blister on my middle finger from throwing the ball. I remember I had a blister on that finger on Labor Day and it bothered me considerably. A ballplayer doesn't pay much attention to minor injuries, but try as he will, a twirler can hardly get the same result from his pitching hand when his fingers are decidedly sore than he can when they are in perfect trim. I know that I unconsciously tried to humor that blistered finger and in doing so no doubt brought the muscles of my back into play in an unusual manner, so that in pitching a fastball to the next man up, I strained my shoulder. I immediately felt it and I couldn't seem to control the ball so well. When I put forth all my strength and tried to get the ball over the plate, it would go outside. When I cut down a little on the stuff I was serving up, the Brooklyn batters would hit me.

The Dodgers scored five runs and won the game.

Alexander said he didn't tell Moran or any of his teammates about the wrenched shoulder in the Labor Day game for a long time afterward. He continued to pitch, however, until the pain was just too great and he had to miss his start in the fifth game of the World Series.

Alexander wrote: "The pitcher knows when he is not right and it is a very disconcerting experience to find yourself, at the critical moment you have been thinking about for months, facing a pennant-winning team with the world's championship at stake, where every eye is watching you, and to know in your own mind that you are not in your best form, not in a position to realize what is expected of you.

"I shall always think of the World Series of 1915 as a peculiar personal disappointment in that I was unable, through lack of condition, to live up to the expectations of my friends."

A week after the World Series was over, Alexander was asked by an interviewer how he developed such a great curveball. He said as a youngster he bought a "How to Curve a Baseball" book and practiced with some of his boyhood chums serving as catchers. When he couldn't find a catcher, he said he'd draw a circle on the side of a carriage house and try to hit it. His problem, he said, was that he couldn't get the ball to curve. He threw the book in the trash barrel but later retrieved it and kept practicing. Finally, he saw the ball bend when he threw it. And with practice, he got better and better.

"A boy or man must have strong wrists to throw curves," he said. "The forearm soon develops and at last a pitcher can go through a hard game and shoot up half curves and not feel the slightest pain in his wrist, forearm, biceps or shoulder. I mix the curves so as to distribute the work among the different muscles of the arm, shoulder and back."[11]

Billy Evans, the great American League umpire, saw Alex pitch for the first time in the World Series and was not as impressed as he thought he'd be. Evans said maybe he had heard so much about the Philadelphia star that nothing Alexander did would have lived up to his reputation. But Evans, who had seen Walter Johnson pitch many times, concluded Johnson was faster. Also, said Evans, Alexander may have felt the pressure of knowing he was the Phillies' only hope of winning the series, a point Hugh Fullerton made in his pre-series analysis.

It may have been any and all of that. Then again, it may just have been a sore arm.

• CHAPTER V •

Nobody Does It Better

"I expect to be just as good as ever."
— Grover Cleveland Alexander

As the World Series excitement eased into the background, one big question surfaced that focused on the immediate future of the Philadelphia Phillies. Was Grover Cleveland Alexander's arm injury serious enough to lessen his effectiveness in 1916 or shorten his career altogether? Alexander provided his own answer when he returned from a hunting trip in Nebraska in January 1916 — his typical way of staying in shape — and wrote a letter to a sportswriter that he was sure would be published, telling everyone he was ready to play.

> Let me tell you that I was glad to hear that Pat had signed for three years and that the baseball war is over.[1] Have just returned from a month's hunting. I did not go very far with the All-Star tourists at the close of last season as I had a pretty hard season during the pennant race and felt that I needed a rest. All the talk about my arm being sore is all wrong. I was just tired from pitching through the season and I guess my arm had done about all it could do, and that is all.
>
> I will be on hand again when the bell rings in April and I expect to be just as good as ever. I took a month's trip into Texas for a hunt and certainly did have a fine time.[2] I hunted at Ferndale Lake and it is a swell place to visit, not only for the good hunting but for the way the people of that place treat you, the family of Robert Huey making it just like home for me. Killifer [sic] and Dugey were there with me and we enjoyed it so much that we will go back again next fall. I had planned to come to Philadelphia after the holidays but my father's health is poor and I have decided to stay here until it is time to go South with the Phillies. Hope the fans in old Philly are well and have had a good winter.[3]

Alex had gone on the Bancroft tour, as he had the year before, but this year he was hit hard in his first few appearances and was worried that he would reinjure his arm. So, with the understanding of his teammates, he left early and went to San Francisco, where he hooked up with his fellow bachelor buddy Killefer for a few nights out on the town. From there, he went to Hot Springs, Arkansas, to enjoy a few days in the spas before getting ready to report for spring training in St. Petersburg. He was about to embark on his greatest season — unthinkable at the time after the year he had just experienced — but the stats he posted in 1916 were not only personal highs. They have not been matched by anyone since then.

As teams made their way north from spring training, the Phillies hooked up with the Washington Senators for an exhibition game on April 16 in the nation's capital. Everything else in the nation seemed far less important. Here's why, as described by Harry Carr, writing for the Washington Bureau of the *Los Angeles Times:* "The Senate debate on free sugar played to empty benches today. Walter Johnson and Grover Cleveland Alexander, the two greatest baseball pitchers in the world, were having a duel." Washington won 2–1 with Johnson pitching three innings, one more than Alexander.

In his prime, nobody had better control than Grover Cleveland Alexander. In 1916, he threw 16 shutouts and had 90 for his career. In 1923, he walked just 30 batters in 305 innings and had a career strikeout-to-walk ratio of better than 2-to-1 (National Baseball Hall of Fame Library, Cooperstown, N.Y.).

The Phillies were looked on as serious contenders to repeat as champions. Their lineup was virtually the same as it had been, and Rixey was ready now to become a 20-game winner — on his way to a career that would see him win 266 games and be the winningest left-hander in the National League until Warren Spahn came along, and later, Steve Carlton. Demaree, now an established veteran, had his best year, winning 19. Boston, with the "Miracle Braves" of 1914 still within memory, was expected to contend, but its outstanding pitcher, Bill James, winner of 26 in 1914, never had another season like that. Consequently, neither did the Braves. This would be the year that Wilbert Robinson's Brooklyn ballclub would finally make its mark. For Robinson, winning a title and dethroning the Phillies would not carry nearly the satisfaction attained by overtaking McGraw's Giants. New York had a mystifying year. The Giants won 17 in a row in one stretch and 26 in a row in another, which remains the major league record for consecutive wins. Yet the Giants finished fourth.

The Phillies and Alexander started 1916 with a 5–4 win over the Giants at Baker Bowl. Alex threw his first shutout in his next start, beating Dick Rudolph and the Braves 4–0. The Dodgers beat him 6–3 on April 26, breaking a Phillie five-game winning streak. Three days later, Alex won a 5–2 decision over Boston. The Phillies finished April in first place with a 7–3 record. Alexander was 3–1.

In May, Alex had a remarkable month. On May 3, he shut out the Braves 3–0 at Braves Field. On May 8, it was the Phillies who went scoreless as Wheezer Dell blanked them 2–0 with Alex taking the loss. On May 13, Alexander shut out the Reds 5–0 at Crosley Field. It was the Phillies' second straight win after a five-game losing streak had plunged them into fourth place. Five days later, Alex threw yet another shutout, blanking the Pirates 3–0 at Forbes Field. It was Philadelphia's sixth straight win and moved them into second place, a game behind Brooklyn. When Alex beat the Cubs 5–3 at Wrigley Field on May 22, it was the first game he had pitched all month that didn't involve a shutout. Four days later, Gavvy Cravath threw Casey Stengel out at the plate, snuffing Brooklyn's chance to score as Alexander threw his fourth shutout of the month in a 1–0 victory. On May 30, Demaree beat the Giants 5–1, ending New York's winning streak at 17. A highlight of the game was Killefer nailing Bill McKechnie three times trying to steal. The Giants were 2–13 when they started their winning streak and finished the month at 21–14, in second place, a game and a half behind Brooklyn. The Phillies were at 20–17, three and a half games out. Not much more could have been expected of Alex. He was 5–1 for the month with four shutouts, three of them in succession. His only loss was the 2–0 shutout to Brooklyn. The Phillies were 8–2 with Alexander in the game and 12–15 when he wasn't in there.

On June 3, Alex continued his mastery of National League hitters with another shutout, his fifth in his last seven starts, in a 2–0 win over St. Louis. This one had some drama. Dode Paskert made a leaping catch at the wall to rob the Cardinals' Frank Snyder of a home run. Nine days later, Alexander took a shutout into the ninth inning against the Pirates at Baker Bowl. Pittsburgh's only run came when Honus Wagner hit a line drive off Alex's ankle, a painful RBI single. But the Phillies won, 2–1, and were in second place, two games behind Brooklyn. On June 15, Alex won another 2–1 decision, this one over Cincinnati. It was Philadelphia's fourth straight win, but they remained in second place, still two games behind Wilbert Robinson's Brooklyn club. Al Demaree pitched well but lost 1–0 to the Reds the next day. Brooklyn won, pushing its lead over the Phillies to three games as Philadelphia headed to Ebbets Field for a big five-game series.

They gained a game on June 19 with Alex winning 3–2, but the day was a somber one for the Phillies. John Dodge, who had been a utility player for Philadelphia in 1912 and 1913, died in a Mobile, Alabama, hospital at the age of 28, the victim of a beaning the day before. Dodge, playing for Mobile in the Southern League, was struck in the head by a pitch thrown by Tom "Shotgun" Rogers of Nashville. A sidelight to the tragedy is that Rogers, though more than likely grief-stricken by the accidental death, threw five consecutive shutouts after the incident, earning him a trip to the big leagues, where he played sparingly for four years for the Philadelphia A's. The Phillies beat the Robins in a doubleheader on June 20, with Rixey and Demaree picking up fairly easy victories, 7–4 and 9–3. Moran's troops had done exactly what they wanted to do. They had won three in a row from Brooklyn and were now one game out with two more games to play in the series. But the next day, Brooklyn turned the tables and took two from the Phillies with Chief Bender and George McQuillan taking the losses. Philadelphia left town having taken the series, three games to two. The ballclub was in its familiar position of being in second place, two games behind the Robins. When Alex beat the Braves, 2–1, on June 23, the win, coupled with a Brooklyn loss, brought the Phillies once again to within a game of Brooklyn. But a five-game losing streak crippled them, with Alex absorbing one of the losses, a 3–0 decision to Boston. On June 30, Alexander lost again, 4–3, to the Giants, the first time he'd lost two straight games all year. As the teams entered July, Brooklyn held a four-game lead over the second place Phillies. Alex had another great month in June. He won five, lost two and allowed two runs or less in five of his seven starts. He was 13–4 for the year. The Phillies were 33–28.

On July 3, Alex lost his third straight game, this one a 5–1 decision to Boston, and the Phillies slipped into third place for one day. He broke his losing streak four days later with his seventh shutout of the season. Once again, Paskert came to his rescue, this time with two leaping catches at the wall, robbing Bob Bescher twice of home runs. They were significant catches because the final score was 1–0. The Phillies traveled to Wrigley Field, where Alex notched another 2–1 victory on July 11, his fourth win by that margin since June 1. His eighth and ninth shutouts came against the Pirates on July 15 and against the Reds on July 20 by scores of 4–0 and 6–0. In the victory over Cincinnati, Alex got as many hits as he allowed, two, and both of his were doubles. He ended the month with victories over the Reds and Pirates, 8–1 and 7–1, and then lost a 5–2 decision to the Cubs. He was 19–6. Despite Alexander's sensational year, the Phillies fell into a syndrome of playing .500 in the last half of July and found themselves in third place, four and a half games behind Brooklyn and a half-game behind the surprising Boston Braves. Without Alex's contributions, the ballclub was 30–32.

On August 2, the Phillies won a great one. They beat the Cubs 1–0 but it took Alexander 12 innings to get his 20th win and his 10th shutout of the season. The game did not lack dramatics. In the top of the 12th inning, Alexander found himself with a man on third and two out. He intentionally walked the next two batters and then fanned Mike Pendergast, his mound opponent, to end the inning. In the bottom of the 12th, Bill Killefer scored the winning run by sneaking home from third base while the Cubs argued a call at third without calling time out. Alexander's 20th win gave him more victories than the Philadelphia A's in the American League, who had managed just 19 wins for the season.

In his next start, Alex got two hits, but the Phillies didn't score and lost to the Cardinals, 2–0, falling five games behind Brooklyn. On August 9, in a doubleheader split with Cincinnati, Alexander threw a three-hit shutout in the first game for his 21st win and 11th shutout. Bender got hit hard in the second game as the Phillies lost, 8–7. Philadelphia put together a six-game winning streak with Alex throwing another shutout against the Giants, 8–0, on August 14. His third shutout in a row and his 13th of the year came on August 18, a 3–0 victory over the Reds. The winning streak ended on August 21 when Alex lost a 6–3 decision in the first game of a doubleheader to Pittsburgh. The Pirates beat Demaree 2–1 in the nightcap and were 3½ game behind the Robins. Alexander finished the month by polishing off Lee Meadows and the Cardinals 7–2 on August 24 and then beat the Cubs 8–2 on August 28. When Jimmy Lavender of the Cubs beat Demaree 2–0 to end the month, the Phillies were 4½ back and were in third place behind Brooklyn and Boston while holding a 67–49 record. Alexander was 25–8 and heading for his second straight 30-win season.

The Phillies started September like a team intent on defending its championship. They swept a five-game series with Brooklyn, knocking the Robins temporarily out of first place, where Boston replaced them. Philadelphia was one game out. The month started with the Phillies blanking Brooklyn twice, and they were 20 games above .500 for the first time all year with a record of 69–49. Alexander and Rixey threw the shutouts. For Alex, it was his 14th shutout of the season, setting a major league record. The loser was Jack Coombs, and the irony was that Coombs held the record for most shutouts. He threw 13 of them for the Philadelphia A's in 1910. The Phillies moved on to Boston and swept the Braves in a three-game series to vault into first place for the first time since April 29. By the time they left town on September 7, they had won eight in a row and Alexander had won his 27th, a 4–2 win over the Braves. They followed the winning streak with a four-game losing streak that knocked them out of first place. Among the defeats was Alex losing to the Giants 9–3 on September 8, but he came back and beat Meadows and the Cardinals again 4–3 on September 12. When Demaree beat the Cardinals the next day, Philadelphia occupied the top spot for another 24 hours. Alex was headed for his 15th shutout against the Cubs on September 16, but the Cubs scored three runs when Joe Tinker got a hit and Luderus botched a ground ball that could have turned into a double play. Still, Alexander survived to win 6–3. In his next start, he was on the short end of a 2–0 loss to the Cubs.

Time was running out for the Phillies, and Moran knew his best chance was with Alex. So on September 23 at Baker Bowl, he started his ace in both games of a doubleheader against lowly Cincinnati, which was in danger of losing 100 games. Alexander won them both, 7–3 and 4–0. The shutout in the nightcap was his 15th of the season. He made short work of the Reds. The game lasted 58 minutes. By September 28, the Phillies had won five in a row and had climbed back into first place in a race to the finish that now included McGraw's Giants, Brooklyn, Boston and Philadelphia. Alexander beat the Dodgers 8–4 on September 28. Moran didn't want to chance having Alex pitch a doubleheader just two days later, so he threw Rixey in the first game and Eppa stymied the Dodgers 7–2. Alex worked game two and was hit harder than he had been in any game all year. He surrendered 11 hits, including a round-tripper to Casey Stengel. Stengel said many years later that getting a homer off of Alexander was one of the highlights of his playing career. On October 2, Philadelphia played yet another doubleheader, and Alex beat Brooklyn in the first game, 2–0, his 16th shutout of the season and 33rd victory. But Milt Stock, playing short for the injured Bancroft, made an error in game two that led to a Brooklyn rally and a 4–2 Robins win. A doubleheader loss the following day to the Braves knocked the Phillies out of the race.

Meanwhile, the Giants won 26 straight games, still the major league record, from September 7 through September 30 and then lost four out of their last five games, including three out of four to the champion Brooklyn Robins. Their lackluster play during the last week of the season so infuriated manager McGraw that he left the ballpark in the middle of an October 2 game against the Robins, saying his players weren't trying hard enough. He was so furious that he didn't show up for the final two games of the year. The players of course denied the allegation, saying they were just in a letdown after winning 26 straight. What lent a tinge of credibility to the situation is that the Giants were out of the race and were in a position to be spoilers. Many of the Giant players still had a strong friendship with Uncle Wilbert Robinson, a former coach with the Giants who left after having a falling-out with McGraw and subsequently got a job managing Brooklyn. If the Giants had swept the Robins, Philadelphia might have edged into first place ahead of Robinson and his Brooklyn club.

McGraw's rantings did not go unheard by Moran of the Phillies, whose team finished just two and half games out. Did the Giants let up against the Robins as their manager claimed? Moran demanded an investigation by the National League. "It's one of the rawest things I've ever seen or heard of in my long career in baseball," he said. "The Giants play their heads off against us, and when they play the Dodgers, they just don't give a damn. When McGraw walks out on his own ballgame, you know something stinks."

This was different from Horace Fogel's mindless ramblings at the end of the 1911 season. This was McGraw, one of the pillars of major league baseball, not a buffoon like Fogel. National League President John K. Tener, a former governor of Pennsylvania, took a cursory look at the situation, but when he interviewed McGraw after the season, the Giant manager had cooled down, and his comments were not nearly as accusatory as they had been. The investigation ended quickly and quietly with no disciplinary actions taken. After the wild finish, the final National League standings were:

Brooklyn	94–60	.610	—
Philadelphia	91–62	.594	2.5
Boston	89–63	.585	4
New York	86–66	.565	7
Chicago	67–86	.437	26.5
Pittsburgh	65–89	.422	29
Cincinnati	60–93	.392	33.5
St. Louis	60–93	.392	33.5

Alexander once more had more than one-third of his team's wins, just as he had in 1915. He had a 33–12 record with 389 innings pitched, 38 complete games, a 1.55 earned run average and 16 shutouts. He was 11–1 in one-run decisions. He came close to having 22 shutouts because on June 12, June 15, June 23 and July 11, he won 2–1 ballgames and on July 23 and July 26 gave up just a single run in 8–1 and 7–1 victories.[4] Though he pitched in cozy Baker Bowl, he actually had a better record at home, 17–6, than on the road, 16–6.

A look at Alex's 16 shutouts:

April 18 — Home — Beat Boston 4–0
May 3 — Away — Beat Boston 3–0
May 13 — Away — Beat Cincinnati 5–0
May 18 — Away — Beat Pittsburgh 3–0
May 26 — Home — Beat Brooklyn 1–0
June 3 — Home — Beat St. Louis 2–0
July 7 — Away — Beat St. Louis 1–0
July 15 — Away — Beat Pittsburgh 4–0
July 20 — Away — Beat Cincinnati 6–0
August 2 — Home — Beat Chicago 1–0
August 9 — Home — Beat Cincinnati 1–0
August 14 — Home — Beat New York 8–0
August 18 — Away — Beat Cincinnati 3–0
September 1 — Home — Beat Brooklyn 3–0
September 23 — Home — Beat Cincinnati 4–0
October 2 — Home — Beat Boston 2–0

Barnstorming tours, such as those put on by Frank Bancroft, were now prohibited, so Alex went back to his beloved Nebraska to hunt and relax and hunt some more — and to contemplate what he thought his services should be worth to the Phillies next year. Before long, he was asked to pitch for a Pittsburg, Kansas, touring team that was in a league actively seeking major leaguers to bolster its roster. The biggest game of the off-season occurred when the Pittsburg crew met up with a team from Webb City, Missouri, that had a pitcher from nearby Coffeyville, Kansas — Walter Johnson. Webb City won the game 3–2, but fans went away knowing they had seen two of the three greatest pitchers of all time. The third was Christy Mathewson, and as Alexander approached the 1917 season, he had his sights on a record held only by the great Giant pitcher — three consecutive 30-win seasons. Johnson in the American League would retire with more wins (406) than either Mathewson or Alexander, but he never won 30 games three years in a row.

Alexander was intent on getting paid in accordance with being one of the game's best. He sought a three-year contract at $15,000 a year. Phillies owner William Baker told the press he was "astonished" at Alexander's greed and offered Alex a one-year contract for $8,000. Meanwhile, Killefer, who had an injury-riddled year, was offered a contract with a $2,000 pay cut, which he rejected. In a move emulated by Dodger pitching stars Don Drysdale and Sandy Koufax almost 50 years later, Alex and "his catcher" staged a joint holdout.[5] As of January 27, 1917, with little more than a month until spring training, Philadelphia's battery mates held fast to their demands.

By February 17, there was still no deal. Baker's offer to Alexander was $7,000 a year and a $1,000 bonus if he won 25 games. Alexander went to Philadelphia to try to settle the matter. After three days of talks, Alex told the press, "Everything's as dark as the weather." Baker said Alexander had not budged from his demand of $15,000 a year. Baker had upped his ante to $10,000. "I think that is all we can afford to pay," said the owner. "He would not even consider a two-year contract at these terms so I made no further attempt to talk business with him."

In the meantime, Bill Pickens, owner of a traveling circus, got hold of Alex and offered him $1,000 a week for 35 weeks to join the circus. He would have to entertain the crowd with some offbeat baseball stunts. Also, he would pitch to any paying customer willing to face him with bat in hand, with an offer of $50 to anyone who got a hit off him. The fact that Alexander would even consider being a sideshow for a circus for huge money was an indication of how much his life was worth to others and of his own self-worth. Many years after his retirement, he would work for a carnival for next to nothing, an indication of how much his worth and self-worth had dropped.

The plot got muddier when Billy Archer, a Cubs catcher who was unsigned, said he was considering hooking up with the circus to be Alexander's battery mate. The whole deal, of course, hinged on Alex. Pickens, an agent for the circus, sent a telegram to Alexander on February 20 asking him if he was interested. Alex wired back, asking for specific terms. Pickens then telephoned Alexander to talk business. He later described the length of the talk by saying it was a $12 phone call.

Baker and Alexander met again and, after much figurative gnashing of teeth by both men, they reached agreement. Alexander would get $12,500 a year plus bonuses that would probably put him close to the $15,000 he demanded. He would go into the 1917 season as the highest paid pitcher in National League history. Mathewson, when at his peak with the Giants, earned $10,000. It was a one-year contract. Killefer, who hit .217 in 1916, signed for an undisclosed amount but without doubt a meager sum compared to the man he handled on the mound.

As the 1917 season approached, the Phillies made few personnel changes. They traded Al Demaree to the Cubs in exchange for pitcher Jimmy Lavender but made no other major deals. The ballclub, which had finished first and a close second under Moran's guidance, was nonetheless getting older. Paskert was still patrolling center field as he had been since 1911. Bancroft was starting his third year of a Hall of Fame career at shortstop. Stock was also starting his third year at third base. Luderus was at first base, where he had been since 1911. Cravath was in right field for the sixth straight year.

Whitted was still in left field, his main assignment since 1915. Niehoff was starting his fourth year at second base. And Reindeer Bill Killefer was once again behind the plate, his station since 1912. Philadelphia was essentially the same team that won the 1915 championship, and they had no reason to believe they couldn't do it again in 1917. They had no idea when they went to spring training that this season would mark the end of an era. Problems were developing that they had no control over. At home, their owner was running out of money. Abroad, a world war was blazing and America was about to jump in.

The Phillies opened the season with Alexander on the mound, as usual, and beat the Dodgers, 6–5, at Ebbets Field. Rixey won the next day in an 11–3 rout, and it appeared that Philadelphia was off and running. But they went to Boston and were swept by the Braves with Alex absorbing a 3–1 loss in the opener. They split the next two games and then lost three more in a row. After just nine games, the Phillies were 3–6, in sixth place and already 4½ games out of first — all of this after a 2–0 start to the season. On April 27, Lavender made his first start and disposed of Giants 5–1 at Baker Bowl. That was the start of a five-game winning streak that pushed the Phillies back over the .500 mark. They were right at .500 with a 6–6 record at the end of April. Alex was 3–2 — not an auspicious start for a man who had won more than 30 games two years in a row and had demanded big bucks or he might join a circus.

He notched his first shutout of the year on May 10, beating his old rival Lee Meadows and the St. Louis Cardinals 1–0. On May 14, he won again, 3–2 over the Pirates. Four days later he surrendered just a single run again in beating the Cubs 3–1 and breaking Chicago's 10-game winning streak. On May 23, Alex got more hits than he gave up. He had two singles and a home run while allowing the Reds just two hits in a 5–1 victory. The win was the sixth in a row for Philadelphia, which had righted its ship in May and was now in first place. Alex continued his string of allowing just one run on May 30 in 5–1 victory over the Giants. As the ballclub entered June, it had crept back into second place, 1½ games behind the Giants, and had a 15–8 mark for the month. Alex was now 8–2 with a six-game winning streak.

On June 2, Alexander allowed just one run for the fourth consecutive game, beating Burleigh Grimes and the Pirates at Forbes Field 9–1 to run his personal winning streak to seven games. On June 6 he hit two triples and shut out the Cubs 4–0. The losing pitcher was Tom Seaton, the old Phillie who bolted to the Federal League in 1914 and was now working for the Cubs. Alexander was sharp again four days later, beating the Cardinals 4–1, and on June 13, beating Cincinnati 3–2. The Reds stopped his winning streak at eight with a 5–4 win on June 17. Philadelphia remained in a seesaw battle with the Giants for first place, and by the end of the month, the Phillies were a solid 37–24, trailing New York by 1½ games. Alex was 12–5.

Philadelphia's season unraveled in July. The Phillies began the month by losing two games to the Dodgers. After splitting a July 4 doubleheader with the Braves, they lost four in a row. Alexander then shut out the Cubs 7–0 but Philadelphia lost the next two games. They remained in second place but had fallen seven games behind the Giants. It got worse. After Alex beat Meadows and the Cardinals again on July 20, the Phillies lost six more in a row, plummeting into fourth place, 11½ games behind New York. They were never in serious contention again, although they ended the month with a four-game winning streak, including a July 31 victory in which Alex once again shut out Meadows and the Cardinals, this time 6–0. In a month that saw Philadelphia win only nine games Alexander won seven of them and had a 19–6 record for a ballclub that was 46–40.

In August, the Phillies still couldn't get anything going. They won two, then lost two, then won two more and lost two more, then won three and lost two. By August 15, they were 7–6 for the month, 53–46 for the year, and while they kept their hold on second place, they were now 13 games behind the Giants. They swept back-to-back doubleheaders from the Pirates at Baker Bowl and then won a fifth straight, also from the Pirates with Alexander picking up his 22nd win. After splitting the next four games, Philadelphia reeled off six straight wins, with Alex getting another shutout in one of them, but on August 29, Meadows of the Cardinals finally got the best of his old Philadelphia nemesis, beating Alexander 4–3. Philadelphia had made a little bit of a run but trailed the Giants by nine games going into September.

Moran, a never-say-die manager who tried to press that attitude into his players, rolled the dice on September 3, as he had about a year before, and had Alex pitch both games of a doubleheader against Brooklyn. The result—his 24th and 25th victories. Milt Stock's homer was all he needed in game one, a 2–0 victory. In the second game, Dode Paskert, the veteran, hit a bases-loaded triple to break the game open on the way to a 9–3 victory. New York won its game, so the Phils gained only a half-game, trailing the Giants now by 8½. Between then and the end of the season, they never got closer than eight games out.

On October 2, with nothing at stake but pride, the Phillies took on the champion Giants at Baker Bowl. After Rixey got cuffed for his 21st loss in game one, 5–2, Alexander came back and won the nightcap, 8–2, over his former teammate Demaree. It was Alex's 30th win of the year, the third year in a row he won 30 or more games, a feat matched in baseball history only by Christy Mathewson.

The Phillies finished second again, this time with an 87–65 record. Pitching wasn't the problem. The four starters gave up an average of less than three runs a game. Alex was 30–13 with a 1.83 earned run average. Rixey won 16 but, with little offensive support, lost 21 even though his earned run average was just 2.27. Rounding out the staff were Oeschger, 15–14 with a 2.75 ERA and Mayer, 11–6 with a 2.76 earned run average. Philadelphia simply didn't get enough clutch hits. Luderus hit .261, down from .281 in 1916 and .315 in the 1915 pennant year. Stock was down to .264, 17 points below what he hit in 1916, his first full season with the club. Paskert hit .251, compared to .279 in 1916. Cravath, who hit 24 home runs and drove in 115 in 1915, had 12 home runs and 83 RBIs in 1917.

The biggest surprise of all was one that no one could have foreseen at season's end. Alex's 30th win, the 8–2 decision over Demaree and the Giants on October 2, was his last victory in a Philadelphia uniform and brought to an end a three-year run that has been unmatched in baseball history since then. In that three-year span, he led the league in wins three times, in earned run average three times, in innings pitched three times, in complete games three times, in strikeouts three times, in shutouts three times and in number of starts twice.

Year	Team	G	GS	GC	IP	W–L	Pct.	ShO	BB	SO	ERA
1915	Phil	49	42	36	376.1	31–10	.756	12	64	241	1.22
1916	Phil	48	45	38	388.2	33–12	.738	16	50	167	1.55
1917	Phil	45	44	34	387.2	30–13	.698	8	56	200	1.83

In his seven years with the Phillies, Alex led the National League in wins five times, in earned run average three times, in complete games five times, in innings pitched six times, in strikeouts five times and in shutouts four times.

• CHAPTER VI •

The Changing of the Uniforms

"Baseball received a knockout wallop yesterday when Secretary Baker ruled players in the draft age must obtain employment calculated to aid in the successful prosecution of the war or shoulder guns and fight."[1]

In December of 1917, Baker went to the National League winter meetings at the Waldorf Hotel in New York with a problem he had to solve. He had a ballclub that wasn't making enough money for him, and things were going to get worse. His meal ticket, Grover Cleveland Alexander, was likely to be drafted into the Army and sent overseas to help America fight "the war to end all wars," as President Woodrow Wilson had called World War I. The Phillies would have 30 potential wins whisked away from them. Worse, from Baker's standpoint, gone too would be the gate receipts that Alex and a pennant contender represented.

So Baker had a serious problem, and he knew only one way to solve it. On December 11, he traded Alexander and Killefer, his battery mate, to the Chicago Cubs for pitcher Mike Pendergast, catcher Bill "Pickles" Dillhoefer and, most important, $55,000 in cash. In interviews years later, Baker admitted that his motivation was simple: He needed the money.

"Pat Moran lost his ballclub today," wrote one Philadelphia sportswriter.

Baker made the deal but was concerned about how the news would be received in Philadelphia. So he threw a party for the Philly writers and broke the news as he wined and dined them.

Charles Weeghman, owner of the Cubs, was elated to go public with the news because he thought he just purchased a championship. This wasn't the first time Weeghman waved a checkbook in search of a great pitcher. Three years earlier, as owner of the Chicago Whales in the Federal League, Weeghman almost landed Walter Johnson, the Senators' great pitcher. But

Washington owner Clark Griffith, who always knew how to play an angle, convinced Chicago White Sox owner Charles Comiskey that he wouldn't want Johnson competing in another league in the same town. So Griffith, with Comiskey's help, was able to make Johnson an offer he couldn't refuse, and he stayed in Washington. Ironically, Comiskey's players would rebel against him in 1919 because of his lack of generosity, leading to the fixing of the World Series in what came to be known as the "Black Sox scandal."

Alex didn't raise a fuss about the trade. In fact, he said he didn't blame Baker for making the deal, considering that he and Killefer were about to be drafted. But he demanded that he get $10,000 of the money going to the Phillies for his services. In what was becoming common practice, he staged a holdout, but this time it was with a new team. Weeghman flew to Omaha to talk to Alex, who had been making $12,500 with the Phillies, the highest salary for a pitcher in the National League. The talks were pleasant but businesslike and ended only with the agreement that talks would continue. Alex said later that one of the unusual aspects of his first dealings with Weeghman was the secrecy Weeghman required. When Alex went to meet him in Omaha, he discovered that Weeghman had checked into a hotel under an assumed name.

Meanwhile, on January 16, 1918, word came from the draft board in St. Paul, Nebraska, that Alex was designated 1-A and would be in the first group of men from that area who would be called up. Undaunted and still looking for the bonus, Alexander arrived in Hot Springs, Arkansas, in February to work out, as he had in years past. He told the press he didn't know whether he was getting in shape for baseball, the Army or working on his farm. In an era long before agents negotiated contracts, Alexander had become adept at taking care of his own business, at least from a financial standpoint, but he had a distinct advantage over others in that regard. He was the best pitcher in the National League.

On March 13, Alex and Weeghman exchanged telegrams and Alex agreed to join the club as it headed for Pasadena, California, for the beginning of spring training although his contract was still up in the air.

James Crusinberry reported on Alexander's actions and attitudes in a *Chicago Tribune* article with a dateline of Newton, Kansas, as the Cubs train headed west:

> Grover Cleveland Alexander, prima donna of the Cubs, is speeding to California with us, eating three a day at the soup stations, taking a hand in the poker game, sleeping in a lower berth and airing himself on the observation platform, but he still maintains he is not one of us.
> When the Cubs' train reached Kansas City this morning, Aleck was there. He already had checked his trunk through to Pasadena and made all preparations for the training trip, but still says he is not one of us. He

conferred with manager Mitchell on the station platform at Kansas City and again in the car, then he took off his coat, his hat and shoes, substituting cap and slippers, and proceeded to be comfortable but still declares he is not one of us.

If this doesn't make him one of us, what t'hell does? Manager Mitchell was empowered by President Weeghman to present a definite proposition to the deluxe hurler. Today he made it, but whatever it was, it wasn't accepted. Alexander said afterwards he and Weeghman were no closer together than before.

Mitchell said he did not know whether Aleck would ride clear to California or hop off at some stop and beat it back to St. Paul, Nebraska Once, Aleck hinted he might do such a thing and another time he said he would go on out and work and get into condition and expect his demands to be met later. There's no telling what a prima donna will do, so we have given up, but our one guess is that he will take the entire training trip and pitch a game of ball for the Cubs in St. Louis on April 16.[2]

After winning 30 games or more for three straight seasons, Alexander was traded to the Cubs before the 1918 season because the Phillies feared he would be drafted into the armed services and be of no use to them. He appeared in only three games for the Cubs before being called into the military. He fought in Germany and came back a year later with issues and illnesses that plagued him the rest of his life (National Baseball Hall of Fame Library, Cooperstown, N.Y.).

Three days later, the Cubs began their workouts in Pasadena with Alex on hand but watching from the sidelines. "They will have to come through with a bonus before I will put on a uniform," he told the press. "So far, they are a long ways from it. They have offered me half of what I demanded and until I am offered the other half, I will either have to sit around here or go back home." He watched his teammates from Bill Killefer's car in the morning and sat under a palm tree and watched the action in the afternoon. In between, he joined the other players on a trip to Cubs stockholder (and future club president) William Wrigley's home where motion pictures were taken of the players picking and eating oranges and enjoying Wrigley's hospitality. Special attention was paid to Alexander in the home movies.

On March 20, while heavy rains fell in Pasadena, confining the Cubs to their quarters in the Green Hotel, many players sat around the lobby, reading newspapers and chatting among themselves. In a conference room nearby, Weeghman, Wrigley and Alexander met behind closed doors. After more than an hour, they emerged and announced that Alex had signed. When the news was announced, "It caused joy in the entire camp," according to one news report. While the ballplayers may have been taken aback by Alex's boldness over his contract, they realized, as ballplayers realized almost a century later, that any one player's victory over ownership is a victory for all of them. Besides, with Alex in the fold, the Cubs were once again bona fide pennant contenders. Terms of the agreement were not announced. The *Los Angeles Times* reported, "Mr. Wrigley and the star hurler disappeared at once in the former's touring car and it was thought possible they went to the bank for a pot of gold for Alec to take back home with him."

Alex had earned $12,500 in his last season with the Phillies. In the deal negotiated with the Cubs, he received a $5,000 bonus instead of the $10,000 he wanted, but he also got a two-year contract for $12,500 that the Cubs would make good even if Alexander went to war. Mitchell announced that Alex would be the opening day starter against St. Louis on April 16.

Four days before opening day, the Cubs got the news they dreaded. Alex was drafted into the Army and was to report for duty April 26. "I am ready to go," he said. "No one will have a chance to call me a slacker." Weeghman called the news "a serious shock" for the ballclub. Then, ever the businessman, he expressed another lament. Weeghman said there was a clause in the deal with the Phillies that if either Alexander of Killefer was called into the armed services 30 days or more before opening day, the deal could be called off. That deadline had passed. Weeghman tried to be patriotic, even in his stress. "While we are sorry to lose him, especially at this time, we are glad to help the government in any way," he said.

J.V. Fitzgerald, in "The Round-Up" column in the *Washington Post*, captured the fears of Cub management. "He is at his best just now and close students of the game looked to him to win more than 30 games again this year and to continue as the king of National League twirlers for several years more. Unless the war ends soon, Alexander may never be able to pitch again. Trench life may not make the average man less able to do his work when he returns to civilian duties but it will certainly end the athletic careers of baseball players."[3]

As promised, Alex got the nod on opening day in St. Louis, matched up against Lee Meadows, the bespectacled Cardinal pitcher he faced many times as a Phillie. St. Louis nipped the Cubs, 5–4. In his next start in Cincinnati, Alexander got his first win of the year in a 9–1 drubbing of the Reds. On April 26, he made his first start as a Cub in Wrigley Field, and he did not disappoint. He threw a two-hitter as the Cubs beat the Cardinals, 3–2. Rogers Hornsby got both hits for St. Louis.

After the game, Weeghman and other Cubs management met with Alexander in Weeghman's office and offered a farewell toast to the man who so complicated their lives—holding them at bay until he got the money he wanted and now leaving them at bay as he went off to war. Alexander responded to the toast, saying, "I am sorry to leave all you fellows, but it looks like a tough fight over there and as if a lot of us must go and help. I don't know whether I shall ever come back to play ball or not, but if I don't, I'll make it necessary for them to dig a lot of holes for the enemy before they get me."[4]

Crusinberry in the *Tribune* summed up Alex's career with the Cubs: "Alexander the Great has come and gone."

He left Chicago on April 27 and reported to Camp Funston near Manhattan, Kansas. Many other athletes were already there, including three other pitchers: Clarence Mitchell of the New York Giants, Winnie Noyes of the Philadelphia A's and Otis Lambeth of the Cleveland Indians. St. Louis Browns outfielder Dutch Wenzel was there, and so was Potsy Clark, who had made a name for himself in college football at the University of Illinois and would later be a coach in the National Football League.

Alex discovered that he was due to go overseas soon, so he had some personal business he had to take care of. A young lady from Omaha, Aimee Arrants, had visited friends in St. Paul one winter and met Alex on a blind date. They immediately took a liking to each other and had kept in touch as best they could. Alex contacted her when he got his Army orders, and they decided to get married before Alex shipped out. On May 31, 1918, the couple were married in the office of Riley County Probate Judge E.E. Morris in Manhattan.[5]

Clarence Mitchell was the best man. Alex got a pass that allowed him to spend his wedding night in a hotel in Manhattan. The next day the 342nd Field Artillery of the 89th Division prepared to head for Camp Mills, near New York City, the staging area for troops that were about to go overseas. Aimee went to New York to be near her husband. Securing a pass for an afternoon, Alex took her to a ballgame at the Polo Grounds.

VI — The Changing of the Uniforms

Before Alex left the country, he made a deal with Weeghman. The Cubs owner agreed to pay Aimee $250 a month every month Alex was gone. For Alex and Aimee, of course, this was security for the young bride. For Weeghman, ever the businessman, this was more than a charitable act. The monthly stipend was an advance on the salary Weeghman expected his pitcher to earn upon his return from the service. Alex also got the $5,000 signing bonus and invested it in Liberty bonds.

The Army's 89th Division was often called the "Middle West Division" because it was made up of so many draftees from Kansas, Missouri, Colorado and Nebraska. It was organized at Camp Funston, Kansas, in September of 1917. In May and June of 1918, the division moved to Camp Mills on Long Island, New York. From there, the units began departing for France with the last of them arriving on July 10. There were some rousing ballgames played along the way with the 89th not having much trouble disposing of pick-up teams they played along the way. But before long, the playing stopped and the fierce fighting began. Alex's 342nd Field Artillery unit was dispatched to Camp Souge, near Boredeaux, for training. On August 5, it was moved by bus to an area called the Toul, where it joined two other field artillery units. On September 12, it engaged in battle again, this time in the St. Mihiel offensive, and helped in the capture of the towns of Beney, Essey, Bouillion ville, Pannes and Xammes.

On October 7, the

As Alexander prepares to go off to war, all eyes appear to be on him as he poses for a picture, standing straight and striking a pose that was much like the one opposing batters saw when he was on the pitcher's mound. Notice that his cap is cocked at an angle the same way he wore his baseball cap over the years (National Baseball Hall of Fame Library, Cooperstown, N.Y.).

division was transported by bus to the Recicourt area, where it became part of the First Army Reserve and where, five days later, it began taking part in the Argonne offensive, one of the last big battles of the war. Gen. John J. Pershing described the fighting this way. "We were no longer engaged in a maneuver for the pinching out of a salient, but were necessarily committed, generally speaking, to a direct frontal attack against strong, hostile positions fully manned by a determined enemy." By October 14, American units had reached and crossed portions of the Hindenburg Line — so named because it was where German military forces had formed a line of resistance against American and French advances. The fighting continued through the signing of the armistice on November 11, 1918, after which the 89th began its march into Germany. On May 19, 1919, division members boarded ships and headed back for New York, where Aimee Arrants Alexander and hundreds of other spouses, other relatives and friends waited to greet their loved ones. After all-too-brief reunions, it was on to Camp Funston, where the division was debriefed and demobilized.[6]

Soldiers who served with Alex remembered him as being a big, strong farm boy athlete, quiet and kind. One, whose name has been lost in the vast reservoir of oblivion, recalled being with Alex in France. "I recall one morning going down to the picket line where the horses were being groomed," he said. "It was raw and snowing. Alex was in charge of the detail. I was standing back and pretty soon he came lumbering over to me. 'Lieutenant,' he said, 'you put on these gloves because you look kind of cold.' Here I was, just over 5 feet 6, weight around 136 and he, 6 feet or better, weighing around 190. I tried to persuade him to keep them for himself but he just wouldn't have it. I mention this only to show his heart."

The soldier said that when their unit went to Germany, he and Alexander were on horseback while most of the soldiers walked. Often, when Alex saw one of his men faltering because of the long journeys, he would get off his horse and offer it to the tired soldier.

Alex's comrade also recalled preparations for a Christmas party in the town of Alsdorf, Germany. Alex had been assigned to put on the party. A few days before Christmas, one of the commanding officers sent for Alex so that they could discuss plans for the party. "We were seated at supper when he came in. I was facing him as he came through the door and the minute I saw him I knew he had been frolicking. Alex came around and saluted the captain. The captain merely sized him up when Alex, like a good soldier, again saluted and beat a hasty, if rather noisy retreat. I saw him the next day and he said he had only been rushing the holiday celebration a bit."[7]

The war was won, and with peace came prosperity and the naïve but optimistic sentiment that this had been "the war to end all wars." It had taken an awful toll — hundreds of thousands of deaths and injuries, and major league baseball had its victims just as every other profession did. On October 2, 1918, Capt. Eddie Grant, who had been the Phillies' third baseman for three years and was traded the year before Alex got there, was killed in Argonne as he tended to several of his troops who had been badly wounded. Grant was the first ballplayer to die in World War I. On October 7, Robert "Bun" Troy, who pitched six innings for the Detroit Tigers in 1912, was killed on a French battlefield. On November 1, Alex Burr, who played one game for the New York Yankees in 1914, was killed in France on his 25th birthday. Eight days later, and two days before the armistice, Larry Chappell, who was an outfielder in more than 100 big league games with the White Sox, Indians and Braves, died of influenza in an Army camp in France.

Both Alex and Christy Mathewson, the winningest pitchers in the National League, came out of the war alive, but both were broken men. Mathewson was gassed and contracted tuberculosis, the disease that eventually killed him at the age of 45. He had transitioned from playing to managing when he was called into service. Alex, on the other hand, was in the peak years of his career, coming off three straight 30-plus win seasons when he answered the call. When he returned, he was, in many ways, a broken man.

He was deaf in his left ear from enduring the sound of bombing for seven straight weeks. He was hit with shrapnel in his right outer ear, an injury that seemed more like a nuisance at the time but might have been what led to the development of cancer in that ear later in his life, an ailment that resulted in amputation of the ear.

(Thirty years after the war, a bum looking for handouts was going around New York City claiming that he was Grover Cleveland Alexander. One donor who became suspicious of the beggar contacted a New York sportswriter to get a description of Alex. The writer asked if the bum had a chunk cut out of his ear the size of a quarter. "No," said the bartender. "Then it isn't Alexander," said the sportswriter.) [8]

His duty on the front lines often meant he pulled the lanyard to fire howitzers at the enemy. This caused damage to the muscle in his right arm — the arm that was responsible for his being the best in the business at what he did for a living in the homeland. He came home shell-shocked and susceptible to two demons that plagued him for the rest of his life — alcoholism and epilepsy. Alcoholism was not considered a disease in those days but rather a sometimes amusing complication of having "one too many." It was socially acceptable. The same could not be said for epilepsy. There was nothing amusing about it, and those afflicted with it were often social outcasts. Alex didn't need any more excuses to drink, but he thought alcohol might help stave off epileptic seizures, so he imbibed more frequently than he might have had he not contracted the disease.

At home, Alex was used to having a couple of beers with the boys after the ballgame. Overseas, it was a little different. "In France, I had hard liquor for the first time," he said. "I had drunk beer all of my life but that was all. Overseas, everybody knew he was going into battle continually and no one knew whether he would be alive tomorrow or not. So a lot of men who had never drunk before drank over there. But fortunately for them, it didn't get a hold of them like it did of me."[9]

Compare these two descriptions of Alexander, the first from Phils manager Pat Moran in 1917, the year before he went to war: "He's an invaluable member of the team because of his splendid character. He is the easiest star pitcher to handle I have ever known. He is always ready for the call of duty. He is a model athlete and one of the cleanest, manliest fellows I have ever known."

Years after the war, teammate "Wild Bill" Hallahan said, "Alex never said much about anything. When he did talk, it was seldom above a whisper. As a rule, you didn't see him around after a game. He would go off by himself and do what he did, which I suppose was drink. That was his problem."

Hallahan also recounted an incident that occurred toward the end of Alexander's career. He said that during a spring training game, some kids in the stands started shooting fireworks behind the ballplayers. He said most of the ballplayers flinched with each bang of the fireworks but that Alexander never budged. Instead, his body stiffened, his fists clenched and his eyes gazed into space as if he were hypnotized. When the noise stopped, Alex turned and had a slight smile on his face, as if to say "it's over now." Twelve years after he had curled up on the ground in Germany and endured seven weeks of bombardments from the Germans, Alex still acted like a man who was shell-shocked.[10]

Then there was the serious matter of epilepsy, which Alexander never acknowledged publicly and there is no definitive record of prior to his entry into World War I. The only ballplayer who ever mentioned it was Hans Lobert, and he did it in an interview about 50 years after he played with Alexander.

Baseball historian Glenn Dickey, writing in 1982, summarized Alexander's plight from the standpoint of dealing with both the illness and people's perception of it: "Epilepsy is an illness that frightens people even now, and that was even more true in Alexander's day. In the climate of the times, alcoholism was more socially acceptable than epilepsy.... It seems likely ... that Alexander tried to hide the fact of his epilepsy and that at least some of his erratic behavior, attributed to excessive drinking, was due to his illness."[11] That is a view that was shared by others, including Aimee Alexander.

When the Cubs got Alexander in the trade with the Phillies, they were getting the best active pitcher in the National League, a great athlete who had won 30 or more games three years in a row and who seemed destined for even greater stardom. What the Cubs got when he came back from the war was a scarred, shell-shocked, half-deaf epileptic and alcoholic whose zest for life, without the inducement of liquor, was left somewhere on a muddy battlefield thousands of miles way.

• CHAPTER VII •

The Cub Years

"It is one of baseball's tragedies that Alex had his own peculiar ideas on keeping in condition."
— Warren Brown

One of the fascinations baseball affords its personnel, fans and historians is the ironies it produces over the years. Cubs owner William Weeghman shelled out $50,000 — some say it was more — to get Grover Cleveland Alexander in hopes that he would bring a championship to Chicago. It turned out that Alexander was hardly any help at all that first year, 1918, because he appeared in only three games before being sent off with the Army, and the Cubs won the pennant without him. Then he came back, played eight more years with the Cubs, and they never won a pennant with him. In midseason 1926, he was sent to the St. Louis Cardinals, and they won a pennant with him.

The 1918 season was cut short by the war, ending on Labor Day by order of the federal government. Chicago finished with an 84–45 record. Hippo Vaughn, a lefty, won 22 games and lost only 10 to lead the pitching staff. Claude Hendrix won 20 and lost 7. Lefty Tyler contributed 19 victories and only 8 losses. The fourth starter, "Shufflin' Phil" Douglas, won 10 and lost 9.

The Cubs lineup had some familiar names. Fred Merkle was the first baseman and hit .297. Merkle represents another irony. Ten years earlier, as a member of the Giants, it was his failure as a base runner to touch second base on an apparent game-winning hit that cost New York a victory against the Cubs. He had been on first when a base hit scored the apparent winning run from third. When Merkle, running toward second, saw the run score, he turned and ran toward the clubhouse. Cubs second baseman Johnny Evers called for the ball, touched second, and Merkle was ruled out on a force play. Now he was playing for Chicago, a team that once again beat out the Giants. Two other familiar names were Dode Paskert, an outfielder who played on the Phillies' 1915 championship team, and Killefer behind the plate, who came over in the Alexander deal. The leading batsman was Charlie Hollocher, who hit .316.

Chicago lost the World Series, four games to two, to the Boston Red Sox in the first year in which the first four teams in the standings of each league got shares of the World Series money in decreasing proportions depending on whether they finished second, third or fourth. The Chicago and Boston players were so incensed by this that they staged a strike between the fifth and six games but returned to finish out the series.

As the ballclub headed for spring training in March of 1919, the Cubs got some welcome news from overseas: "Alexander has left station en route to the United States," came word from Gen. John Pershing in a cable from Germany, where the 89th Division went after the armistice was signed. Alexander arrived in New York aboard the French liner Rochembeau, and his presence caused quite a stir.

"The scenes that followed his arrival caused the eyes of the French and Belgian soldiers on board, as well as those of many American civilians, to well nigh pop out of their heads," the *Chicago Tribune* reported.

"They got something of a jolt, then, when photographers by the score boarded the vessel and dragged a freckle-faced sergeant of the artillery, laden with all the clumsy paraphernalia of the doughboy of the A.E.F. (American Expeditionary Force) from the hold to the boat deck to be photographed again and again. As the big pitcher was pushed and hauled to the upper deck, the hundreds of troops below, recognizing the freckled-countenance, cut loose with an uproarious cheer."[1]

Later that same day, Alex told the press, "I'm afraid I'll not be ready to go in on April 23, opening day. Give me seven more days and I'll be in shape. I'll be pitching real ball by May 1."

Until Alex was ready, Vaughn, Hendrix, Douglas and Martin had to keep the Cubs in the running. Douglas was a veteran pitcher who couldn't outpitch Alex, but he could outdrink him, and there is no reason to think the two of them didn't put it to the test in barrooms throughout the National League. Cub president Bill Veeck, Sr., saw the potential for disaster with his two pitchers pairing up in taverns after ballgames. On July 25, Veeck traded "Shufflin' Phil" to the New York Giants for Dave Robertson. Douglas had a couple of good years with the Giants, winning 14 in 1920, 15 in 1921 and two in the 1921 World Series against the Yankees. But all the while, Giants manager John McGraw tried to cope with Douglas's excessive drinking. At one point he hired former ballplayer Jesse Burkett to escort him to and from the ballpark. Another time, McGraw arranged to have Douglas hidden away—for all practical purposes, kidnapped—so he could dry out.

In August of 1922, Douglas was 11–4 and leading the National League with a 2.63 earned run average but was still creating big problems with his drinking. McGraw fined him and suspended him. A dejected Douglas sent a letter to Les Mann, an outfielder with the Cardinals, who had been Douglas's roommate several years back with the Cubs. In the letter, he told Mann he didn't want McGraw to win the pennant and, with a little "inducement," he could be persuaded to leave the team. Mann turned the letter over to league officials who contacted Commissioner Kenesaw Mountain Landis. Douglas was banned from playing professional baseball ever again.[2]

Another of Alexander's teammates on that 1919 Cub ballclub was also destined for big trouble. Lee Magee was a reserve outfielder, a second baseman and a schemer. He was no relation to Alex's former teammate Sherry Magee. In 1920, Lee Magee admitted to Cubs officials that when he was with Cincinnati two years earlier, he bet against the Reds before a game and then tried to fix the game so the Reds would lose, but Cincinnati won in 13 innings. The Cubs suspended him. Magee sued the ballclub and lost. Subsequently, newly appointed Commissioner Landis banished him for life.

Hippo Vaughn drew the opening day assignment and got the Cubs off to a good start with a 5–1 decision over the Pittsburgh Pirates. Pittsburgh bounced back to win the next two games, 6–5 and 6–3. Lefty Tyler was the winner in a 7–1 decision over St. Louis, but the next day Jakie May of the Cardinals won a pitcher's duel over Vaughn and the Cubs, 1–0. Phil Douglas then threw a shutout as the Cubs ended April by beating St. Louis, 4–0, and had a 3–3 record going into May. Nobody realized it at the time, but the Cincinnati Reds, off to a 6–0 start, were about to run away with the National League championship and win the most controversial World Series in history—a series most Reds thought they would have won even if eight members of the Chicago White Sox hadn't conspired with gamblers to throw it.

All of that was still in the future as Lefty Tyler won his second straight start, downing the Pirates 4–2 at Forbes Field on May 1. When Vaughn won a 2–1 decision the next day, the Cubs had their first three-game winning streak of the young season. Next they split a four-game series with the Reds. Alex made his first start of the year on May 9 and lost a 1–0 heartbreaker to Cincinnati. Chicago won its next two games but then lost six in a row. Alex dropped a 3–2 decision to Rube Benton and the Giants on May 13 and lost 4–3 to Jeff Pfeffer and the Brooklyn Dodgers on May 18. He had his first really bad outing of the year on May 23 when the Phillies knocked him around in a 7–2 loss. Then on May 30, Jakie May of the Cardinals beat him in a 5–4 decision. The Cubs entered June with a 15–16 record and found themselves in fifth place, 7½ games behind the Reds.

Alex, who had never experienced a losing season, was 0–5. While he had pitched well in all but one game, he wasn't the brilliant taskmaster of years past and was certainly one of the reasons why the Cubs were floundering at about the .500 level. He got his first win on June 2, beating Pittsburgh 7–0 for his first shutout of the year in the first game of a doubleheader. When Douglas shut down the Pirates 2–1 in the second game, Chicago went over the .500 mark at 17–16 and would not be below .500 again for the rest of the season. On June 8, Alex picked up his second win with a 7–2 victory over the Braves at Wrigley Field. He threw his second shutout of the year four days later as Chicago defeated Philadelphia, 3–0. The Cubs had now moved into third place and had a six-game winning streak, and Alexander had won three in a row. But they lost three out of four to the Giants, with Alex losing in relief in a 15-inning game on June 15 and notching the only win of the series, a 7–2 decision over Red Causey on June 17.

Alexander was 4–6 and starting to turn his season around. More important, the Cubs were starting to show some signs of life and were in third place, six games behind the Reds. But a big problem had developed. Alex felt as if his right arm were about to fall off. He had never experienced anything like it in his career, not even in the World Series of 1915 when he had the sore arm. This was different. This was, in all probability, war-related. Cub trainer Fred Hart said that he was "muscle-bound"—not like a weightlifter with bulging biceps but like a man whose muscles had bound up on him, causing extreme pain. It was the result of Alex's spending seven weeks in Germany yanking the lanyards of howitzers and now using different muscles in the same arm to throw a baseball day after day. What he needed, said Hart, was rest.

While Alex rested, the Cubs made some front office moves. Fred Mitchell had been serving both as club president and field manager. On July 6, Wrigley divested Mitchell of his front office responsibilities so he could concentrate solely on what was happening on the ballfield. Bill Veeck, Sr., became president. Three weeks later, Veeck disposed of Shufflin' Phil Douglas, making him McGraw's problem in New York. In return, the Cubs got Robertson, a hard-hitting outfielder who led the National League in homers in both 1917 and 1918 with 12 each year. He hit none with the Cubs in what was left of the 1919 season.

Alexander returned to the mound on July 15 and picked up his fifth win, beating the Braves 7–2 at Braves Field. On July 23, he and Douglas each threw shutouts as Chicago took care of Brooklyn twice at Ebbets Field. It was Douglas' last outing with the Cubs. On July 27, Alex threw another shutout, this time beating the Cardinals 4–0 in St. Louis. Alex was now 7–6 with four shutouts. He was barely above .500 but had an earned run average under 2.00. Entering August, the Cubs found themselves in third place, 10 games behind the surging Reds.

Alexander lost his first two starts in August, 2–1 to the Phillies and 2–0 to the Braves, but, despite the losses, lowered his earned run average. On August 10, he finally got another win, and this time it was Alex getting the shutout, his fifth of the season in beating the Giants 2–0 and evening his record at 8–8. His next start was vintage Alex, mowing down the Dodgers 2–0 for his second straight shutout and sixth of the season — and doing it in 70 minutes. He got his ninth win on August 16, beating the Giants and his old teammate Phil Douglas 4–3 at the Polo Grounds. After the game, Douglas disappeared for a while and later said evil spirits had gotten a hold of him and forced him to join some buddies—in Tennessee. That earned him the first of many suspensions from McGraw.

Alex closed out the month with a 10–2 decision over the Phillies on August 22 and then split shutout decisions, losing 1–0 to the Braves and Joe Oeschger at Braves Field on August 26 but getting the best of Frank Woodward and the Cardinals, 1–0, on August 30. September was a month in which ballclubs played out the season and geared up for next year. Cincinnati was running away from everybody, including the Cubs, who were in third place but 17½ games behind the Reds. Alex finished out the year by winning four and losing three in September. In his three losses, the Cubs got him five runs. Of his four wins, two were shutouts and one, a 3–0 decision over the Braves on September 21, took 58 minutes.

Alexander was 16–11. Nine of his wins were shutouts, and his 1.72 earned run average was not only best in the National League but remains the best Cub earned run average ever. A comparison of numbers is evidence enough that Alex had not yet returned to the form that made him the dominant pitcher in the National League before the war. In 1917, he had 44 starts and one relief appearance. In 1919, he had 27 starts and three relief appearances. In 1917, he pitched 388 innings and had 34 complete games. In 1919, he had 235 innings and 20 complete games.

In 1920, baseball embarked on some changes that brought to an end the so-called "Dead Ball Era" and gave rise to the home run as a more prominent weapon in the sport's offense. It was more of a change in rules than of baseballs. Prior to 1920, it was common for one ball to be used for an entire game if possible because of the expense of replacing it. If a ball was hit into the crowd, a new ball was put into play. Otherwise, the same ball was used no matter how scuffed or dirty it became. The result was that it was often difficult for a hitter to see as darkness set in, and it was definitely difficult to pick up the spin of the ball as it left the pitcher's hand. Another advantage for the pitcher was that as a game got into the later innings, the ball got softer and more difficult to hit long distances.

Another new rule that favored hitters was the banning of "trick pitches" such as the spitball and shine ball. Pitchers who relied on the spitter to make their living were allowed to use it until the end of their careers. No one coming into the majors could use it. The leagues even went so far as to publish lists of spitball pitchers who could continue to use the pitch. In the American League, they were Doc Ayers and Dutch Leonard of the Detroit Tigers, Ray Caldwell and Stan Coveleski of the Cleveland Indians, Urban Shocker and Allen Sothoron of the St. Louis Browns, Allen Russell of the Boston Red Sox, Jack Quinn of the New York Yankees and Red Faber of the Chicago White Sox. In the National League, two of the pitchers allowed to throw spitters had ties to Grover Cleveland Alexander. Clarence Mitchell of the Brooklyn Dodgers was best man at his wedding, and Shufflin' Phil Douglas of the New York Giants was his teammate the year before with the Cubs. Others allowed to continue throwing it were Burleigh Grimes of the Dodgers, Dick Rudolph and Dana Fillingim of the Boston Braves, Bill Doak and Marv Goodwin of the St. Louis Cardinals and Ray Fisher of the Cincinnati Reds.

The American League felt the impact of the new rules immediately because of one man, George Herman "Babe" Ruth," the former Red Sox pitcher who was converted into an outfielder because of his great hitting strength. Now a New York Yankee, Ruth hit the astounding total of 29 home runs in 1919 and then, with the rule changes in effect, walloped 54 in 1920 on his way to hitting 714 in his career. The National League saw no such domination. Cy Williams of Philadelphia, aided by the Baker Bowl short right field wall, led the league with 15 homers.

Alex and other ballplayers had to contend with another rule change, this one affecting their lives off the field. Prohibition went into effect in 1920, banning the sale of alcoholic beverages. This didn't mean ballplayers couldn't drink. It just meant the drinks were a little harder to find, but it wasn't long before athletes knew where the speakeasies were in the cities they visited, and they were often treated like royalty when they made their way in. Alex justified his drinking by telling people he could pitch better with a hangover.[3]

He was not affected by the spitball ban because he didn't rely on trick pitches. Even at the age of 33, he still had the same sidearm delivery, a live fastball, a curveball with changing speeds and an unequaled ability to nip the outside corners of the plate to both right-handed and left-handed batters. His ability to throw complete games in 90 minutes or less was not prompted by a desire to go have a drink as much as it was by his being intent on keeping hitters off balance. He never wanted to give hitters much time to think between pitches.

The 1920 season was played under the shadow of gambling accusations on relatively small levels, such as Lee Magee's admitting that he single-handedly tried to fix a game a couple of years past, and on huge ones, such as the revelation that was to come, implicating eight members of the Chicago White Sox in conspiring to fix the 1919 World Series. For all of his off-the-field indiscretions with alcohol, Alexander was never accused of gambling. In his playing days, he was too frugal with his money to part with it in such a manner. Alcohol was his vice of choice. When his playing days were over, he didn't have any money to gamble.

The Cubs got off to a slow start in 1920, losing three in a row to the champion Reds and then losing to the Cardinals 2–0. Alex was 0–2 after the first week of the season. Hippo Vaughn registered the Cubs' first win in a 9–6 victory over the Cardinals on April 19. Alexander's first win was a 4–3 victory over the Reds in the home opener at Wrigley Field on April 22, but Chicago lost three more in a row to fall to 2–8 and was already in sixth place, 4½ games out of first. They would tumble to seventh by the end of the month. In May, they reeled off a seven-game winning streak at the start of the month and a nine-game winning streak at the end of the month and found themselves in first place entering June with a record of 24–16. A big reason was Alexander, who put together an 11-game winning streak beginning on April 22 and running through May 31, including a win in relief of Claude Hendrix on May 2.

But the Cubs followed their nine-game winning streak with a 10-game losing streak that included Alex losing a 5–1 decision to Bill Doak and the Cardinals, ending his string of 11 wins in a row. Rogers Hornsby hit two triples to lead the St. Louis attack. Alex also lost to his old buddy and teammate, Rixey of Philadelphia, but stopped the Cubs' losing streak as well as his own with an 8–1 victory over the Braves. By the end of June, the Cubs were 34–31 and in third place, three games behind Brooklyn. Alex was 13–6 and destined to have his best year from the end of the war to the end of his career.

On July 1, Alexander won his 14th game with a 1–0 shutout of the defending champion Reds, but the headline of the day went to another great pitcher, Walter Johnson, who threw the only no-hitter of his career for the Washington Senators. When their respective careers ended, Johnson was second in all-time wins with 417; Alex was third with 373. Johnson was second in career shutouts with 110; Alex was third with 90. Johnson had the one no-hitter; Alex came within one out of one but never had a no-hitter.

By the end of July, Chicago had fallen below .500, a status the Cubs would have most of the rest of the year. Only Alex and Hippo Vaughn were steady on the mound. The bullpen couldn't hold many leads. Speed Martin was 4–15, Paul Carter was 3–6 and Abraham "Sweetbreads" Bailey was

1–2, a combined record of 8–23 for three men who often entered games that were tied or when the Cubs had the lead.

On August 15, Alex threw a 1–0 shutout against Cincinnati. The next day, Claude Hendrix got pummeled as the Reds beat the Cubs 9–1. But once again, attention was on an American League game, one that had tragic consequences. In a game between the New York Yankees and Cleveland Indians, Yankee right-hander Carl Mays beaned Indian shortstop Ray Chapman, who died from the injury, the only fatal injury in major league baseball history. The Chapman beaning reinforced baseball management's resolve to make sure all balls used in games were clean and unscuffed and that pitchers refrained from doctoring the ball or throwing trick pitches. There was no indication that Mays did anything unsavory or that a different baseball would have prevented the tragedy. Nonetheless, baseball used the incident as an object lesson.

The most bizarre event of the season for the Cubs occurred on August 31 in a game against the eighth-place Phillies. Hendrix, the veteran right-hander, was scheduled to pitch for the Cubs against Lee "Specs" Meadows, the former Cardinal pitcher. Prior to the game, Cub president Veeck received messages that the fix was on, that gamblers had heavy money on the lowly Phillies to win the game. Rather than jump to any conclusions or point any fingers, Veeck talked to manager Fred Mitchell. They decided to change the pitching rotation and move Alex up to pitch on August 31. The Phillies won the game anyway, 3–0. When the game came under investigation, and because Hendrix had been removed from the lineup by the Cubs, there was speculation that he was involved in the alleged fix, an allegation that was never proved. Nonetheless, the Cubs released him at the end of the season and he never pitched in the major leagues again. Veeck said later it might have been gamblers' intentions to leak information about the August 31 game so that the Cubs would change the rotation and prevent Alex from pitching in a later game in which gamblers had high stakes. At any rate, Philly manager Gavvy Cravath, when informed about allegations of the fix, said, "Jeez, I don't know why they have to bring a thing like this up just because we win one. Gee, we're likely to win a game most any time."[4]

(Seven years later, Cravath was out of baseball and won election as a magistrate judge in California despite having no legal training or background. He remained a judge for 36 years and said he based many of his decisions on the principles of sportsmanship he learned in baseball.)[5]

The biggest repercussion of the August 31 ballgame was that a grand jury in Chicago was empaneled to look into the accusations of gambling on that game and in baseball in general. Chicago sportswriter Hugh Fullerton and others had been sniffing around trying to put all the pieces together on their gut feeling that the 1919 World Series had been fixed. When testimony was taken about gambling influences in baseball, those in the know began to connect the dots, and the Black Sox scandal exploded. In December of 1920, baseball owners, needing a czar to control the game, found one in Judge Kenesaw Mountain Landis. He imposed lifetime bans on eight Chicago White Sox players even though a jury had found them not guilty of participating in a fix. In separate, unrelated actions, Landis also kicked out Magee, the Cubs reserve who admitted trying to fix a game two years earlier, and Shufflin' Phil Douglas, who drank and wrote himself into oblivion.

Alex finished the year at 27–14 with a 1.91 earned run average. Vaughn was 19–16. The rest of the staff was 29–39. Robertson, the slugger acquired for Douglas, led the club with 10 home runs. In this, the first year after the "Deadball Era," Paskert was next in home runs with five.

After the 1920 season, Alex went the rest of his career without striking out 100 batters. Perhaps it was his age or his now famous and continuous "lack of attention to training," and maybe it was his war injuries that were taking hold. Or maybe it was a combination of all three. Whatever it was, Alex, or "Ole Pete" as he was now being called, relied more and more on finesse to get him through ballgames, but he often saved those fewer strikeouts for key situations.

His days of barnstorming between seasons were over, but Alex and many other great ballplayers of the era found a lucrative "winter job" in the unlikely town of Attleboro, Massachusetts, and its neighbor, North Attleboro. Each year for several years, the adjoining communities engaged in friendly but competitive baseball games with teams made up of the town's athletes and would-be athletes. The nature of the rivalry changed in 1919 when some rich businessmen approached Attleboro manager Dan O'Connell, who was friends with some big league ballplayers, and convinced him to hire some major league players to be on the Attleboro team. Money was no object, they assured him.

Soon North Attleboro, which had its share of civic pride and wealthy sportsmen, joined the bounty hunt for good ballplayers. In 1919, Walter Johnson showed up long enough to pitch and win the final game of the series for North Attleboro and pick up a check for $500 for his efforts. In 1920, Attleboro backers wanted revenge. They sent for Alex and offered him what North Attleboro had paid Johnson the year before, $500 a game. Alex pitched in the second game of the series, after Bob Shawkey of the Yankees beat Lee Meadows of the Cardinals in the first game. As it worked out, North Attleboro recruited and signed mostly American League players while Attleboro hired National League stars. Alex did his part by coming out the winner in a 6–2 decision, facing a lineup that included Eddie Collins, Harry Heilmann and Stuffy McGinnis. His teammates were no slouches. Attlesboro had Frankie Frisch, Sam Rice and Dave Bancroft. As the teams prepared for the rubber match, Attlesboro brought in Burleigh Grimes, Rogers Hornsby and George Sisler. Grimes never got a chance to pitch. Alexander was the starter and winner of an 8–2 decision. He left town $1,000 richer — or that is to say he received $1,000 in pay, $500 for each of the two games. How much he left on the bars of speak-easies is not recorded.[6]

Two events occurred in the off-season involving people close to Alex. The Cubs, disappointed in the sixth place finish, took the difficult step of firing Fred Mitchell, the man who had served Wrigley as both general manager and field manager, and replaced him with Johnny Evers, the old second baseman whose best known trait beyond his baseball skills was his apparent inability to develop any people skills. Also, on March 31, 1921, Frank Bancroft, whom Alex got to know through the worldly baseball tours he sponsored, died in Cincinnati.

The Cubs opened the 1921 season on April 13 with a 5–2 victory over the Cardinals at Wrigley Field, a game in which Specs Toporcer of the Cardinals made his major league debut. Not surprisingly, Alex was the starter for the Cubs and benefited from Bob O'Farrell's three-run homer to get the win. But Ol' Pete felt a twinge in his arm in the middle innings and was removed for a pinch hitter. The injury may have sprung from an incident in pregame ceremonies when a photographer, hustling to get the shot he wanted, accidentally crashed into Alex, knocking him down. He didn't pitch again for nearly a month.

After the opening day win, Chicago won its next two games before absorbing a 14–2 clobbering by the Pirates, who beat them again the next day. The Cubs then went to St. Louis and beat the Cardinals twice to increase their record to 5–2, including a 4–0 mark against St. Louis in the young season. When the ballclub headed for Cincinnati, Alex, whose arm was still hurting, took a detour and went instead to Youngstown, Ohio, and to the offices of the legendary John D. "Bonesetter" Reese, a former steel mill worker who became so adept at assisting injured co-workers by manipulating their bones and muscles with his hands that he eventually went into the business full time. In today's world, he would be considered a chiropractor. In his era, he was a bonesetter and considered a quack by the established medical community of Youngstown and surrounding areas. The young bone specialist tried to appease his critics by going to medical school at Case University in Cleveland but had to drop out because he could not stand the sight of blood. But his instructors there recognized his talent for working with bones and ligaments and wrote glowing letters of recommendation for him. Eventually, he earned the respect of physicians who acknowledged that Reese possessed skills they did not have. For his part, Reese showed respect for his colleagues by refusing to treat patients with acute illnesses.

His reputation for treating athletes started innocently enough. One of his patients was Jimmy McAleer, a Youngstown boy who was an outfielder with the Cleveland Spiders in the early 1900s. McAleer was so impressed with Reese that he told teammates and other ballplayers about him. Word spread so quickly that in 1903, the Pittsburgh Pirates offered Reese the job of team doctor, a position he turned down because he would have had to leave Youngstown. So instead, athletes came to Youngstown to see him. Cy Young came. Christy Mathewson came. Walter Johnson came. Ty Cobb came. In all, 28 future Hall of Famers, and more than 50 ballplayers altogether, made the trek to Youngstown to have their aching bones treated and twisted into place at the hands of Bonesetter Reese. And in April of 1921, Grover Cleveland Alexander made the journey in which, he said later, Reese saw him for three minutes, snapped a tendon back into place, and charged him $10.[7]

The Cubs, minus Ol' Pete, lost two out of three at Cincinnati, then lost three in a row to Pittsburgh to fall under .500 for the first time in the season at 6–7. They were right at .500 and 9–9 when Alexander returned to the mound and bested his old Philadelphia teammate, Stan Baumgartner, 6–2, at Baker Bowl. When Hippo Vaughn and Speed Martin also notched victories over the Phillies, the Cubs were riding a three-game winning streak and were three games above .500. No one could have foreseen that as being the high point of what was to become an extremely bleak season. Alex didn't pitch again for two weeks, when he came out on the losing end of a 10–7 decision to the Cardinals. The Cubs were still a .500 ballclub at 15–15, but already in the young season they were nine games behind the Giants. The loss to the Cardinals was the second of what was to become a seven-game losing streak that pushed the ballclub into sixth place and out of contention for the rest of the season.

Alexander's arm, while mended by Bonesetter Reese, didn't have the strength of previous years, and Alex was relegated to once-a-week duty. He started on June 4 and lost a 4–3 decision to the Dodgers. On June 11, he and the Cubs beat Boston 6–3 at Wrigley Field, giving Chicago a modest two-game winning streak. Five days later, Alex showed signs that he and his arm were returning to form as he went all the way in a 13-inning, 5–4 win over McGraw's Giants. He finished June with a 6–3 decision over the Cardinals on June 21 before getting knocked out of the game in an 11–3 loss to the Pirates on June 26. In July, the Cubs struggled with a lack of consistency that was becoming the hallmark of their season. When they got good hitting, the pitching faltered. When their pitchers came through, they got no hitting. Alex's month was a good example. After beating the Cardinals and Jess Haines on July 1, he won a 6–2 decision over the Reds, then lost 1–0 to the Giants and 2–1 to the Braves before beating the Dodgers and the Phillies in consecutive starts, 10–0 and 6–2, and then was the victim of a shutout again, this time 3–0 to the Dodgers and Burleigh Grimes.

On August 7, Evers was fired. The Cubs were 43–59, in sixth place, 22 games behind the Giants. The new manager was Bill Killefer, the veteran catcher who for years had been Alexander's personal battery mate. Killefer was a respected player and a knowledgeable baseball man. He was a tough competitor but not mean-spirited like Evers. The dream-come-true version of the conversion would have Alex going out and winning one for his old buddy making his managerial debut. But Alexander got rocked as the first place Giants beat the Cubs 7–2 in a game in which the New York third baseman was knocked unconscious when a hard-hit ground ball took a bad hop and hit him in the face. It was rough going for Killefer as the ballclub lost two, won one and then lost six in a row, including an 8–6 loss to Boston in which Alex gave up a home run to Walter Cruise that went all the way out of Braves Field. Alexander finished August with a 6–1 decision over Brooklyn on August 24 and a 4–2 loss to the Giants. By this time, the Cubs were in seventh place, 28½ games behind New York.

The pattern that plagued the Cubs and Alex all year continued in September. His first four decisions of the month were all shutouts. In two, he blanked the opposition, beating the Reds and his old teammate Rixey 7–0 on September 2 and the Phillies 10–0 on September 14. In between, he lost to the Cardinals 1–0 on September 6 and to the Pirates 8–0 on September 10. He made his last start of the season on October 1, losing to Cincinnati 5–3 and finishing the year with a 15–13 record.

Alex's earned run average was a career high, 3.39, attributed possibly to his lack of arm strength early in the year and to the first year of the so-called "live ball" that upped batting averages of many players. His strikeout total for the year dropped to 77, 96 fewer than the previous season and the first time in his career, except for the war years, in which he did not strike out 100 batters. Though he had a few good years still left in him, Ol' Pete never struck out 100 batters again.

The Cubs started the 1922 season with some new faces and high hopes. Killefer started his first full season at the helm and was grooming a young catcher named Leo Hartnett, who made a name for himself with his chatter long before he did with his bat. "Gabby" Hartnett developed into a Hall of Famer but settled for a .194 average in limited duty while he was learning his trade as the backup catcher for Bob O'Farrell. The ballclub got out of the gate fast, with Alex topping Eppa Rixey in a 7–3 decision at Crosley Field in Cincinnati on opening day, April, 12. They won again the next day, and after an off day, lost two. In between, on April 14, the city and the ballclub mourned the loss of Cap Anson, one of the Cub all-time greats, who died in Chicago. The Cubs won eight of their next nine, and when first baseman Ray Grimes hit a two-run homer on April 26 to beat the Cardinals, Chicago found itself in the unfamiliar spot of being in first place. On April 30, St. Louis pounded Alex in a 10–0 victory. As they entered May, the Cubs were 11–5. But Alexander, who won his first three starts, got belted again on May 7 as the Cubs lost to the Pirates, 11–5. In that game, Walter Mueller, in his first major league at bat, homered on the first pitch he saw from Alex, who was knocked out in the second inning. When he lost his next two starts, to Lee Meadows and the Phillies in a 4–0 shutout and Jesse Barnes and the Giants by a 5–4 margin, Alex was a .500 pitcher at 3–3. He rebounded with wins over the Braves and Reds and had a no decision in a 2–2 tie against the Reds in a game called by darkness. The Cubs hung around the .500 mark for most of June, and when Alex won his first two starts in July, beating the Pirates and the Braves, the Cubs moved to 37–36 in the midst of what would be an eight-game winning streak. They had a seven-game winning streak in August but won about as many as they lost the rest of time and finished in fifth place with an 80–74 record.

The season had its share of exciting and zany moments. On July 23, Grimes set a major league record when he homered in a 4–1 win over the Dodgers, giving him at least one RBI in 17 consecutive games. It was right about that time that Alex gave a newspaper interview in which he told reporters why hot weather didn't bother him, even at the ripe old age of 35. "My early training helped me stand the heat," he said. "When I was a youngster, I used to follow a reaper under a hot Nebraska sun for $1.10 a day. I had one experience when I was a boy which I will never forget. I wanted to earn a little money for the Fourth of July, so I went to work for a farmer and planted corn all day, for which he gave me ten cents."

On August 25, the Cubs and Phillies hooked up in a contest that still ranks as one of the most bizarre in baseball history. Chicago "edged" Philadelphia 26–23, still the most runs scored in a major league game. The Cubs scored 14 runs in the fourth inning to take a 25–6 lead and then had to withstand a furious charge by the Phillies, who had the bases loaded in the ninth inning when the final out was made.

Alex didn't pitch after September 9, when he and the Cubs lost to the Pirates 7–4 at Forbes Field. That was the first loss in what became a five-game losing streak. On September 16, with the Cubs in fifth place, 12 games out of first, Ol' Pete was given the rest of the season off, except of course for his appearance in the annual City Series against the White Sox. He won 16 games in 1922, one more than he had in 1921, but he lost 13, his strikeout total dropped to 48, and his earned run average was the highest of his career, 3.63. It was small consolation that the well-rested Alex threw a shutout against the White Sox.

Alex still exhibited remarkable control on the mound, but the same could not be said about him once he got off the field. Aimee, a stand-by-your-man kind of woman, often said her husband's problems were due more to epilepsy than to alcohol and blamed his behavior as an aftereffect from the beaning he had received as a base runner before he got to the big leagues that left him unconscious for 36 hours. She also said the trauma of his service in World War I affected him for the rest of his life.

"Alex never had any regrets," Aimee told Frank Finch of *The Sporting News*. "Oh, he might suffer from temporary pangs of remorse after a binge but he was a very stubborn man. He would rarely admit to my face that he was sorry but used to leave little apologetic notes under my pillow, in my purse, and places like that. Once in a while he would take me in his arms and say, 'Aimee, I don't mean to worry you.' Then he'd proclaim his intention to reform. Alex was not the malicious type. Alcohol was just something he couldn't handle."[8]

As for Alex, when he was winning, he made no excuses for himself. He laughed and told people he pitched better with a hangover. When he was losing, he told the same people that he couldn't help it, that his father had been a heavy drinker and it was just a habit he picked up that he couldn't shake. In the press, it was politely referred to as "breaking training" or some sort of paraphrase. In America, it was the Roaring '20s, when heroes' weaknesses were winked at rather than scorned or pitied. Alexander told sportswriter Bob Broeg there would be times he would get up in the morning and have a couple of belts of whiskey in his hotel room. Then he'd brush his teeth and have a third shot, he said. "And there were mornings on the road when I'd get to the elevator and go back to my hotel room and have a fourth shot before going down for breakfast," he said.

His old friend Killefer, now his manager, tried to look the other way as much as he could. But one morning Alex literally stumbled into the Cubs clubhouse. He was humming, which, for those who knew him, was a telltale sign that he had been drinking. Killefer was irate. "You're still pitching," he told his star. "Who says I wasn't, Bill old boy," replied Alexander. He went out and threw a one-hitter against the Phillies, and did it so quickly he was still drunk when the game was over, according to Tom Sheehan, one of the Philly players who batted against him.[9]

In 1923, William Wrigley greatly expanded the ballpark named for him, increasing the seating capacity to 33,000. What he needed was a ballclub that would fill the seats with satisfied customers. Grover Cleveland Alexander, 36 years old, lacking the fastball he once had and lacking the off-the-field discipline that he never really had, was still the ballclub's best bet to be a pennant contender. They opened the season on April 17 at home against the Pirates and Killefer let Alex watch the action from the dugout and bullpen. He went with Earnest Preston "Tiny" Osborne, whose physical appearance belied his nickname. A shade under 6 feet, 5 inches tall and weighing 215 pounds, the tall, slender right-hander gave hitters a formidable figure to look at as he took his windup and fired the ball to the plate. In the forgettable 1922 season, Osborne was a pleasant surprise, winning nine, losing five, in what was his rookie year. Osborne pitched well in the opener but lost a 3–2 decision to the Pirates. Alex took the mound the next day and stifled the Pirates in a 7–2 Cub victory. It was the start of a seven-game winning streak, the sixth of which found Ol' Pete winning his second start, a 7–3 decision over the Cardinals. But the Cubs followed their seven-game winning streak with a five-game losing streak. At the end of April, the ballclub was in familiar territory with a 7–6 record.

Alex lost a 2–1 decision to Pittsburgh on April 27, then lost 3–2 to the Cardinals on May 3 and 4–1 to the Giants on May 8. Though he had lost three in a row, he was drawing attention for a more positive reason. Heading into mid-May, Alexander had not walked a batter all year. On May 13, he evened his record at 3–3 by beating Dazzy Vance and the Dodgers 5–2. Once again, he didn't walk anybody, his sixth straight start without issuing a base on balls. Four days later, the string was broken when Alex walked three batters in

Bill Killefer was Alexander's catcher with Philadelphia and with the Cubs and was one of his managers with the Cubs. When Ol' Pete got in Joe McCarthy's doghouse, Killefer was a coach with the Cardinals and was said to have been instrumental in convincing St. Louis to pick him up for the stretch drive in the 1926 pennant race (National Baseball Hall of Fame Library, Cooperstown, N.Y.).

a 7–4 win over the Phillies. Alexander still holds the major league record of most innings without issuing a walk from the start of a season — 52. Bill Fischer of the Kansas City A's went 86 innings without issuing a pass, and Christy Mathewson of the Giants and Randy Jones of the San Diego Padres each went 68 innings without walking anybody, but those were all midseason accomplishments.

The Cubs were better than they had been in the past few seasons, and Killefer got more than he expected from Alexander, who won 22 games and lost only 12 for the season. He lowered his earned run average to 3.19, and his 72 strikeouts were about the same total as two years earlier. The remarkable statistic was that Alex walked only 30 batters all year in 305 innings — about one walk every 10 innings. He didn't walk a batter until May 17 and walked only 27 after that. Vic Aldridge won 16 games for the second year in a row and lost only nine. Osborne didn't live up to expectations, winning eight and losing 15. The Cubs had a little more offense, with four players in double figures in home runs: Hack Miller had 20, Bob O'Farrell and Bernie Friberg each had 12, and Arnold "Jigger" Statz had 10. Put it all together and it was a fourth place team, a big disappointment to Wrigley and Killefer, particularly since Alex had rebounded so well from two sub-par years.

As spring training began in 1924, Alex and the rest of the baseball world received a jolt with the news that Pat Moran died in Florida while preparing to get his Cincinnati ballclub ready for the coming season. In the early years, Moran had been the guy who gave Alex his first big break, by convincing Phillies manager Red Dooin to keep him on the squad in 1911. Four years later, Moran was the manager and Alex was the ace of the staff as the Phillies won their only pennant. He is remembered also as being the manager of the Cincinnati Reds team that beat the Chicago White Sox in the 1919 World Series tainted by revelation that eight Chicago players had conspired with gamblers to "fix" the series. Not surprisingly, Moran always said the Reds would have won it anyway. For Alex, he had lost two old friends within the space of about a year — Frank Bancroft, who put together such spectacular barnstorming tours a few years back, and now Moran, his mentor, his manager and, like Alex, a man who was often the last one to leave a bar at closing time. His death certificate listed the cause of death as Bright's Disease. The unofficial cause, in the minds of many, was alcoholism.

The 1924 season opened on April 15 with the Cubs losing to the Cardinals 6–5 at Sportman's Park. Alex watched from the bench as Rogers Hornsby went 2 for 5, a .400 percentage to start the season. No one would have guessed that his opening day performance actually lowered his batting average for the season. Hornsby was to hit .424, still the best ever. Alexander got his first win, and the Cubs evened their season record the next day with a 13–4 victory. On April 21, he lost to the Reds, now managed by Jack Hendrix, 2–1, but turned around eight days later and beat Lee Meadows, now pitching for Pittsburgh, also by a 2–1 score. He beat the Cardinals 4–1 at Wrigley Field on May 4 and got the best of Burleigh Grimes and the Dodgers on May 10, with the Cubs outlasting Brooklyn 7–5. He followed that up with wins over the Giants 6–4 on May 15 and 8–6 over the Phillies on May 21. Though he lost to Pittsburgh 5–4 on May 27, Alex entered June with a 7–2 record and seemed well on his way to another 20-win season. On June 25 at Pittsburgh, he was clipped by a line drive on his pitching arm. He stayed on to eke out an 8–7 victory, but X-rays later showed a fractured wrist.

Alex spent much of the summer of '24 working with young Cub pitchers in the bullpen and trading stories with his speakeasy buddies after the ballgames. When he was injured, the Cubs were in second place, 2½ games behind McGraw's Giants. When he returned to the hill on September 1, Chicago was in fourth place, 9½ games behind the Giants.

On September 20, Alex beat the Giants 7–3 in 12 innings for his 300th major league victory, a game in which an error by second baseman George Grantham, a notoriously poor fielder, prevented him from winning in nine innings. The Giants featured a lineup with seven future Hall of Famers—shortstop Fred Lindstrom, second baseman Frankie Frisch, right fielder Ross Youngs, center fielder George Kelly, first baseman Bill Terry, left fielder Hack Wilson and shortstop Travis Jackson. The milestone 300th win was hardly mentioned in the newspapers of the day. Individual statistics were not as glorified in those days as they were in years to come, except for the Herculean achievements of a brash Yankee slugger, George Herman Ruth.[10]

Chicago	AB	R	H	*New York*	AB	R	H
Adams, ss	7	1	1	L'strom, 3b	4	0	1
H'thcote, cf	4	1	2	O'Con'l, rf, cf	2	1	0
Grantham, 2b	5	0	1	Frisch, 2b, 3b	6	1	2
Fitzg'd, rf	6	1	1	Nehf, rf	0	0	0
Friberg, 3b	5	1	3	Youngs, rf, 2b	5	0	3
Grigsby, lf	5	3	1	Kelly, cf, 3b	6	0	3
Hartnett, c	6	0	4	Terry, 1b	6	1	0
Cotter, 1b	6	0	2	Wilson, lf	6	0	2
Alexander, p	6	0	1	Jackson, ss	6	0	3
Totals	50	7	16	Gowdy, c	5	0	0
				Barnes, p	2	0	0
				(a) S'worth	1	0	0
				Jonnard, p	0	0	0

VII—The Cub Years

Chicago	AB	R	H	New York	AB	R	H
				(b) Bentley	1	0	1
				(c) McQ'lan	0	0	0
				Ryan, p	0	0	0
				(d) Snyder	1	0	0
				Maun, p	0	0	0
				Baldwin, p	0	0	0
				Totals	51	3	15

(a) batted for Barnes in seventh
(b) batted for Jonnard in ninth
(c) ran for Bentley in ninth
(d) batted for Ryan in eleventh

```
Chicago      0 1 0 0 0 1 1 0 0 0 0 4 — 7
New York     0 0 1 0 0 0 0 1 1 0 0 0 — 3
```

Errors—Adams, Heathcoate, Grantham, Friberg, Hartnett, O'Connell, Kelly, Jackson. Doubles—Wilson. Triples—Hartnett. Stolen base—Frisch. Sacrifices—Heathcoate, Grantham. Double plays—Jackson, Frisch and Terry; Adams, Grantham and Cotter. Left on base—New York 13, Chicago 12

	IP	H	R	BB	SO	
Alexander	12	15	3	1	5	(W)
Barnes	7	10	3	1	1	
Jonnard	2	0	0	0	2	
Ryan	2	1	0	2	2	
Maun	⅓	4	4	0	0	(L)
Baldwin	⅔	1	0	0	0	

Umpires—Klem and Wilson. Time: 2 hours, 30 minutes

When Alexander got hurt, his ballclub had a record of 36–22. In his absence, the Cubs were 32–37. Alex went 3–3 the rest of the way and finished with a 12–5 record and an earned run average of 3.03. For the first time in his big league career, except for the three appearances in 1918, Ol' Pete went through a season without throwing a shutout. The Cubs finished fifth with an 81–72 record, 13 games behind the Giants.

On October 27, 1924, Veeck made a trade that was to affect the history of the Cubs for many years to come, and in more ways than one. Chicago traded veteran pitcher Vic Aldridge, a minor league first baseman named Al Niehaus and George Grantham, the stone-fingered infielder, to Pittsburgh for veteran shortstop Walter "Rabbit" Maranville, first baseman

Charlie Grimm and veteran pitcher Wilbur Cooper, a 20-game winner for the Pirates in 1924. Maranville and Grimm were fun-loving athletes whose off-the-field antics wore thin on Pirate owner Barney Dreyfuss, who didn't appreciate Grimm's banjo-playing and Maranville's cavorting around in the clubhouse. Maranville gave Alexander a new drinking buddy until Maranville became manager for a short stint — short because of Alexander, he would later say. Grimm became the regular first baseman for a decade and then managed the club to three pennants, in 1932, 1935 and 1945. His 1938 ballclub also won the championship, but Grimm quit early in the year and turned over the reins to Gabby Hartnett.

Maranville broke in with the Boston Braves in 1912 and was the shortstop on the "Miracle Braves" team of 1914 that went from last to first in half a season and then beat Connie Mack's mighty A's in the World Series. He was known as a slick fielder, adequate batter, outstanding drinker and a world-class flake. As with Yogi Berra a generation later, it is hard to separate fact from fiction in stories told about Maranville, partly because, like Berra, he enjoyed his reputation and rarely denied any story told about him. It is said that he once swam across a river fully clothed because he could get to the other side of it faster that way than by driving around it. He earned his Hall of Fame credentials with his glove. In 1914, when he played shortstop for the Braves, the second baseman was Johnny Evers, legendary second baseman of the Cubs a few years before. There weren't any poems written about Maranville and Evers, but the record shows that each turned more double plays in 1914 than Tinker and Evers did with the Cubs. Ten years later, Maranville was still graceful and efficient in the field. In 1923, playing for Pittsburgh, he led all shortstops in the National League in double plays. In 1924, still playing for Pittsburgh, he led all second basemen in double plays.

Grimm knew Alexander by reputation both on and off the field. He recalled a time in which Alex tried to make it as an insurance salesman in the off-season. Wrigley, trying to help out his pitcher — and perhaps trying to keep him occupied and out of trouble — offered to purchase a huge policy. The Cubs were in spring training on Catalina Island at the time. Grimm said Alex was so thrilled with landing the big policy, he couldn't help himself. He went down to a bar called The Hurricane to celebrate. Naturally, he was recognized by most of the patrons, many of whom bought him a drink. By the end of the evening — actually the early morning hours— Alex got involved in what Grimm described as "some sort of jam" that apparently was the talk of the island by daybreak. Wrigley was among those who heard about it and scrapped the insurance deal with Alex.[11]

Sportswriters had covered for Alex for years, partly because his pitching heroics seemed to prove that he could handle the liquor that was never far from his grasp. But as the years took their inevitable toll on his athletic abilities, those who had to deal with Alex found it more and more difficult to sluff off his alcohol problems with innocent phrases like "John Barleycorn" and "lack of attention to training rules."

Biographer Kavanagh writes, "Ol' Pete knew he had a problem with alcohol. The trauma of front-line service had changed him from a cold-beer-after-the-game casual drinker to one who would hide bottles of booze and drink to ward off epilepsy. It was his opinion that an alcoholic edge held the sneak attacks of his ailment at bay."[12]

He still had some good pitching years left in him. But the epilepsy that he tried to hide, and the alcoholism that he could no longer hide, were wearing him down, and while some good days were still to come, most were well behind him.

• CHAPTER VIII •

Managerial Merry-Go-Round and McCarthy

"His resolve to go home early grew weaker as his pitching years faded. There would always be a saloon somewhere with someone to talk to about how great the old days had been."
— Jack Kavanagh

Ol' Pete showed no signs of going downhill on opening day of 1925. On April 14, he mowed down the Pittsburgh Pirates 8–2 at Wrigley Field and came close to hitting for the cycle, lacking only the triple. Quin Ryan, broadcasting from the roof of the grandstand, called the play-by-play for WGN in the first radio broadcast of a regular-season Cubs game. Alex didn't pitch again until the following Sunday, April 19, when the Cardinals beat him 6–0. The Cubs lost four in a row in mid–April but came back to win five in a row between April 23 and April 27. By the end of the month, they were 8–6 and in third place, with Alexander posting a 2–2 record.

Alex went two weeks without a start and then won a 4–2 decision over the Phillies at Baker Bowl on May 14 to break a six-game Cub losing streak. When they lost four more in a row, including Alex getting clipped 5–2 by the Giants, they had lost 10 out of 11 and found themselves in seventh place, already 10 games out of first on May 18, barely a month after the season had started. One of the problems for the ballclub was that Maranville, who Veeck and Killefer hoped would team with Grimm to inject some life into the team, broke his leg in a spring training game on March 15 and didn't play once the regular season started until May 24. On May 23, Veeck tried once again to shake up the troops. He traded backup catcher Bob O'Farrell — backup only because Hartnett was playing so well — to the Cardinals for catcher Mike Gonzalez and infielder Howard Freigau. Gonzalez, a Mexican who didn't speak good English, wasn't much of a ballplayer, but years later, as a scout, he added to memorable baseball lexicon when he scribbled a note saying a particular prospect was "good field, no hit."

VIII — Managerial Merry-Go-Round and McCarthy

In Maranville's first game back, Alex tamed the Reds 5–1 at Crosley Field. Four days later, he watched from the bench as his teammates had their biggest offensive outpouring of the year, scoring 12 runs in the seventh inning en route to beating Cincinnati 13–3. In the big inning, four Cubs players had two hits each — Grimm contributing a single and a double, Barney Friberg smashing a double and a triple, and winning pitcher Wilbur Cooper and outfielder Arnie Statz each getting a pair of singles. That was the high point of another disappointing month, and the Cubs entered June still mired in seventh place. By July 7, with no turnaround in sight, Veeck dismissed Killefer, the congenial manager and Alexander's friend and confidante going back to their glory days as battery mates on the great Phillies teams. The new manager was a surprise to most of the Cubs and to most of the rest of the baseball world. Veeck named Maranville to lead the club for the rest of the year. He was a brash, bawdy veteran, in stark contrast to his predecessor. Maranville had spent the first six weeks of the season being an erstwhile manager and coach from the sidelines while he waited for his leg to heal.

Alexander lost to Dazzy Vance and Brooklyn 4–2 in Maranville's debut. That night, the new manager and a couple of his players objected to the rates they were being charged by a New York City cabbie. When the cabbie objected to the objections, tempers flared and Maranville and company wound up in jail temporarily until they were bailed out in night court. On the field, the Cubs continued to play at a pace that kept them in seventh place. On September 1, Alex lost a 2–0 decision to Boston, pushing them 24 games out of first place. By this time, Maranville had made as many headlines off the field as he had on the field, including a recent incident in which he reportedly deposited the contents of a spittoon onto passengers of a train. He was relieved of his duties as manager, though he remained as a player until he was released at the end of the season.

Perhaps more significant than the firing of Maranville was the role that Alexander may have played in it. Maranville had been a drinker for much of his career, and although he was eccentric and at times wild, he always showed up for work and didn't let it affect his play. He knew of Alex's fondness for liquor and put up with it. But he blamed Alex for the circumstances that led to his firing.

According to Maranville, Alexander didn't show up at the ballpark on a day he was scheduled to pitch in Philadelphia. Veeck was at the game. He wrote a note telling Maranville to fine him $250 and for both of them to report to Veeck's office upon their return to Chicago.

Maranville said when they arrived at Veeck's office he told Alex to tell the truth about what happened but instead, in Maranville's words, "Alex told a pack of lies." And Veeck knew it. Veeck told Alex that the lies not only cost him an additional $250 but they had cost Maranville his job. George Gibson replaced the Rabbit as Cubs manager.[1]

Gibson was a veteran, having managed the Pirates in 1920 and 1921, guiding them to fourth and second place finishes. The Bucs were 32–33 in 1922 and in fifth place when Gibson was terminated. He would return to manage the Pirates in 1932 and 1933, compiling two more second place finishes, and then was let go in 1934 with his team in fifth place with a 27–24 record. He finished out the 1925 season with the Cubs.

When the season was over, the Cubs were in last place with a 68–86 record, and it hadn't really mattered who was managing. Chicago was 33–42 under Killefer, 23–30 under Maranville and 12–14 under Gibson. Alex finished at 15–11, not bad for an eighth place team, and tops on the team in victories.

Wrigley and Veeck never intended for Gibson to be the Cubs manager over the long haul. He was a veteran and he was available to finish out the season. He finished his major league managerial career with a .546 percentage and had some good teams. The rap against him in Pittsburgh was that he wasn't much of a disciplinarian, not the best resume for someone who was going to have to oversee the likes of Maranville, Alexander and a clubhouse full of underachievers.

The Cubs brass had gone along with Killefer, the former Cubs player who had a loose clubhouse and a losing ballclub, and with Maranville, who turned out to be an experiment that didn't work, and then Gibson, the willing caretaker when there was no loftier goal than to see the season through to the end. As the 1926 season loomed, the Cubs chose as their next manager a man with no major league managerial experience but someone with a stellar record in his hometown of Louisville. His name was Joe McCarthy. He knew how to win and he knew how to keep a ballclub in line, at least in the minor leagues. The Cubs were willing to give him a try in the major leagues if he was willing to leave his comfortable surroundings in Louisville, where he had won seven consecutive American Association championships. Louisville was home and McCarthy's job was secure—but it wasn't the big leagues. Chicago was. McCarthy agreed to come. Thus the rocky relationship was about to begin between Grover Cleveland Alexander, the veteran pitcher who didn't care much for training rules or discipline, and Joseph Vincent McCarthy, a rookie manager two months younger than Alexander and someone who was going to have to prove early on that he could take control and keep control of a big league ballclub.

Alex's off-season was divided between trying to deal with his ever-more-apparent drinking problems while convincing the media and the public that he was finding new ways to stay fit. In January, 1926, *Chicago Tribune* sportswriter Irving Vaughan did a piece on Alex extolling the virtues of bowling. "Nothing like it for an arm," Ol' Pete told the writer, who watched him perform at a bowling alley on Chicago's north side.

"Gripping the heavy ball is great stuff for the fingers—and the fingers are important in any kind of pitching. Also helps the wrist and that too plays its part. It takes strong fingers and wrists to get the spin that makes a ball hip or hop. The arm merely produces the speed," he said.

Alex, who had been subsisting for years by stashing bottles in little hideaways he'd find in clubhouses, would also, from time to time, agree to go into a hospital or clinic and try to take the "cure." Veeck and the Cubs picked up the tab. In the winter between the 1925 and 1926 seasons, he checked himself into the Keeley Institute in Dwight, Illinois, about 50 miles south of Chicago, and stayed for three months, leaving only to take the train to Chicago to sign his contract for the 1926 season. That chore completed, he took the train back to Dwight. The institute was founded in 1879 by Dr. Leslie Keeley, who had become interested in the problem of drunkenness in soldiers and tried to find a cure for it. With the help of chemist friend, John Oughten, Keeley came up with a concoction he called his "Gold Cure for Drunkenness" and began marketing it at $9 a bottle. The Keeley Institute became so popular that it expanded to other states and the "cures" expanded to include solutions to the tobacco and opium habits. Alex paid the institute out of his own pocket in hopes of not only curbing his alcoholism but staving off any problems with his new manager. It didn't work in either instance.

The trouble began in spring training. Alex's wife was with him on Catalina Island, and Aimee recalled years later how she saw right away that McCarthy and Ol' Pete were not going to hit it off.

"Ever since we'd been with the Cubs, Alex and I had eaten at the same table in the Hotel St. Catherine at Avalon," Aimee told interviewer Frank Finch in a *Sporting News* story published May 2, 1951, six months after Alex's death. "One morning, we came down for breakfast and McCarthy, who was the only manager Alex ever had trouble with, was sitting at our table. He didn't even ask us to sit there," she said.

Alex hurt his ankle in spring training and was hospitalized for several days. First reports were that it was broken. McCarthy had to pass the hospital every day to get to the ballpark but never stopped to see Alex, she said. The Cubs had a different version of what happened. They thought the ankle injury might just be a sprain. They ordered a second X-ray when Alexander got back to the mainland. Doctors determined that what appeared to be a sprain might just be an aberration that frequently showed up in the

X-rays of very active people. To test their theory, Alex's other ankle was X-rayed, and it showed up the same as the first X-ray. Alex was told to turn in his crutches and get on the train. When it was time to break camp at Catalina, the players' wives who were there left before the players did and headed home. The ballplayers then started barnstorming their way home. Alex made the trip but "began hitting the bottle but good," in Aimee's words. When the ballclub arrived in Kansas City for some games, McCarthy sent Alex on to Chicago.

The Cubs opened the 1926 season at Crosley Field in Cincinnati. McCarthy tabbed Wilbur Cooper as the opening day pitcher in a game the Cubs lost 7–6. The next day, Charlie Root stymied the Reds in a 9–2 Chicago victory. Losing pitcher was Carl Mays, the man who six years earlier threw the pitch that killed Ray Chapman. Alexander got the nod in game three and lost a 2–1 decision to Red Lucas, the great-hitting Cincinnati pitcher, who tripled to drive in the winning run. Alex's next start was the Wrigley Field home opener, and Ol' Pete didn't disappoint. The Cubs beat the Reds 4–2. He lost another tough one on April 27, this one to Johnny Morrison and the Pirates 2–1. In his next start, on May 2, the Cubs won their fourth straight—and all were come-from-behind wins, as Chicago beat St. Louis 6–5.

Joe McCarthy was a successful minor league manager at Louisville and became a Hall of Fame manager with the New York Yankees. But in 1926, he had never managed a big league club when the Cubs hired him. When Alexander continually broke training rules, he provided McCarthy with a way of showing Alex and the rest of the ballclub who was boss. He suspended Alexander. A month later, Alex was with the Cardinals (National Baseball Hall of Fame Library, Cooperstown, N.Y.).

Six days later at Wrigley Field, Alexander prevailed again as the Cubs beat the Giants 6–4. It was his third win of the year and his last win in a Cubs uniform. Writing in the *New York Times,* sportswriter Harry Cross said this:

"The shadow of Alexander hovered over the Giants like Banquo's ghost. His easy swinging

VIII—Managerial Merry-Go-Round and McCarthy

motion sent the ball soaring over the corners of the plate, and when the ancient arm began to weaken in the sixth, his stout heart carried him through. An inspiring figure was Alex the Great as he stood unmoved in the face of New York's vicious blows."

No one knew at the time, of course, that it was to be Alex's last win in a Cubs uniform.

On May 22, Alexander was honored by the Cubs and their fans and was presented with a new car, a Lincoln sedan, in appreciation for his many great years with the ballclub. Little did the fans know that their hero was losing control of his life and his career for the same reasons he was not a good candidate to use the gift they had presented to him. When the Cubs made an eastern road trip in early June, Alex stayed behind, missing games in Pittsburgh, Brooklyn, New York and Boston. When he joined the team in Philadelphia, he was in no condition to pitch. He had broken training rules by his excessive drinking, a circumstance that had caused Mitchell and Killefer, Maranville and Gibson to look the other way when they saw it. Not McCarthy. He saw Alex's antics as insubordination and a way of testing the leadership and guts of a rookie manager. McCarthy responded with a typewritten message, dated June 15, 1926, written on the stationery of the Hotel Adelphia in Philadelphia where the Cubs were staying: "This is to officially advise you that you have this day been indefinitely suspended without pay for violating rules of training, drunkenness and not appearing in uniform. Secretary Seys has been advised to furnish you transportation back to Chicago."

Jimmy Cooney, the Cubs shortstop, recalled in an interview how Alexander sniffed ammonia between innings of ballgames because he thought it staved off epileptic fits and used to hide liquor bottles in the lockers of rookies to try to fool McCarthy. Sometimes during games, he would sneak into the locker room to have a belt or two.[2]

Alexander, suspended for the first time in his career, took the train back to Chicago to await his fate. He didn't have to wait long. On June 22, the Cubs asked waivers on their 39-year-old problem child. The St. Louis Cardinals, perhaps to the delight of one of their newest coaches, Bill Killefer, signed Alex. He joined a team managed by another no-nonsense manager, this one with a world of major league experience, Rogers Hornsby.

When Alexander's name came across the waiver wire, Branch Rickey, the Cardinals' straight-laced general manager, was out of town, working on establishing the ballclub's farm system, a Rickey innovation in baseball that all other teams would eventually emulate. Cardinals owner Sam Breadon saw that Alexander was available and sent a wire to Hornsby to see if he was interested. Rickey, a man who refused to work on Sundays and didn't drink anything stronger than orange juice, might not have been inter-

HOTEL ADELPHIA
EUROPEAN PLAN
400 ROOMS   400 BATHS
ABSOLUTELY FIREPROOF

CHESTNUT STREET AT THIRTEENTH

PHILADELPHIA, PA.

June 15, 1926

G. C. Alexander,
Chicago Cubs,
Chicago, Ill.

Dear Sir:—

    This is to officially advise you that you have this day been indefinately suspended without pay for violating rules of training, drunkenness and not appearing in uniform.

    Secretary Says has been advised to furnish you transportation back to Chicago.

                          Manager

This letter, typed by Joe McCarthy on the stationery of the Hotel Adelphia in Philadelphia, informs Alexander he has been suspended. It is the beginning of the end of his day with the Chicago Cubs.

ested. But he wasn't available and Hornsby didn't reply to the wire. So Breadon made the decision on his own to acquire the aging pitcher.[3]

Meanwhile, McCarthy had some explaining to do to the fans of Chicago who had honored Alexander less than a month earlier and were pretty much oblivious to all the problems Alex created for himself off the field. At the time of the suspension, McCarthy told the press, "Alexander hasn't pitched for a month and recently has been no help to the team. He has stayed away from the field, not appearing in uniform here (Philadelphia) or at Boston. If a man doesn't report and work out, he can't keep his arm in shape. I'm not going to stand for that stuff. I don't intend to let Alexander or any other player break up my ballclub." So Alex, who once said of McCarthy, "I'm not going to take orders from any bush manager," was headed for the fourth-place Cardinals. It was, as Bill Henry said in a column in the *Los Angeles Times* on June 24, "one of the most startling bits of (baseball) news in a long time."

Breadon was willing to take the chance that Alex would behave and perhaps even help the Cardinals move up in the standings. He gave himself a little insurance, though, with a directive that was a condition of employment: Aimee had to travel with the team when the Cardinals went on the road. She said later she couldn't keep Alex away from liquor all the time, but she kept him in good enough condition to work and, in turn, she said, he didn't give her any trouble.

The Cardinals didn't have to wait long to get a return on their investment. On June 27, 37,718 crowded into Sportsman's Park to watch Ol' Pete make his first start for St. Louis against McCarthy and the Cubs. It was, as *Chicago Tribune* writer James Crusinberry reported, "by far the biggest crowd that ever saw a game of ball in St. Louis." Alex and the Cubs won 3–2. Several newspaper accounts of the game mentioned the word "revenge" and how McCarthy watched from the third base coaching box as Alex mowed down the Cubs hitters.

Alex had joined a team that was exciting and at times explosive but was sputtering along in fourth place, behind Pittsburgh, Cincinnati and Brooklyn. He became the fifth member of that ballclub to eventually be elected to the Hall of Fame. (First baseman Jim Bottomley, second baseman Hornsby, outfielder Chick Hafey and pitcher Jesse Haines were the others.) They didn't lack for team leadership. Including Hornsby, four of the squad would spend part of their careers as Cardinal managers. (The others were catcher Bob O'Farrell and outfielders Billy Southworth and Ray Blades.) Third baseman Les Bell didn't make it to the Hall of Fame and never managed the Redbirds, but he did hit .325 to lead the club in hitting. Eccentric rookie Flint Rhem, whose excessive drinking ruined a promising career, won 20 games. Other starters were Haines, Bill Sherdel and Vic Keen.

On July 2, Alex had his second strong outing in a row but had no decision to show for it, leaving the game before Pittsburgh scored the go-ahead run in winning 3–2. On July 6, Alexander pitched well again, and took a 2–1 lead into the ninth inning against Cincinnati. But Wally Pipp, the first baseman most famous for being replaced by Lou Gehrig in the Yankees lineup the year before, hit a homer off Alex to tie the game, and the Reds got three runs off him in the 11th to capture the victory. Five days later, Alex tamed Boston 7–2. In Brooklyn, on July 16, a large crowd assembled to see what they hoped would be a great pitching duel between Alex and Burleigh Grimes. It didn't materialize as both got clobbered and neither got the decision in an 8–7 Brooklyn win

On July 22, Alex once again pitched eight strong innings but weakened in the ninth, giving up the decisive two runs in a 5–3 loss to the Giants. He didn't pitch nearly as well in his next outing but got the win anyway, a 9–5 victory over the Phillies. By the end of July he was 3–2 with the Cardinals with two no-decisions. But the Cardinals as a team had started to jell just in time for the stretch drive. Alexander absorbed a 7–2 pasting at the hands of the Giants on August 1 and got a save on August 5 when Hornsby used him in relief to protect an 11–9 win over Brooklyn. Two days later, he started against Brooklyn and hooked up once again with Burleigh Grimes. This time Ol' Pete was hitting the corners and keeping hitters off balance in recording a 3–0 shutout. On August 14, he had the chance to beat McCarthy and the Cubs again but lost 3–2 with the winning run scoring on his throwing error. Being used now as both a starter and a reliever, Alex was showing signs of his old form as he picked up two more saves. He then got a no-decision in a 2–2 tie with the Pirates in a game that was halted for two hours by rain and finally stopped by darkness.

St. Louis put together eight-game and six-game winning streaks in August to put the Cardinals in the heat of the race for the National League flag. But their September schedule was a nightmare for a pennant contender. After September 1, they didn't play another home game. Instead, they traveled the entire National League circuit, first to Chicago, then to Cincinnati, Pittsburgh, Boston, Philadelphia, New York, Brooklyn and then back to Cincinnati for the final games of the season.

On September 2, Alex once again went up against the Cubs. He beat Charlie Root 3–0 for his eighth win as a Cardinal, his second shutout and his second win over his old teammates. The Cards were in the thick of the pennant race, and Alex was contributing mightily on the field. Off the field, Aimee Alexander was contributing just as mightily by not letting her husband be too far out of her sight.

On September 5, Alex beat Cincinnati 7–3 to propel the Cardinals into first place. After the game, Hornsby, plagued by back problems all year, made a quick trip to Youngstown to get an "adjustment" from Bonesetter Reese, the doc who had helped Alex and so many other athletes with his chiropractic maneuvers. After the Cards split a Labor Day doubleheader in Pittsburgh, the top of the standings looked like this:

St. Louis	80–57	.583
Cincinnati	77–56	.578
Pittsburgh	73–57	.561

Alex didn't win any more games but picked up another save before the season ended. The Cardinals went to Boston where the seventh-place Braves roughed up Alex and got 18 hits in an 11–3 win. The next day, the two teams split a doubleheader with Haines tossing a shutout and the Cardinals winning 2–0, but Johnny Cooney bested Rhem in the second game 4–3. The next day, Alex was used in relief, and Cooney, playing first base, drove in the winning run in the 14th inning for a 5–4 Boston victory. The Cardinals and Reds were tied for first place, but only for a day. On September 14, with St. Louis having an off day, Cincinnati beat Brooklyn to move into sole possession of first place. The Cardinals moved on to Philadelphia and Alexander's old haunt, Baker Bowl, for another oddity in scheduling — a six-game series. While the Cards did not clinch the pennant mathematically in

Alexander was 38 when he joined the Cardinals and helped them to get to the World Series twice. He won his 373rd major league game with them in 1929 and celebrated a little too much after the game. He was suspended for the rest of the season and never won another big league game. Had he won just one more, he would have the National League record instead of being tied with Christy Mathewson (National Baseball Hall of Fame Library, Cooperstown, N.Y.).

Philadelphia, they clinched it in spirit by walloping the Phillies in the first five games by scores of 9–2, 23–3, 10–2, 10–1 and 7–3. While St. Louis was winning 10–1 on September 17, Frankie Frisch, a future star Cardinal, homered in the 10th inning to help the Giants beat the Reds, pushing St. Louis back into first place to stay. The Cardinals moved on to Brooklyn, splitting two games with the Robins. In the second of the two, St. Louis won 15–7, with third baseman Bell leading the attack with three triples and a double. On September 24, Rhem won his 20th game and the Cardinals clinched the pennant in a 6–4 win against the Giants at the Polo Grounds, the first National League championship in the history of the franchise. In that last month, playing nothing but road games, the Cardinals were 13–11.

Alex won 9 and lost 7 for the Cardinals, but his ability to both start games and come in from the bullpen added depth to the pitching staff and helped bring that first championship to St. Louis. His totals for the year, including his work with the Cubs, were 12 wins and 10 losses and an earned run average of 3.05, including a 2–1 record as a relief pitcher with two saves.

It was a title full of ironies. Hornsby, the great second baseman and manager, was incensed that owner Breadon had scheduled exhibition games in Buffalo and Rochester in September and said so publicly. While Hornsby was at the helm for the Cards' first championship, his days were numbered. Breadon traded him to the Giants shortly after the World Series. For Alex, it was his first championship since 1915. The Cubs had gotten him in 1918 in hopes of winning a pennant. They won it, but Alex was off at war. When he returned, they never won it. And now, the year they "sold him down the river," as Crusinberry put it in the *Chicago Tribune,* he was part of a championship team with the Cubs' archrivals on the other side of the river in St. Louis.

The celebration in St. Louis would have to wait. The New Yankees won the American League crown. Since the Cardinals were already in New York, where the World Series would start in a few days, the team remained there rather than going home. The Yankees were a formidable crew, one year away from having a team that many historians have deemed the best in baseball history. Babe Ruth hit .372 with 47 home runs and 145 RBIs. Rookie Tony Lazzeri, a second baseman, hit .275 with 18 homers and 114 RBIs. Lou Gehrig, the "Iron Horse" first baseman, hit .313 with 16 home runs and 107 RBIs. Bob Meusel and Earl Combes joined Ruth in the outfield, and Marty Koenig and Joe Dugan were at short and third respectively. Pat Collins, a relative no-name compared to the others, did most of the catching and handled pitchers like Herb Pennock, who was 23–11, Urban Shocker, 19–11, and Waite Hoyt, was 16–12.

As already noted, the Cardinals had many stars—Hornsby, Bottomley,

Southworth, Hafey, Haines, O'Farrell and Ol' Pete Alexander. But for Breadon, the most valuable player for the Cardinals during the last two months of the season might very well have been someone who never put on a uniform — Aimee Alexander.

• CHAPTER IX •

A Strikeout for the Ages

"He was always hitting the corners. Even in batting practice, he never gave you anything good to hit at."
— Chick Hafey, describing 39-year-old
Grover Cleveland Alexander

New York was a bustling city in 1926, run by a free-wheeling mayor named Jimmy Walker who would be forced to resign six years later in the midst of scandal and allegations of corruption. Not far away, in Philadelphia, six million people attended the World's Fair held in conjunction with the sesquicentennial of the signing of the Declaration of Independence.

Throughout the country, The Roaring 20's were in full swing with couples dancing the Charleston, sneaking into speakeasies and listening to the first record album of an up-and-coming clarinetist and band leader, Benny Goodman. America was a nation at work. The unemployment rate was 1.8 percent, the gross national product was growing, and it cost two cents to mail a letter. Richard Byrd and his pilot, Floyd Bennett, became the first men to fly over the North Pole, and Sinclair Lewis won the Pulitzer Prize for fiction for his novel *Arrowsmith*. Antifreeze was used in automobiles for the first time, and Henry Ford, the man who made automobiles, established the eight-hour day, 40-hour workweek for his employees. The National Broadcasting Company (NBC) and Book-of-the-Month Club both made their debuts, Gertrude Ederle became the first woman to swim the English Channel, Bobby Jones won the British Open golf tournament, and Gene Tunney won a 10-round decision over heavyweight boxing champion Jack Dempsey. Before the year was out, movie idol Rudolph Valentino, magician Harry Houdini and circus founder Charles Ringling had died. Perhaps the most telling comment to describe the temperament of the times came on April 7, as the baseball season was about to begin, when Emery Buckner, the U.S. attorney for the eastern district in New York, told a Senate Committee that bootlegging was a $3.6 billion business in the United States.

In 1926, the St. Louis Cardinals were thought of as outsiders, at least in terms of baseball glory. They and their American League counterparts, the St. Louis Browns, were the only teams west of the Mississippi River, and neither had ever been to a World Series. The Cardinals as a team hit 90 home runs. Four players in the Yankees' starting lineup, Ruth, Gehrig, Meusel and Lazzeri, combined to top that total, with Ruth alone contributing 47, more than half the St. Louis total. This was the Yankees' first trip back to the World Series since 1923. Their awestruck opponents were expected to be easy pickings for the Bronx Bombers.

On the eve of the World Series, Hornsby received shattering news. His mother had died in Texas. It was emotionally crushing for him, but so was the idea of leaving his team as they were about to embark on the greatest

Rogers Hornsby managed the Cardinals when Alexander joined the team. Alex helped St. Louis win the pennant and the World Series. Alexander always thought Hornsby contributed to the myth that Alex was either drunk or hung over when he struck out Tony Lazzeri and then shut down the Yankees the rest of way in the seventh game of the World Series (National Baseball Hall of Fame Library, Cooperstown, N.Y.).

and most important experience of their collective professional lives. Hornsby had always been a warrior. Now he was a general, about to lead his troops into their biggest battle. To abandon them now would be unthinkable, like Gen. Custer leaving Little Big Horn or Grant or Lee or Stonewall Jackson turning their backs on the men they were called to lead. Hornsby stayed. The funeral was postponed until after the World Series.

The Rajah picked Wee Willie Sherdel to pitch the first game. Standing 5 feet, 10 inches tall and weighing 160 pounds, Sherdel didn't overpower anybody, but the left-hander kept them off balance with his stuff. He had been a Cardinal his entire career and in 1925 led the National League in winning percentage at .714 with his 15–6 record. He had been a steady performer in the pennant year, winning 16, losing 12. A highlight of his career had come two years earlier, when, in a relief role, he came in to face Johnny Mokan of the Phillies. Philadelphia had runners on first and second. Sherdel went into his stretch, checked the runners, and then delivered to the plate. Mokan bunted the ball in the air and it was snared by Bottomley, charging in from first base. He whirled and threw to shortstop Cooney covering second, who doubled up the runner there and then threw to first, where Hornsby alertly covered the bag. It was a 3–6–4 triple play on one pitch.

His mound opponent for the opener was left-hander Herb Pennock, a 25-game winner and future Hall of Famer who won 240 games in the majors without an overpowering fastball but with a great deal of finesse. One baseball writer commented that Pennock succeeded because he knew the weakness of every batter in the American League and pitched to that weakness. Over the course of his career, he gave up more hits than innings pitched and didn't rack up many strikeouts. But in 22 years in the big leagues, he walked an average of only two batters per nine innings pitched. If he needed an out to get out of a jam, he found a way of getting it. Pennock broke in with the Philadelphia A's in 1912. On April 14, 1915, he came within one out of throwing the first opening day no-hitter, giving up only a single to Harry Hooper with two outs in the ninth. Six weeks later, A's owner Connie Mack put young Pennock on waivers, and the Red Sox, victims of the opening day one-hitter, pick him up. He pitched for the Red Sox until 1923, when he was traded to the Yankees. On June 4, 1925, Pennock and the Lefty Grove of the A's hooked up in one of baseball's greatest pitching duels, with the A's winning 1–0 in 15 innings. In characteristic style, Pennock gave up four hits and no walks. On September 25, 1926, he pitched the pennant clincher for the Yankees, a 10–2 win over the St. Louis Browns.

A crowd of 61,658 jammed into Yankee Stadium on the afternoon of October 2, 1926, as the Cardinals made their World Series debut before a hostile audience that was twice the size they were used to at Sportsman's Park in St. Louis. The Cardinals jumped on Pennock early. Taylor Douthit doubled past Ruth in right field and scored when Bottomley dumped a blooper over third baseman Joe Dugan's head into left field. St. Louis had a 1–0 lead before the Bronx Bombers had even come to bat. But the Yankees tied it in their half of the first without getting a hit. Sherdel, perhaps nervous as the game got started, walked Meusel, Combs and Ruth. When Gehrig hit into a force play at second, Meusel scored the tying run. Sherdel then settled down, pitched out of the inning and was not nicked for any more runs until the sixth. Ruth singled, Meusel moved him to second with a sacrifice bunt, and Gehrig drove him in with a base hit. That was the last scoring of the game. Bottomley got a base hit in the ninth off of Pennock, the first hit he had allowed since Bottomley's RBI single in the first. The Yankees won 2–1 to take a one-game lead in the series. In the locker room after the game, some of his teammates sympathized with Sherdel over his "hard luck." Hornsby overheard them and said, "The hell with yapping about hard luck. That one's over. We'll even it up tomorrow."[1]

An even bigger crowd, 63,600, showed up for game two, a game the Cardinals had to win. If they fell two games behind, the odds were not good that they would be able to overtake the Murderers' Row gang. For the biggest game of his managerial career, Hornsby turned to his old warhorse, Alexander, who had been on his good behavior for the most part since joining the Cardinals—and having his wife as his roommate. But Ol' Pete did have his moments. Wild Bill Hallahan, a rookie pitcher with the Cardinals in 1926, recalled one incident.

"Alex liked to go out before a game and work in the infield, generally around third base. One day we were taking batting practice and there's Alex, standing at third, crouched over, hands on knees, staring in to the plate. A ground ball went by him and he never budged, just remaining there stock still, staring in at the batter. Then another grounder buzzed by and the same thing. He never moved a muscle. Then someone ripped a line drive past his ear and he still didn't move. That's when Hornsby noticed him. Roger let out a howl and said, 'where in the hell did he get it?' meaning the booze, of course. 'Get him out of there before someone gets killed.'"[2]

Alexander's mound opponent in game two was Urban Shocker, one of the best but least-heralded pitchers of his era, partly because of his dour, strictly-business personality, partly because his best years were with the St. Louis Browns, who were always out of the glare of a lot of publicity and, toward the end of his career, because he was not colorful on an extremely colorful Yankee team. Shocker broke into baseball as a catcher. During those days, a foul ball bent his ring finger back so far that it never was quite right again. It had a permanent crook in it, something he said later helped him develop a special grip on the ball when he was pitching. Shocker had four sensational years with the Browns: 20–10 in 1920, 27–12 in 1921, 24–17 in 1922, and 20–12 in 1923. When he dropped to 16–13 the next year, the Browns peddled him to the Yankees, where he had his only .500 season, 12–12 in 1925, when the Yankees finished seventh. In 1926, he bounced back and fell one short of another 20-game season, finishing at 19–11. Like Pennock, he was not overpowering but got the ball over the plate, allowing only about two walks per game. Shocker would have one more good year, going

18–6 in 1927. A year later, he would be dead at the age of 38, the victim of pneumonia and heart disease. But on Sunday, October 3, 1926, he was matched up with Grover Cleveland Alexander in what was expected to be another thriller between two veterans.

Ol' Pete didn't help himself when he made a wild throw in the second inning after giving up singles to Meusel, Lazzeri and Dugan. He was down 2–0. Alex gave up another base hit to Combs in the third and then retired the next 21 batters. The Cardinals tied the game in the third inning when Douthit got a bunt single, Southworth followed with a single, Hornsby sacrificed the runners over to second and third, and Bottomley drove them in with a base hit. The game remained tied for the next three innings. In the seventh, Southworth broke the game open with a three-run homer into the right field stands. Thevenow also homered, but his didn't make it out of the park. He hit a shot into right field that lodged in a groove in the wooden fence. A bewildered Ruth could not find the ball while Thevenow circled the bases. The Cardinals won the game 6–2 behind Alexander to even the series at a game apiece.

Richard Vidmer described Alex's performance this way in the *New York Times:* "Youth will be served, the prophet says, but youth will be served in different ways. Yesterday, Yankee youth was served a brand of pitching they couldn't solve. They saw elusive curves and tantalizing twisters, slow sinkers and some a little slower. They saw them but they couldn't hit them."[3]

The Cardinals boarded the train for St. Louis to prepare for their first home game since Art Reinhart beat the Pirates on September 1. When they arrived, they were greeted with a hero's welcome the likes of which had not been seen in St. Louis since the troops started coming home from World War I. The next day, they sent Jesse Haines to the mound to prove they deserved the adulation. Haines had a blazing fastball and developed a knuckleball that he actually threw with his knuckles on the ball, as opposed to today's pitchers who throw more of a "fingernail ball." Haines was a kind fellow but he was a tough competitor who often showed anger when things didn't go right on the field. He and Alex went back a long way. On September 1, 1920, when Alexander was still with the Cubs, he and Haines hooked up in a 17-inning game in which both pitchers went all the way and the Cubs won 3–2. On July 17, 1924, Haines threw a no-hitter against Boston, the first no-hitter in the 20th century for St. Louis. His 210 career wins in 18 years were the most by a Cardinal pitcher until Bob Gibson passed him about 50 years later.

The Yankees went with Dutch Ruether, a much-traveled left-hander whom they had picked up from the Washington Senators on August 27. Ruether had a reputation of being a bit of a flake who didn't turn his back on trouble. But he had a solid major league career that included a brief stint with the Cubs in 1917, then several productive years with Cincinnati, including 1919, when he was 19–6 with the Reds' pennant winner and won the first game of the World Series against the Chicago White Sox, a victory that became tainted when it was learned eight Chicago players conspired to lose the World Series in the famous "Black Sox" scandal. Ruether also pitched for Brooklyn before heading to Washington and finally the Yankees. He was 14–9 with the 1926 ballclub. On October 5, he took on Haines and the Cardinals in boisterous Sportsman's Park, filled to capacity with 37,708 fans. It was to be Haines' day as the big right-hander tossed a 4–0 shutout and hit a two-run homer off Ruether, who needed relief help from Bob Shawkey and Miles Thomas before it was over.

In the fourth game, the Cardinals went with their 20-game winner, Flint Rhem, a man who knew what to do with a fastball on the field and a highball off the field, one of the few players who could match Grover Cleveland Alexander drink for drink in a saloon. He was no match for Waite Hoyt and the Yankees. The Bronx Bombers, who had trouble getting good swings off of Sherdel, Alexander and Haines, with their assortment of off-speed pitches and knuckleballs, feasted on the fastballs of Rhem. He managed to strike out Combs and Koenig in the first inning, both on fastballs, but couldn't get the high hard one past Ruth, who hit the first pitch over the right field wall. In the third inning, Rhem tried to fool the Babe with an off-speed pitch and Ruth smashed it over the roof in right center field. By the sixth inning, Rhem was gone. Herman Bell faced Ruth and gave up what was believed to be the longest home run ever in Sportsman Park, a drive that went into the center field bleachers. Sportswriter Fred Lieb said the ball traveled well over 500 feet "and still had plenty of carry." When the sun went down on St. Louis that night, Ruth had World Series records for home runs, RBIs, total bases and slugging percentage in one ball game. The Cardinals fought valiantly and matched the Yankees in hits with 14 but lost the game 10–5. The series was even at two games each, but the Cardinals had a casualty. Douthit collided with Hafey going after a fly ball and separated his shoulder. He did not play again in the series.

The fifth game was a rematch of the opener, with the two lefties, Sherdel for the Cardinals and Pennock for the Yankees, taking the mound. The contest was scoreless until the fourth inning when Bottomley doubled and crossed the plate on Bell's single. The Yankees tied it with a cheap run off Sherdel. Pennock got a double to right, only because Hafey fell going after the fly ball. With Combs batting, catcher O'Farrell caught Pennock straying too far off second and fired a throw that would have nailed him, but Thevenow could not hold on to the ball. Combs then walked and Koenig singled to tie the game. Les Bell's double and O'Farrell's single in the seventh inning allowed the Cardinals to regain the lead. In the ninth, with St. Louis three outs away from victory, Gehrig hit a pop fly that Thevenow backed up to gather in when a gust of wind blew it away from him for a double. Gehrig scored on a base hit to tie the game. Koenig led off the Yankee tenth with a single and advanced to second when Sherdel, facing Ruth, threw a wild pitch. Hornsby then directed Sherdel to walk Ruth intentionally. After the Babe's three-homer output in game four, Hornsby told his pitching staff, "That big guy doesn't get any more good balls to hit." Meusel advanced both runners with a sacrifice bunt. Hornsby then had Sherdel intentionally walk Gehrig to get to Lazzeri and to load the bases. Lazzeri hit a sacrifice fly to right for what proved to be the game winner. Final score: Yankees 3, Cardinals 2. The Yankees needed one more win to eliminate St. Louis. The two teams headed back to New York.

October 9 was a cold Saturday in the Bronx, more like football weather. Hornsby, who had a funeral to go to after the series was over, was in no mood to give up. "Knock the ball down the pitcher's throat and don't concede a thing," he told the players in the locker room before the game. And once again, he put the ball in the hands of Grover Cleveland Alexander. The Yankees went with Shawkey, who had an off year in 1926, starting just 10 games and compiling an 8–7 record. But his career with the Yankees had been brilliant. They got him from the A's in 1915 in Connie Mack's fire sale of players after having lost the 1914 World Series to the "Miracle Braves." Shawkey responded by winning 24 games in 1916 and losing 14. In 1919, he was 20–11 and was 20–12 in 1922. He was a warhorse who was used to winning big games. But the Cardinals heeded their manager's advice and came out swinging. They scored three in the first inning and three more in the seventh en route to a 10–2 victory as Alex mowed down the Yankees, comforted by having a lead from the opening inning. Alex struck out six, walked two and scattered eight hits in the complete-game victory. Lester Bell, the Cardinals' leading hitter during the regular season, had two singles, a homer and four RBIs to lead the attack.

The weather was cold, rainy and bleak on October 10, less that ideal conditions for the seventh game of the World Series. It had rained most of the night, the air was chilly and the field and grandstands were wet as the players arrived at Yankee Stadium. All of these conditions, plus an erroneous morning radio report that the game had been postponed, contributed to the crowd being down to nearly half to what it had been in previous games in New York, 38,093. Those who braved the elements sat on wet seats and saw one for the ages.

Hornsby had gotten the most out of his pitching staff and had maneuvered it so that Haines, the knuckleballer and winner of a 4–0 shutout earlier in the series, would be on the mound again to throw his fluttering slow stuff to one after another of the Bronx Bombers. Huggins chose Hoyt, winner of game four and the ace of the staff in 1926. In the regular season, he won 22 games and lost only 7. The 22 wins were tops in the American League, and he also led the league in earned run average, 2.63, and winning percentage, .759. He pitched for the Yankees for 10 years and won 157 while losing 98 before finishing his career as a relief pitcher in the National League. His lifetime mark of 237–182 combined with his ability to win big games earned him a place in the Hall of Fame. But for years afterward, because of what happened in the seventh game of the 1926 World Series, he was heard to say jokingly, "Hey, I also pitched in that game."

The Yankees took a 1–0 lead in the third inning on a Ruth home run. In the Cardinal fourth, after Hornsby grounded out, Bottomley singled to left and Bell reached when Koenig mishandled his ground ball. Hafey hit a pop fly into short left field. Meusel came racing in, Koenig back-pedaled from short, and the ball dropped between them for a base hit. Since the runners had to hold up in case the ball was caught, they each advanced just a base, loading the bases. O'Farrell ripped a Hoyt pitch on the line to left center. Meusel and Combs both went after it and nearly collided. Meusel nearly caught it but couldn't hold on. Bottomley scored to tie the game and the bases remained loaded. Thevenow then got a clean single to center, scoring Hafey and Bell.

Thevenow was one of the earliest examples of what has now become almost a World Series expectation—heroics coming from an unexpected source. In years to come, the names of Dusty Rhodes and Bill Mazeroski and Gene Tenace and Jim Lehritz would become part of the legend. In 1926, little Tommy Thevenow helped set the standard. A light-hitting shortstop, Thevenow hit two home runs in his 14-year career, and they came in the same week—inside-the-park home runs on September 17 and September 22, 1926. He then went homerless in his next 3,351 regular-season at bats. So his game two home run—the one Ruth couldn't find in the outfield fence—was a pleasant surprise. His single in the fourth inning of game seven, which drove in two runs, contributed to an overall series in which he hit .417 with 10 hits in 24 at bats—this from a man whose lifetime batting average was .247.

In the sixth inning, the Yankees got one of the runs back when Dugan singled and came around to score on Severeid's double but was stranded at second. In the seventh inning, Combs led off with a single and went to second on Koenig's sacrifice bunt. Hornsby, determined that Ruth would not be the man to beat him, ordered Haines to intentionally walk him even though it put the lead run on base. Haines pitched carefully to Gehrig, too carefully in fact, and walked him to load the bases. Hornsby called time out and walked in from his second base position to the pitcher's mound. In conferring with Haines, the veteran showed him his pitching hand and the blisters that had formed on his knuckles to the point where they were bleeding. Hornsby made a decision that has become part of baseball folklore. He looked to the bullpen and motioned for 39-year-old Grover Cleveland Alexander, who had pitched nine innings just the day before, to come in to pitch to Tony Lazzeri, the rookie second baseman who had driven in more runs than Gehrig during the regular season (114 for Lazzeri, 112 for Gehrig).

As a big league ballplayer, Lazzeri was a hero in the Italian-American community, and he would become an important but lesser known cog in the "Murderers' Row" that trampled American League pitching for the next few years. In 1925, playing for Salt Lake City in the Pacific Coast League, aided by a 200-game schedule, Lazzeri hit 60 home runs, drove in 222 runs and scored 202 runs. In his major league career, he would have seven 100-RBI seasons, and on May 24, 1936, he became the first big league player to hit two grand slam home runs in the same game. On this day, however, cold, rainy Sunday, October 10, 1926, he was a 23-year-old rookie with his best days ahead of him and was about to face Alexander, a grizzled 39-year-old one-time superstar whose best days were behind him.

Tony Lazzeri was a rookie with the Yankees in 1926 and went on to have a great career with the Bronx Bombers. But he is remembered in baseball history as the man Pete Alexander struck out with the bases loaded in the seventh inning of the seventh game of the World Series (National Baseball Hall of Fame Library, Cooperstown, N.Y.).

Alex took his time strolling in from the bullpen to the mound. Some say he was drunk. Some say he was hung over. One story has it that he was sipping whiskey from a bottle he had stashed in the bullpen. Another has it that he was dozing when the call came for his services. Aimee Alexander contended to her dying day that her husband was neither drunk nor hung over. She told sportswriter Frank Finch in a 1951 interview, "After Alex won the sixth game, Hornsby said to him, "Now, Pete, don't celebrate too much. I may need you tomorrow. Well, Alex celebrated and so did most of the other players, but he definitely was not drunk during the seventh game. Hornsby told me years later, 'The biggest mistake we made, Aimee, was not denying the story from the start. At the time it made good reading, so we let it go.'"[4]

In John P. Carmichael's anthology of player reminiscences titled *My Greatest Day in Baseball,* Alexander described the circumstances and gave insight into why his actions coming in from the bullpen made his behavior suspect. The Yankee Stadium bullpens in those days were under the bleachers and out of view of the playing field, which meant the players in the bullpen couldn't see what was happening on the field. There was a telephone in the bullpen, and it was used to summon Alex.[5]

Some accounts say he did not warm up. Alex says he had time for "a few quick tosses." Then he took the long walk in to the mound and saw the bases loaded and Lazzeri waiting to bat. Alex said he said to himself, "Take your time. Lazzeri isn't feeling any too good up there. Let him stew."[6]

In his two previous games, Ol' Pete had pretty good luck against Lazzeri with breaking stuff, so he started him off with a classic Alexander low-and-away curveball that Lazzeri took for a called strike. Lazzeri was set up now for a fastball. Alex delivered, but Lazzeri was also thinking fastball. He turned on it and walloped it into the left field bleachers—but foul. How far foul depends on whose account of it you believe. It was close enough to take the breath away from the Cardinals momentarily. Lazzeri was set up again but this time for another curveball, another one low and outside. This time, Lazzeri lunged at the ball rather weakly for strike three. In modern day parlance, it would be said that on that particular pitch, Alex made him look bad. The old man toppled the rookie. Alex was the king of the hill. Later, he would reflect on the ball Lazzeri hit foul and say, "A few feet made the difference between a hero and a bum."

In the eighth inning, clinging to the 3–2 lead, Ol' Pete set the Yankees down in order, and he got the first two batters, Combs and Koenig, in the ninth. All that stood between Alex and a World Series championship was George Herman "Babe" Ruth. Some accounts have it that Hornsby stuck to his earlier promise that Ruth would not be a deciding factor. Therefore, Alex was not to give him anything good to hit at, and if he walked, so be it, even if he did represent the tying run. This theory is borne out by the fact that Ruth walked four times in five at bats in the final game. Alex's version is a little different. After the Babe walked on a 3–2 pitch, Alexander approached the plate and asked umpire George Hildebrand how close the pitch was to being a strike. Hildebrand reportedly said "it was this much outside" and put his thumb and forefinger so they were a fraction of an inch apart. "If it was that close," Alexander reportedly said, "I'd have thought you'd given an old guy like me a break." He then went back to the mound to concentrate on Meusel, the next batter. As Alex delivered, Ruth inexplicably broke for second base. O'Farrell, who had one of the best arms in the league, gunned him down for the third out. Hornsby put the tag on Ruth to wrap up the World Series for the Cardinals.

What made Ruth try to steal second under those circumstances? Maybe he thought it was the Yankees' only chance to score off Alex, who had been having his way with Yankee hitters for about a week now. Ruth said afterwards, "Just to see Old Pete out there on the mound, with that cocky little under-sized cap pulled down over one ear, chewing away at his tobacco and pitching baseballs as easy as pitching hay is enough to take the heart out of a fellow."[7]

James Harrison wrote in the *New York Times,* "Alexander wrote finis to the hopes of the surging Yankees with an old hand but a steady one. Fate made a hero of Alexander and a victim of Hoyt. Fate was the scene shifter who set the stage in the seventh, out upon which Alexander shuffled. His hat was perched on one side of his head, and he was slowly chewing a quid of tobacco. He was a quaint, almost humorous figure with his jaunty cap, his old man's gait and his quizzical fans, but when he wound up his arm and threw, the Yanks had reached the end of the trail."[8]

In its lengthy account of the game, the Associated Press pointed out that Haines, and not Alexander, got the win. "But the glory belongs to Alexander who was sold down the river a short time ago as a Chicago Cub discard."

Alex's strikeout to end the seventh is a part of baseball history. The story of how it happened lives on, partly because of the baseball glory it represents, partly because so many people who saw it have different views about it, and so many who didn't see it but have reported on it have given it what in today's vernacular would most assuredly be called "spin."

Alexander himself said years later, "There must be a hundred versions of what happened.... It used to be that everywhere I went, I'd hear a new one, and some were pretty far-fetched, so much so that two or three years ago I ran into Lazzeri in San Francisco and said, 'Tony, I'm getting tired of fanning you.' And Tony said, 'Maybe you think I'm not.'"[9]

Hornsby too told the story many times. Unlike Alex, the Rajah did nothing to dispel the rumors that Alex might have been drunk or hung over when he came into the game. In an article he wrote, as told to J. Roy Stockton for *Look* magazine in 1953, Hornsby said, "People have asked me many times about what happened that day, in that seventh-inning clutch, when Alexander was called from the bullpen to relieve Haines. They wanted to know what I said and what Alex said and whether he had a gin bottle out there in the bullpen. Well I left my position at second base and walked out to meet him. Naturally, I wanted to get a close look at him, to see what shape he was in. And I wanted to tell him what the situation was, in case he was dozing."

Dozing? In the seventh inning of the seventh game of the World Series? That was his manager's concern. Would he have had that same concern with any other pitcher on the club or, for that matter, any other player? The implication is clear. Hornsby knew from experience that Alex might have "broken training" the night before. He said he told Alex the situation, that the Cardinals were winning 3–2, that the bases were loaded with two out and that Lazzeri was the batter. "Alex didn't say much," according to Hornsby. He said not to worry about him and that there was nothing much to do except "give Tony a lot of hell." And he proceeded to strike him out.[10]

Alexander said later his biggest thrill in the series was not the strike out but watching O'Farrell gun down Ruth trying to steal second, the play that ended the game and the series. "I don't think I ever saw a better peg in my life than the one O'Farrell threw then," said Alex.

Third baseman Bell was standing on the mound when Alexander came in and overheard the conversation between manager and pitcher. He said Hornsby talked for a moment or two and then said, "Who am I to tell you how to pitch?" Alexander then conferred with O'Farrell and told him he not only had to get Lazzeri, but had to retire Dugan, Collins and whoever would pinch-hit for Pennock in the eighth and then Combs and Koenig in the ninth. If he did that, he said, "when the big son of a bitch comes up, the best he can do is tie the ballgame." Bell was amazed that Alex already figured out that Ruth would be the last hitter in the ninth if he retired everybody else — which he did.

"He was nearly 40 years old, but doggone, there wasn't another man in the world I would have rather seen out there at that moment than Grover Cleveland Alexander," said Bell. "So when you hear those stories about how Alex didn't think he might have to pitch the next day and was out all night celebrating and how he was hung over when he came in (to pitch), that's a lot of bunk. I saw him around the hotel the night before, for goodness sakes. I don't say he didn't have a drink, but he was around most of the night.... Everybody knows that he was a drinker and that he had a problem with it, but he was not drunk when he walked into the ballgame that day. No way."

Bell said a lot of aspects of that strikeout were exaggerated as the story was told time and again. For one thing, he said, there was never a doubt that the ball Lazzeri hit into the left field stands was foul. There was no drama to it. Alex busted a fastball inside, Lazzeri got around on it and pulled it. It was hit hard but hooked right away and was foul all the way, said Bell.[11]

Flint Rhem, the Cardinals' 20-game winner, fancied himself as the next Alexander, both in pitching and drinking. When reflecting on Alexander's pitching heroics years later, Rhem said he and Alex were both in the bullpen sharing a bottle of whiskey during that seventh game and that when Alex got the call, he handed the bottle to Rhem and got ready to go in the game. No other player in the dugout or bullpen that day remembers seeing Alex drink. That, coupled with Rhem's penchant for wanting to be like Alex and the fact that his memory was tainted by alcoholism, makes his account suspect. Four years later, when the Cardinals were in the thick of a pennant fight with the Dodgers, Rhem disappeared and was gone for several days without anyone knowing his whereabouts. When he returned, he had the look of a man who had been out on a bender. He told his teammates he had been kidnapped by gamblers and forced to drink bootleg liquor. Rhem lasted 12 turbulent years in the majors, winning 105 games, 268 fewer than Alex, the man he so admired.

George "Specs" Toporcer was a reserve Cardinals infielder in 1926 who watched from the bench as Alexander came in to pitch. "Inevitably, one question always arises whenever there is discussion on this series. What was Alec's condition that day?" said Toporcer. "All I can say in reply is simply this: Whether he obeyed Hornsby's edict of the night before, I don't know. To me, he appeared the same as he did on any other day of the season. He was a steady drinker. It is possible he had a few drinks the night before, perhaps even that morning. It was impossible to tell. But he certainly was not intoxicated in the true sense of the word. Of that I am certain."[12]

But then this from O'Farrell, Alex's catcher, in a January 25, 1976, interview with *St. Louis Post-Dispatch* Sports Editor Bob Broeg: "Alexander had celebrated the night before and he was snoozing in the bullpen. We called him Old Low and Away because of his remarkable control.... Old Low and Away threw that sharp, short curve of his and Lazzeri struck out."

O'Farrell also had an explanation for why Ruth, representing the tying run, tried to steal second and was thrown out (by O'Farrell) to end the game. The catcher said it was unlikely, the way Alexander was pitching, that the Yankees were going to get two straight hits off him to score the run. To that point, they hadn't come close to getting one hit. By advancing to second, it would take only one hit to tie the game.

Haines said he didn't notice anything unusual about Alex when Ol' Pete came in to replace him. "I always say: He pitched two good innings, didn't he? I got to give the old fellow credit. Alec was always calm, no matter what the game was. He was never jubilant. That's the way he was. I would never say a word against him. A man comes out and pitches two and a third innings and then they accuse him of being drunk. I would never do that. He couldn't do that, pitch like that, if he was drunk."[13]

Eppa Rixey, Alex's old teammate with the Phillies, said he ran into Alex long after he retired at an old-timers gathering in Cincinnati in which Bucky Walters was being honored. Alex was not a part of the program, but when he was spotted in the audience, he was called on to say a few words. Rixey said Ol' Pete brought down the house when he got up and told the crowd, "Folks, I'm so damn tired of strikin' out Lazzeri...."

• CHAPTER X •

Forty Years Old and Counting

"There are two famous Nebraskans — me and William Jennings Bryan. The difference between the two of us is that he drinks orange juice."
— Grover Cleveland Alexander

Alex acknowledged his drinking problem because, particularly late in his career, he had no choice. It was public knowledge. He did not talk about his battles with epilepsy because epilepsy was thought of as something far more peculiar than alcoholism. In the 1920s, the public could more easily accept a man who sometimes had a few too many drinks than they could a man who had unsightly seizures caused by a disease that some thought came from the devil. Aimee Alexander said doctors told her that Alex's epilepsy might have been the result of his being unconscious for 36 hours after he was struck in the head with a ball when he was breaking up a double play in Galesburg, or it could have occurred as an effect of hearing at close range the booms of the big guns in Germany during World War I that left him deaf in one ear.[1]

There are few references by players to Alex's epilepsy. Hans Lobert, Alex's second baseman in Philadelphia, mentioned it to Lawrence Ritter in his interview for Ritter's book *The Glory of Their Times*. Lobert, looking back 50 years, said he remembered he and other players holding onto Alex when he had a seizure in the dugout. There is no other account of Alexander suffering from epilepsy that early in his life or having an attack on the field that early in his career. But "Specs" Toporcer witnessed two incidents late in Alex's career.

"The first happened in a dining room while we were coming north from spring training," he said. "The other happened right on the ballfield. Pitching against the Phillies one afternoon, it struck him just as he was going into his windup. He automatically went through with the pitch, arching the ball to the plate, while Don Hurst, the Philly batter, froze in amazement. Curiously enough, the ball cut the heart of the plate for a called strike.

Such was the nature of his marvelous control. When it is considered that Alex spent a year in service at the height of his career, was a chronic alcoholic and suffered from epilepsy, it borders on the fantastic to recall that he was a winning pitcher in the majors until the age of 43. Too, it was always a puzzle to me how a man whose fingers would tremble whenever he held his arm outstretched could have the remarkable control and steel nerves which he displayed."[2]

When the Cardinals took the train back to St. Louis from New York, there was the expected festive mood from winning the World Series, but there was also plenty of black coffee available for Alex — enough to float a battleship, said Hornsby — as the locomotive chugged closer and closer to its destination, where big crowds waited to greet their heroes, winners of the first baseball championship in city's history.

For Alex and Aimee, it was then home to Nebraska, where another celebration awaited them in St. Paul, the little hamlet with 1,600 residents, who were not content to call their hometown hero Alexander the Great. To them, he was Alexander the Greater, conqueror of the New York Yankees. After the final out was recorded, the town went wild, with people dancing in the streets and the local band assembling in front of the home of Alex's widowed mother, Martha Alexander, to serenade her. Elsewhere, plans were being made for a festive parade and cookout that would rival anything ever done even on the Fourth of July. The press reported that women were scurrying around, getting recipes for Alex's favorite dishes. On October 27, 1926, the grand celebration took place. Twenty-thousand people packed the streets of St. Paul. City officials gave speeches lavishing great praise on Alex, and he was presented with a charm for his watch by the local Masonic Lodge. That was followed by the community's biggest barbecue ever, with 12,000 sandwiches served. Naturally, there was a ballgame between the men of Ord and Howard County, and it didn't take much coaxing to have Alex pitch a few innings. His niece, Elma O'Neill, said the game didn't last too long, because they couldn't find a catcher who could hold on to Alex's fastball. The day concluded with a street dance that lasted until midnight. All in all, it was a day fit for a king, for indeed that's what Alex was to his friends and neighbors. It was a day that Alex would remember for the rest of his life and would one day be a bittersweet memory.

Alex was besieged with requests for interviews and public appearances all winter. He even got calls from theatrical agents in Omaha who wanted to book him as part of an entertainment package. He was humble and polite in telling all comers what he could and couldn't do. One of the things he couldn't do, most of the time, was turn down a drink if it was offered to him. He described his feelings about the media and public frenzy this way:

"It's great to be a champion, but it's hell, too." And he said he didn't think he always got a fair shake from the press concerning his favorite off-the-field pastime.

"Sure I always drank, but not as much as they say. I don't claim it has done me any good and I don't believe it has done me any harm. I will say that I don't think I would have done any more in baseball if I had never taken a drink," said Alex. "You know, a baseball season is long and you cannot keep in strict training all the time — but I would not recommend my way to anybody else."[3]

The Cardinals' euphoria from being World Series champs didn't last long. On December 21, 1926, Sam Breadon in effect fired Hornsby by trading him to the New York Giants for infielder Frankie Frisch and a pitcher named Jimmy Ring. This was an outgrowth of a feud between Breadon and Hornsby over the exhibition game in September that Breadon insisted the Cardinals play in New Haven, Connecticut, on an off day. Hornsby vehemently objected because the team was in the heat of a pennant race. They needed the day off to rest, and besides that, Hornsby didn't want to risk any injuries not only to his starters but to his bench as well. Breadon told Hornsby he understood the circumstances but that he had made a deal long ago with George Weiss, owner of the New Haven club (and later general manager of the great Yankee clubs in the 1950s). To Breadon, a deal was a deal. In the heat of the argument, Hornsby accused his boss of being more interested in making a few bucks from an exhibition game than in winning the National League pennant. That remark stung — and it stuck. Breadon decided on that day that Hornsby had to go. He would pick his time. December 21 turned out to be the time.

St. Louis fans did not react well. Hornsby was the greatest hitter in the National League, and he had just led his club to its first championship. Some fans threatened to boycott the Cardinals in 1927. Vandals hung black mourning crepe at the front entrance of Breadon's home. Sportswriter Jim Gould said he would never see another Cardinal game while Breadon was the owner, and he kept his pledge for many years.

For Alex, it was the dismissal of another manager who, like Killefer on the Cubs, had put up with him and his habits because he was winning ballgames. There is no way of knowing whether Alexander noticed the similarity between Hornsby's situation with Breadon and his own circumstance with McCarthy six months earlier. In each case, the head man saw the necessity of showing the star player who was boss — and both times it was the star who was sent packing.

Breadon offered the managerial job to Killefer, but Killefer turned it down out of loyalty to Hornsby. So Breadon approached O'Farrell, the popular catcher who had gunned down Babe Ruth to end the World Series. O'Farrell accepted. As spring training 1927 approached, a new era was beginning in St. Louis, one that would eventually bring more championships, the formation of the "Gas House Gang" and a few more managerial changes. For Alex, the immediate change was no more Catalina Island in the spring. The Cardinals trained in Avon Park, Florida. And no more Aimee to support him on the field and baby-sit him off the field. Wives were not allowed at the Cardinal training camp, so Avon Park became a new playground for the man who arrived as a World Series hero, someone for whom many a townsfolk was willing to buy a drink.

On February 26, Alex turned 40, and while he probably celebrated the occasion, there are no reports of anything unseemly taking place. He was optimistic about the future and downplayed his age. "Of course we can't figure very far ahead on account of the possibility of being hurt," he told the Associated Press in March. "But if I am lucky enough to keep whole, I ought to go on quite a while yet. My legs are still good and my arm never gives me any trouble. "The older pitchers have one big advantage over the youngsters. They know more about it. They ought to, most of us learned in a hard school — experience," he said.

Alex said that when he was younger, he had a lot more "stuff" and loved to show it to batters and dare them to hit it. As he grew older, he said, it became more important to have good control, to know the batter's weaknesses and to exploit them. Throw it where you want to throw it, not where the batter wants you to throw it, said the old master. "The best place for him is the worst place for me, so I try to keep it out of there," he said.

O'Farrell tabbed Alex as the Cardinals' opening day pitcher April 12 against his old teammates, the Cubs, at Wrigley Field. But he got hammered and Charlie Root pitched well as Chicago won the season opener 10–1. In his next start, he beat Cincinnati, as he usually did, in a 2–1 Cardinal victory at Crosley Field. St. Louis had begun the season with a six-game road trip and won half the games. Then they came home and won seven out of 10, with Alex winning his second straight 2–1 decision, this one over Vic Aldridge and the Pittsburgh Pirates. Then, a strange thing occurred. Alexander, who had gone through his career pretty much injury free except for the sore arm in the 1915 World Series and the problems that sent him to Bonesetter Reese a few years later, was sidelined not by injury but by two illnesses usually associated with children — measles and tonsillitis. He was out for 10 days.

His next start was at Pittsburgh on May 5, and again he hooked up with Aldridge and again he came out the winner as the Cardinals won 4–2. They were now 12–6 and had won nine out of 12 since their 3–3 beginning.

At New York on May 12, Alexander suffered his first loss in a month. Even at age 40, he was usually pitted against the ace of whoever the Cardinals were playing. This time it was Burleigh Grimes, and Alex came out on the short end of 3–2 ballgame. He took another tough loss, 4–3, at Philadelphia on May 17 to even his record at 3–3 despite pitching consistently well since opening day. In his first six starts, the Cubs had scored only 14 runs. They bounced back in his next two starts with 8–5 and 11–3 victories over the Cubs and Cincinnati. Heading into June, Alex was 5–3 and, more important, the Cardinals were 22–16 and in second place, four games behind the Pittsburgh Pirates, who were being sparked by the Waner brothers, Lloyd and Paul, "Big Poison" and "Little Poison." The Breadon haters, keeping track of Hornsby and Frisch, saw that in mid–May, Hornsby was hitting .425 and Frisch was at .365.

On June 5, Alex threw his first shutout in two years and his first in a Cardinal uniform as St. Louis defeated Brooklyn 8–0 in the first game of a doubleheader at Sportsman's Park. Haines didn't fare as well in the second game, and Brooklyn won 6–1, breaking the Cardinals six-game winning streak. At this point in the season, one thing was apparent. Flint Rhem, who had won 20 games for the pennant-winning Cardinals the year before, was struggling to keep on a pace to win half that many in 1927. And he was drinking himself into oblivion. Before his career was over, he would have many infamous drinking escapades. In 1927, he was a late arrival for a game. When he showed up, he told O'Farrell he had been out with Alex the night before and that people kept buying Alex drinks. In order to keep Ol' Pete out of trouble, Rhem said, he grabbed the drinks intended for Alex and got rip-roaring drunk in order to protect Alex.

On June 11, Alexander won his fourth straight game, beating the Phillies 4–2 on the eve of the biggest series of the year in St. Louis. The New York Giants were coming to town. It would be the first appearance of Hornsby in St. Louis since he had been traded. Breadon was no fool when it came to drama and publicity. He delayed the ceremony in which the World Series rings were distributed until the weekend of the Giants series. A special guest that day was Col. Charles A. Lindbergh, a Missouri National Guard captain who earlier in the year had become the first man to fly solo across the Atlantic Ocean in a plane called The Spirit of St. Louis. There was no shortage of heroes on June 18, 1926, when Breadon, Lindbergh, Alexander and his teammates and Hornsby were all honored. It was not lost on Breadon or the crowd that Hornsby was the only one wearing a visitors uniform. When the ceremonies ended and the game began, Alexander took the mound, held Hornsby to a double in four at bats and beat the Giants and Freddie Fitzsimmons 6–4.

Between June 21 and July 7, the Cardinals experienced a six-game winning streak and a six-game losing streak, with Alex winning one and losing one in that span. He threw his second shutout of the year on July 11, a 7–0 win over Philadelphia, but then lost five days later when Brooklyn shut out the Cardinals 3–0. He split two other decisions in July, and with a win over Philadelphia 6–3 on July 28 behind Jess Haines, the Cardinals hit a season high 15 games over .500 at 55–40, and St. Louis was in the heart of the pennant race, in third place, 2½ games behind the Pirates and 1½ games behind the second-place Cubs. Alex won a 6–2 decision over the Giants on August 2, a 4–1 decision over the Braves on August 6, a 2–1 decision over the Pirates on August 11, a 5–3 decision over the Pirates on August16, an 8–2 decision over the Phillies on August 20 before finally losing a 2–1 decision to Brooklyn in the second game of a doubleheader on August 29. He was 5–1 for the month and hadn't allowed more than three runs in any of the games, tantalizing batters with pinpoint control and using the old Alex theory of throwing the ball where he wanted to throw it, not where the batter wanted to hit it.

"Don't count us out yet," Alex told the press. "The Cubs are out in front now but we are right after them. Injuries to O'Farrell, Southworth, Frisch, Thevenow and Blades have handicapped us or we would have stepped away from the field long ago. When we return to St. Louis, just watch our smoke."

When Flint Rhem threw one of his best games of the year in beating the Dodgers 3–1 on August 31, four teams were in the thick of the pennant race with 2½ games separating them. The Cubs had sneaked into first place, a game ahead of the Pirates. The Cardinals were in third place, two games out — but the three teams were tied in the loss column. The Cubs were 73–50, the Pirates 71–50 and the Cardinals 69–50. The fourth place Giants, 2½ games back, had a record of 70–52. The Cardinals went into Pittsburgh on September 2 with a chance to overtake the Pirates and zero in on the Cubs, but it didn't work out that way. The Bucs beat Alex 5–3 and then jumped on Haines early on September 3 on their way to a 14–0 pasting of St. Louis. The Cardinals then traveled to Wrigley Field for their most important stretch of games of the season, three versus the Cubs at Chicago followed by four more with the Cubs at home. Sherdel hooked up with Charlie Root in a pitching duel on September 4, and Sherdel came out on top 2–1. In a doubleheader the next day, Rhem lost 6–1, but Haines salvaged the day and the series with a 2–0 shutout in the second game. Then it was on to St. Louis, where Alex won a laugher 13–1 on September 6. The two teams split a doubleheader the next day, and then Sherdel came out on the losing end of an 11–7 series finale. The Cardinals had won four out of the seven games with Chicago, the last time the two teams played each other. But while the Cubs and Cardinals were beating each other up, the Pirates continued to win and the Giants moved ahead of both Chicago and St. Louis in the standings. Pittsburgh remained on top, but now New York was second, a half-game out, Chicago was third, two games out, and the Cardinals had slipped to fourth but were still only 2½ games out of the lead. The championship was still up for grabs.

Brooklyn saw a little of the "smoke" Alex talked about when the Robins came to St. Louis. The Cardinals swept a four-game series. The next stretch was crucial, seven straight games with the Giants. Alex won a 6–3 decision on September 14, but the Cardinals lost four out of the six other games with New York. Meanwhile, similar to what happened when the Cubs and Cardinals played each other, the Pirates continued to win and increased their lead on both of them. The Cardinals swept a five-game series from the Phillies at Wrigley Field, and a 6–5 win over Boston on September 22 gave them a six-game winning streak. Alex lost a tough one 3–2 to Boston to end the streak, but then the Cardinals won six more, including Alex's 21st win of the season. When it was all over, the Cardinals had compiled a record of 23–11 from September 1 on, but they would look back with dismay to the two-game series on Sept 2–3 when Pittsburgh swept them, because the Pirates were 23–10 down the stretch to win a great pennant race. The Pirates, with the Waner brothers, Pie Traynor and KiKi Cuyler, earned the right to play the New York Yankees, who had evolved into what many historians think is the greatest team in baseball history. Essentially the same team that the Cardinals beat in seven games the year before, the Bronx Bombers disposed of the Pirates in four straight.

Injuries crippled the Cardinals at three key positions. O'Farrell played only 61 games behind the plate, and Blades played the same limited number in the outfield. Shortstop Thevenow broke his leg early in the season and managed to get into only 29 games. At 21–10, Alex had the last great year of his career. Haines led the staff with 24 wins while losing only 10. Sherdel posted 17 wins against 12 losses while the erratic Rhem, winner of 20 in 1926, slipped to 10–12 in 1927. Frisch did what he could to make Cardinal fans accept him as Hornsby's replacement, hitting .337 to lead the club. He scored 112 runs and stole 48 bases. Hornsby hit .361 for the Giants, but he lasted in New York for only a year, being shipped off to Boston prior to the 1928 season. (Why would a .361 hitter be dealt? The same reason a pennant winning manager was traded the year before. With Hornsby, a team got a lot of player but often more personality than management wanted to put up with.) Hafey hit .329 and Bottomley finished at .303. Bell, leading percentage hitter on the championship team, dropped to .259.

Despite missing a second straight National League pennant by just 1½ games, Breadon decided to change managers. He had no hard feelings toward O'Farrell. In fact, in firing him, he gave him a $5,000 raise to go back to catching full time. Breadon thought the Cardinals would be stronger with O'Farrell just concentrating on catching and hiring a manager with some experience. He had a man with those credentials on his coaching staff—Bill McKechnie, who took the Pittsburgh Pirates to a World Series championship in 1925. That was only the first of many changes for the Cardinals. Bell, whose best year in the majors was 1927, was traded to Boston. O'Farrell got off to a bad start and was traded to the Giants on May 10. The next day, general manager Branch Rickey filled the catching gap by acquiring Jimmy Wilson from the Phillies. Perhaps the deal that pleased Alex the most came in June when Rickey purchased Clarence Mitchell, the only left-handed spitballer in the majors, from the Phillies. Mitchell was not a great pitcher and is remembered in baseball lore for two things unrelated to pitching. Playing for Brooklyn in the 1920 World Series, he hit the ball that resulted in Bill Wambsganss's unassisted triple play. He also hit into a double play in the same game. Five putouts in two at bats remains a major league record. The other distinction is that he was Alex's best friend in baseball and the best man at his wedding. Now they were teammates.

On February 26, 1928, Alex observed his 41st birthday in Avon Park, Florida, by accepting gifts from friends and well-wishers and by giving some advice to young pitchers coming up. Ol' Pete's advice hadn't changed much over the years. "I attribute my long service to the Phillies, Cubs and Cardinals to good control," he told the press, "plus a pretty fair knowledge of where the ball ought to be pitched. I have made it a point to study every batsman I face and now I know just about what kind of balls to serve them to obtain the best results. By perfecting my control and knowing where to pitch to a majority of batters facing me, I seem to get by."

Going into the 1928 season, the Cardinals were considered one of the favorites. They had come within two games of being two-time National League champions and might have accomplished the feat had it not been for injuries to Thevenow, O'Farrell and Blades. Their hopes rested on getting through the season pretty much injury free plus a resurgent year for the eccentric Flint Rhem and another good year from the ageless wonder, Grover Cleveland Alexander. They got a chance to see what they were made of from the opening gun, starting the season with a two-game series with the Pittsburgh Pirates. Haines won a 14–7 laugher on opening day, April 11, where the hitting was good and the pitching wasn't. The following day, Ol' Pete took the mound and reminded old-timers of his days with the Phillies as he breezed to a 5–0 shutout, the 90th shutout of his career and, as it turned out, his last.

After the game, reporters asked him how he had managed to survive so long in the era of the "lively ball," which had been around for about eight years. "I have come to the conclusion that the great increase in batting in the big leagues isn't due to the quality of the ball," he said. "It's caused by the mania to make home runs. Every hitter is trying to knock the ball out of the park.

"Some time ago, I determined it was a cinch to pitch against the sluggers. All you have to do is to keep the ball over the outside corner of the plate and make them hit into the wrong field. Don't let them pull the ball. Make them push it. If the ball really is lively, it shouldn't bother a man who knows how to pitch. It's the new style of batting and the poor judgment of numerous pitchers, especially the youngsters, that are responsible for the high averages in both leagues. The ball is all right if you know what to do with it."

The Cardinals went through April winning just about as often as they were losing. Alex found himself in a familiar situation, often being matched against the other team's best or near-best pitcher. After winning the 5–0 shutout in which his mound opponent was Burleigh Grimes, he lost a 3–2 decision to Guy Bush and the Cubs, then was the winner in a 7–2 victory over Eppa Rixey of Cincinnati and finished the month as the loser to the Cubs and Sheriff Blake in a 6–5 ballgame. The Cubs were 8–7 and Alex was 2–2.

May didn't get any easier for Alex. His control was still his meal ticket, but his strikeouts were fewer, as were his complete games, and he needed a little more time between starts. Plus, he kept being matched up against the aces of the National League. On May 1, he dropped a 6–3 decision to Red Lucas and the Reds. On May 6, he beat Dazzy Vance and the Dodgers 4–2. He beat Philadelphia on May 11, lost to the Giants on May 18 and then was the winner against the Cubs 8–7 on May 21. He didn't make another mound appearance until June 6, when he came out on top of an 11–6 decision over the Giants when his mound opponent was his old teammate Vic Aldridge. The Cardinals ended May by downing the Pirates in three out of four games at Forbes Field. As play entered June, 3½ games separated the top four teams, with Cincinnati on top, the Giants in second, 2½ back, the Cubs in third, 3 games out, and St. Louis in fourth, 3½ behind the Reds. The first two months were a good indication of what kind of race it would be. The Cardinals came out of the box fast with their two wins over the Pirates and were tied for first with the Giants on April 15. Then McGraw's bunch had the lead until April 26, when Brooklyn crept on top for a couple of days before relinquishing the lead to the Reds. The Reds and Cubs were tied for first place on May 15 and 16, and the Cubs led from May 17 through May 22, after which Cincinnati regained the lead and held it through June 14.

The Cardinals started June with a three-game winning streak, including Alex beating Vic Aldridge of the Giants again, 11–6, on June 6, Alexander's first start since May 18. Rhem lost a tough one 4–3 the next day, and St. Louis split the next two games with New York. Then the Cardinals traveled to Brooklyn and Boston, where they won eight in a row and moved into first place on June 16. Alex had a great month. After winning over the Giants on June 6, he was again the winner on June 11 in an 8–1 decision over Boston and won a 6–2 decision over Cincinnati on June 17. He was pressed into service two days later and got the win in a 9–4 victory over the Reds. The schedule called for the Cardinals to return to Cincinnati the next week, and Alex won yet another one over the Reds, this time 7–4, on June 24. His only loss for the month came on June 30 when Burleigh Grimes of the Pirates bested him 4–3, but the Cardinals went 20–6 for the month and were out of first place for only four days from June 16 on.

St. Louis won 17 and lost 11 in July, with Alex on pace for another 20-win season, winning four out of five decisions. But in the dog days of August and September, he won only 5 and lost 6 as the Cardinals won their second championship in three years and once again faced the New York Yankees in the World Series. At one point in the season, he was 11–3 but finished at 16–9 — respectable by anyone's standards but outstanding for a 41-year-old. On September 20, Alex took the mound in a game against the Giants in which his mound opponent was a kid named Carl Hubbell, whom McGraw brought up from the Texas League in July. Alex had him beaten as the Cardinals led 4–2 after seven innings. But Shanty Hogan hit a grand-slam off Ol' Pete in the eighth and Hubbell and the Giants prevailed 7–4. It was Hubbell's 10th win. He would go on to win 243 more in a 16-year career that included a stretch of 24 consecutive wins and his remarkable feat in the 1934 All-Star game of fanning Babe Ruth, Lou Gehrig, Al Simmons, Jimmy Foxx and Joe Cronin consecutively.

Hubbell, who was 25 at the time, reflected on that game many years later. He said he had heard that Alex never had thrown a pitch above a batter's waist and after watching him pitch, and believed it. "He could throw a ball through the eye of a needle," said Hubbell.

The St. Louis pitching staff was much the same as the one that had faced the Yankees in the 1926 World Series. Sherdel had his best year in the majors and led the staff with a 21–10 mark. Steady Jess Haines had another 20 win season and lost only 8. Alex contributed his 16–9 record, and Rhem rebounded from 1927 to go 11–8. Mitchell, acquired early in the season, picked up 8 wins while losing 9. At bat, the Cardinals couldn't offer any

"Murderers' Row" as the Yankees could, but they had some heavy hitters and had improved defensively. First baseman Bottomley hit .325 and had 31 homers to tie for the league lead with Hack Wilson and had 136 RBIs to lead the league. He also hit 20 triples to lead the league. Hafey, the dependable outfielder, hit a team-high .337 and had 27 home runs and 111 runs batted in. Frisch and outfielder George Harper hit .300 and .305 respectively. St. Louis was strong up the middle with Jimmy Wilson behind the plate replacing O'Farrell, Frisch and Rabbit Maranville, a midseason acquisition, at second and short, and Taylor Douthit, the best defensive center fielder in the league.

The Yankees came into the World Series crippled. Ruth had a sore ankle and Lazzeri had a sore arm. Earle Combs and Herb Pennock, stalwarts on the pennant winners in 1926 and 1927, were out with injuries. The Cardinals thought they were primed to once again climb to the top of the baseball world. A crowd of 61,425 filled Yankee Stadium on October 4 as Willie Sherdel and Waite Hoyt hooked up in the first game. Sherdel pitched well, but Hoyt pitched better, giving up only a solo home run to Bottomley as the Yankees won 4–1. Meusel had a two-run homer, Ruth had a single and a double and Gehrig had two hits and two RBIs to provide all the offense the Bronx Bombers needed.

The second game had all the makings of a repeat of the 1926 series. In '26, after losing the first game, the Cardinals sent out the old master, Ol' Pete, to tame the Yankee bats, and he did. Any thoughts of a repeat performance were dashed in the first inning of the 1928 game when Gehrig launched a three-run homer and the Yankees chased Alex with four more in the fourth on their way to a 9–3 victory. They had beaten a 41-year-old warhorse who wasn't at his best. Years later, George Pipgras, the Yankee starting pitcher, offered a possible reason why. He told author Donald Honig that he and Alexander were asked to pose for a publicity picture before the ballgame. "I put out my hand for him to shake and he reached for it and, I swear, missed it by a foot he was so drunk. Either that or he had a wicked hangover," said Pipgras.[4]

Before the series started, a reporter asked manager McKechnie how Alex was behaving. "Pretty good — for him," said McKechnie. "He was only out of condition six or seven times during the season and then it usually came just after he had pitched a good game."

The scene shifted to St. Louis, but there was no wild celebration this time. When the Cardinals won in 1926, it had been their first championship. In 1927, they almost won it. In 1928, they were back on top. So the uniqueness was gone, replaced by high expectations. Had the Cardinals won the first two games, it might have been different. But coming home down two games to none gave game three more of a sense of taking care of business than jubilantly returning home. And who better to take care of business than Haines, the 20-game winner. If Alex was the heart of the pitching staff, Haines was the backbone. His mound opponent on October 7 was Tom Zachary, whom Yankee manager Miller Huggins had picked up off of the Washington scrap heap. Pitching for the Senators the year before, Zachary put his name in the record books by giving up the 60th home run to Babe Ruth. Now Ruth was a teammate. But it was Gehrig who did most of the damage, hitting two home runs off Haines as the Yankees rolled to their third straight win 7–3.

It was up to the lefty Sherdel to try to avoid the sweep. His mound opponent was Waite Hoyt. Sherdel pitched well, as he had almost every time he faced the Yankees in World Series play, and headed into the seventh inning leading 2–1, with a Ruth home run being the only score against him. In the seventh, Sherdel thought he had struck Ruth out, but umpire Cy Pfirman ruled that strike three was a quick pitch and disallowed it. Ruth hit the next pitch out of the park to tie the game. Gehrig followed with a homer. After another base hit, McKechnie lifted Sherdel and called on Ol' Pete, just as Hornsby had two years before. But this time Lazzeri doubled. Before the inning was over, the Yankees had scored four runs. In the eighth inning, Ruth homered off Alex, his third home run of the game. Alex gave up two runs on four hits in 2⅔ innings, and the Yankees won 7–3 to make a clean sweep of the Cardinals. In 1926, Hornsby made the decision to pitch around Ruth, who walked 12 times in the seven games. McKechnie elected to takes his chances pitching to him. Ruth hit .625 with three doubles, three home runs, four runs batted in and nine runs scored in the four games. Gehrig hit .545 with four homers and nine RBIs. The Cardinals scored 10 runs and gave up 27. The Bronx Bombers had clearly lived up to their name.

• CHAPTER XI •

The End of the Road

"He was more to be pitied than censured."
— Specs Toporcer

America took a roller coaster ride in 1929, and so did Grover Cleveland Alexander. By year's end, the bottom had fallen out of what each had going for them. The country was still enjoying the Roaring '20s with its speakeasies, booming economy and a decade of peace. Herbert Hoover was sworn in as President of the United States. Postage stamps had a two-cent value and the newest one, picturing adventurer George Rogers Clark, was the largest in physical size ever printed. In February, Americans were enthralled with the news of gangsters killing gangsters in what came to be known as the St. Valentine's Day Massacre in Chicago. Later in the year, penicillin was used for the first time to fight disease, the Museum of Modern Art opened in New York, William S. Paley founded the Columbia Broadcasting System (CBS), the Philadelphia Athletics beat the Chicago Cubs in the World Series, and Notre Dame was the best college football team with a 9–0 record. On October 29, stock prices plummeted on the New York Stock Exchange, resulting in a market crash the likes of which were never experienced before or since. Fortunes were lost. Dreams were dashed. The nation was plunged into The Great Depression.

Alexander's fortunes began to crash in January when the love of his life (besides booze and baseball), Aimee, his wife and helpmate for almost 11 years, filed for divorce, charging "extreme cruelty." She was too nice to go into detail about the cruelty, but she testified that he had tried to "take the cure" six times and had failed each time. He couldn't live without alcohol, and because of that, she could no longer live with him.[1]

The divorce papers were filed in Lancaster County District Court in Lincoln, Nebraska. Alex had taken up residence in the Hotel Lincoln, where he had been for about 30 days and would stay until he left for spring training. The *Omaha World-Herald,* the state's largest newspaper, reported that

XI—The End of the Road

Alex was hoping for reconciliation—and so were the citizens of Lincoln. Alex was a frequent visitor in the off-season and was, of course, well known. The newspaper reported, "There is regret here that the matrimonial bark of the Alexanders has struck a reef, and folks generally share with Grover his hope that the wreck may be floated and the happy marital relations of the Alexanders resumed."[2]

There was trouble in St. Louis, too. Breadon, disgusted that his team was swept in the World Series, decided to replace McKechnie. In effect, he sent him to the minor leagues, giving him the job of managing the Rochester, New York, Redbirds, the Cardinals' top farm club. In doing so, he promoted the Redbirds' manager, Billy Southworth, moving him up to manage the big league club. Southworth was not as harsh as Hornsby in his managerial style, but he was a much tougher taskmaster than McKechnie had been. In his playing days, Southworth had been managed by McGraw, Hornsby and other tough, often irritable men, and some writers thought he tried too hard to be like them in his first managerial effort. He joined the Cardinals with much the same onus as McCarthy had with the Cubs in 1926— a rookie manager with a veteran club. Instead of trading an icon to show who was boss, as McCarthy had done, Southworth laid down some stringent rules as soon as he arrived at training camp, including not allowing wives on a trip to Miami, where the Cardinals played an exhibition game.

When Alex headed for spring training at Avon Park, his life off the field was in shambles, but he was coming off a 16–9 season with the National League champions, and Breadon was willing to grant a $17,500 contract to see if Alex had yet another good year left in him. Things were different now, though. No longer was Aimee at arm's length, and no longer was his drinking masqueraded in the press as "breaking training," or more whimsically, "battling John Barleycorn." It was publicly acknowledged that Alex had a drinking problem. The epilepsy was not as widely known, though Aimee said in later years that some of his seizures were mistaken for drunkenness. Gone were the carefree days of going to Warm Springs and then heading for spring training on his own. He boarded the train in St. Louis with his pal Clarence Mitchell and they rode rails to Florida to prepare for the 1929 season. As it turned out, Mitchell had to come to Alex's defense almost from the moment they got off the train. As onlookers gathered around Alex, it was obvious he had a gash on his face. Alex said he cut his face when he fell in a skiing accident. Mitchell assured everyone the story was true. Alex skied during the off-season to help build up his arms and legs, he said. Some doubted the story but no one challenged it. Ol' Pete celebrated his 42nd birthday on the train to Avon Park but was on his good behavior, refraining from celebrating the event in the club car.

Alex started the 1929 season with 364 wins. He needed eight to tie Christy Mathewson's National League record of 372 and nine to top it. Alex was aware of it but not many others across America were, because record-keeping was slower in those days and there wasn't the media hype about impending record-breaking that characterized almost every baseball season a half-century later. At the time Alex was pursuing Mathewson's mark, the record book showed Matty with 372 wins. Statisticians combing baseball box scores came up with another win for him about 20 years after he died and long after Alex retired.

Aimee wasn't there to baby-sit Ol' Pete, so the Cardinals came up with another plan. They had hired Charles "Gabby" Street as one of Southworth's coaches. Gabby was a colorful character who spent several years in his playing career as Walter Johnson's catcher with the Washington Senators. He was perhaps best known for a stunt in which he caught a ball dropped from the top of the Washington Monument — on his 15th try. Now the man who at one time was the catcher for Walter Johnson was assigned to be the babysitter for Grover Cleveland Alexander — to keep track of him as best he could off the field.

Alexander sits alone next to the water cooler late in his career. He pitched in the major leagues until he was 43, a remarkable career under any circumstances, but especially since he battled alcoholism and epilepsy through much of it. Within a decade, he would be trying to earn a few bucks by telling baseball stories in an arcade featuring sword swallowers and flea circuses (National Baseball Hall of Fame Library, Cooperstown, N.Y.).

Alex got the opening day assignment in Cincinnati April 16, a cold day that kept the crowd down and bundled up. His mound opponent was Red Lucas, who was no stranger, and Alexander came out on top, allowing five hits in a 5–2 victory. At Chicago on April 22, Pat Malone shut out the Cardinals 3-0, saddling Alex with his first loss. He lost a 6–2 decision to the Pirates on April 28 and was knocked out of a game and did not get the decision in a 9–7 win over the Giants on May 5. It wasn't until May 9 that Alex registered his second win of the year, beating Boston 5–1. On May 13 at Philadelphia, the Cardinals staked him to an 8–2 lead, but he could not hold it and the Phillies eventually won the game 10–9. On May 17, he lost again, this time at Pittsburgh 6–2. He finally got a laugher and beat the Reds 12–1 on May 21. He closed out the month by getting a no-decision in a game in which he was knocked out early and a win against the Reds—and Lucas— again on May 30 by a score of 5–1. Frank Funkhouse took down the Phillies 8–1 on May 31 to give St. Louis a 26–15 record. More important, the Cardinals were in their familiar first-place perch, a game ahead of the Pirates, 1½ games ahead of the Cubs. But Alex was struggling. It was more than just a matter of tiring, of not completing games. He was not holding leads. His record was 4–2, but almost all of his performances were shaky.

Things didn't get better in June. He was sent to the showers in the second inning of an 11–8 loss to Brooklyn on June 4 and then was hit hard but managed to get his fifth win in a relief role on June 10 when St. Louis beat Philadelphia 10–9. On June 15, he once again was removed and did not get the decision when the Cardinals beat Boston 5–4. St. Louis was 34–19 and in first place but without much direct help from Alex. After the game, Alex got word that Aimee had almost drowned in an accident in Lincoln, Nebraska, where she had been fishing with friends. She had fallen into a river. A 13-year-old boy, Richard Paul, son of her fishing companion, Nebraska Adjt. Gen. H.J. Paul, pulled her out, but she was unconscious and had to be resuscitated. She made a full recovery.

In Alex's next start, on June 20, the Cubs knocked him out in the first inning in a game Chicago eventually won 7–6. The drubbing also knocked Alex out of the starting rotation as the Cardinals continued to battle the Cubs, Pirates and Giants for the National League lead. The only mound appearance he made for two weeks didn't count in the standings. On June 26, the Cardinals filled an open date with an exhibition game in Galesburg, Illinois, where Alex began his professional career in 1909. Galesburg residents hadn't forgotten him. When the Cardinals arrived in town, they were treated to a parade after which local politicians gave welcoming speeches and recalled with pride the days when Grover Cleveland Alexander graced their dusty pitching mounds. Of course, there was a ballgame featuring the locals, and Alex took it easy on them as he pitched a couple of innings.

On July 1, the Cardinals headed east for a road trip. Alex stayed behind. The official line was that he was suffering from lumbago and was admitted to St. John's Hospital in St. Louis. Skeptics say that was a cover story, that Alex really went back to the Keeley Institute in Dwight, Illinois, to dry out. He didn't start another game until July 18 at Boston. By that time, the Cardinals were in a free fall. From the time they hit their season high of 15 games above .500 at 34–19 on June 15, they had won 8 and lost 23 and were a .500 ballclub. When Alex returned to the mound on July 18, his teammates got five runs in the eighth inning to bail him out and give him a 6–4 win.

Within days of Alex's return, Breadon decided to make another managerial switch. This time, he sent Southworth packing to Rochester to gain experience managing that ballclub and brought back the veteran McKechnie to see if he could resurrect the major league team. Alex got his second straight win on July 23, beating the Phillies 8–2 at Sportsman's Park. He got hit hard in a 10–5 loss to McGraw's Giants on July 28. But he bounced back on August 1 and was the winner in a 5–2 decision over Brooklyn, his 372nd victory, tying him with Mathewson as the winningest pitcher in National League history. His first crack at breaking the record came in Pittsburgh on August 8, but his defense deserted him in a 5–1 loss to the Pirates. The Cardinals made two errors in the fourth inning, allowing the Bucs to score four runs.

Sometimes fate plays unusual games. Alexander's lumbago, or whatever it was, prevented him from surpassing Mathewson's mark earlier in the season. Breadon's decision to switch Southworth and McKechnie helped put Alex back in the starting rotation in July. Then two errors prevented the Cardinals from nailing down the all-time wins record for Alex in Pittsburgh. Those circumstances, among others, brought the old warrior to Baker Bowl in Philadelphia, the home field for him when he broke into the major leagues in 1911, where he had three straight 30-win seasons in 1915–1917, where he threw a record 16 shutouts in the 1916 season and where he had become the only Phillies pitcher to win a World Series game in 1915. And, just as the magic moment of his career—the strikeout of Lazzeri in the 1926 World Series—came in a relief role, so did his 373rd career victory.

Neither the Cardinals nor the Phillies were going anywhere in the National League race when they hooked up for a doubleheader on the afternoon of August 10. Sherdel and St. Louis breezed to a 7–1 victory. Haines had trouble in the second game, but Cardinal bats came to life and the two teams battled to a 9–9 tie when McKechnie summoned the bullpen and called for Alex. "Just hold 'em and we'll win the game for you," the manager is reported to have told his aging pitcher as he gave him the ball. Alex

XI—The End of the Road

pitched three innings of scoreless relief, and St. Louis pushed across two runs in the 11th to win the game. Alex was officially king of the hill — the pitching mound — with more wins than anyone in the National League and anyone in all of baseball except for Cy Young and Walter Johnson. The achievement was noted in the newspapers, but with more than a month left in the season, the assumption was that more wins would be forthcoming.

His next start was to be in New York on August 17, so Alex asked McKechnie for some time off to go fishing with friends. He promised to stay away from liquor, but McKechnie waved him off, as if to say "don't make promises you can't keep." The only pledge McKechnie wanted from Alex was that he would be at the Polo Grounds ready to pitch on the day of his next start. Alex could fulfill only part of the promise. He showed up at the ballpark, but only after Gabby Street found him in a hotel where he had checked in on his own. He was obviously feeling the effects of several days of heavy drinking, but he insisted he could pitch. His opponent that day was young Carl Hubbell, and he was no match for the Giants lefty. Alex gave up seven hits before being knocked out in the third inning of a game the Giants won 9–5.

Two days later, the soft-spoken McKechnie, nicknamed "Deacon Bill" because of his Christian attitude and behavior, suspended Alex for breaking training rules. The kind-hearted manager fretted for many years about how Alex had forced his hand and how the great pitcher's utter lack of self control had cost him an even more exclusive spot in baseball's record books.

"Don't let it go to your head," McKechnie warned him when Alex asked for some time off after breaking Mathewson's record. "Please don't do anything foolish. I'm warning you. If you're not back here on time, you'll get a ticket somewhere else." McKechnie said Alex told him not to worry, that he was just going to see a friend. The friend, as it turned out, was his old pal alcohol, and they had a long visit, as *New York Times* columnist Arthur Daley put it.

"Our season still had six weeks to go when I disciplined him," McKechnie told reporters several years later. If only he had stayed sober on that trip, he could have won five or six more games in 1929 and would have had that National League record all by himself."[3]

But he didn't stay sober, so instead of being with his teammates in New York, Alex boarded a train bound for St. Louis and the next day met with Breadon in the executive offices at Sportsman's Park. Alex, at age 42, was like a boy being sent to the principal's office. Breadon talked to him behind closed doors and sent him home to Nebraska without docking him any pay.

Breadon told the press, "Alexander has done too much for this club and for St. Louis to be shuffled out into the cold. He is not even under suspension. The winter will take care of the situation satisfactorily in some way.

Alexander has been a great pitcher and a likeable fellow and I feel that he can still be of service to us."

Ol' Pete was grateful. When he emerged from Breadon's office, he told reporters, "Mr. Breadon told me to straighten up with a long rest and all would be all right — that my pay would go on and I would not be suspended. It is certainly wonderful. Mr. Breadon never has taken a nickel of my salary since I have been with the club and I am going to try to show my appreciation. Maybe I am not good enough to win 25 games a season again but I will be in there holding my own to the tune of 15 victories or more. I expect to regain my best condition and to pitch for the club next year."[4]

News of Alexander's latest run-in with management was bad news for baseball fans in St. Louis. Westbrook Pegler, the renowned writer who began his career as a sportswriter, was in St. Louis covering a game at Sportsman's Park in which the Browns beat the Philadelphia A's, 2–1. Pegler drifted from his account of what he considered a boring game to report the following:

> As if the customers here had not enough to depress them, they have fallen to brooding over the case of Grover Cleveland Alexander, who has been detached from the Cardinals and sent home. Old Aleck seems likely to become a problem for the local chamber of commerce as it is now remembered that he did much to keep the name of the town in the daily datelines of many cities in the World Series of 1926.
>
> Although he has broken training in a violent way several times this season and certainly has not been very useful to the Cardinals, it is now recalled that this trait was the very one that brought him to St. Louis in the first place.

This grand diversion into the psyche of St. Louis Cardinal fans was followed by a return to the original subject, the St. Louis Browns-Philadelphia A's ball game.[5]

Alex went home to Nebraska to fish for bullheads and sort out his life while his Cardinal teammates finished out the season. Now his life off the field was his entire life, and it was not a pleasant one. On September 25, he appeared in court in Grand Island, Nebraska, charged with drunken driving. He had been arrested after a six-mile police chase. He paid fines and was sent on his way, probably saved from harsher penalties because of his reputation as a ballplayer. On October 3, his divorce from Aimee became final. She emerged from court with H.J. Paul, her friend from the Nebraska National Guard and the man whom she was with when she nearly drowned the previous summer. She had testified that she continually tried to help Alex but that she now thought he would never quit drinking. Later, she confided to friends that she hoped the divorce would shock him to his senses. Grover Cleveland Alexander went into the winter of 1929 with his career and his marriage in shambles.

XI—The End of the Road

It didn't get any better on December 11 when Breadon, one of Alex's staunchest supporters, traded him to the Phillies. Breadon had been the man who rescued Alex from the scrap heap in 1926. Then Alex rescued the Cardinals. Breadon had put up with Alex's "training violations" and had never fined him or suspended him without pay because he wanted to believe in him, and he was grateful to the end for Alex's part in bringing the Cardinals their first championship. Perhaps in anticipation of public reaction, and, as writer Pegler had predicted, the sense of being criticized no matter what he did, Breadon explained the trade by saying he thought a change of scenery would be good for Alex. In essence, he was trying to say he was doing Alex a favor by getting rid of him.

The deal had some noteworthy ironies. Alex, the broken-down pitcher, was returning to the team and the city where he had developed into, in the view of many, the best pitcher of his generation. Now William Baker, the man who peddled Alex in 1918 because he needed the money, was getting him back for almost nothing. A further irony was this: Philadelphia was getting the winningest pitcher in National League history—but the player they were most interested in was the throw-in in the deal, a catcher named Harry McCurdy, who was known as a slow-footed backup catcher but compiled a .280 lifetime batting average playing for several teams in a ten-year big league career. The Phillies needed a catcher because their starting backstop for the past two seasons, Walt Lerian, was killed in an automobile accident on October 22, 1929, in his hometown of Baltimore. The *New York Times* was prophetic in its assessment: "Alexander, athletically aging and in ill health last season, gives little promise of being an effective and dependable hurler."

In Grand Island, Alex got in trouble again. On January 15, 1930, police charged him with drunkenness, possession of liquor and disorderly conduct. His companion, identified as Mary B. Madon of St. Paul, Nebraska, was also fined. On January 17, Roy H. Masonnof of St. Paul filed suit against Alex, calling him a "love pirate" for stealing the affections of his wife. Mrs. Masonoff was the "Mary Madon" in Alexander's vehicle two days earlier and, as her husband contended in the court papers, it wasn't the only time she and Alex had been in his vehicle, or in other places, for that matter. Masonoff was no fool. He knew his wife was fooling around with one of baseball's highest paid talents. He sought $25,000 in damages. Alex had known the woman since childhood, and at one time they had been sweethearts. He had been dating her since his divorce was final. The "love pirate" matter was later settled to everyone's satisfaction without the benefit of public record to learn the details.

When Alex reported for spring training in Leesburg, Florida, he joined a team full of high hopes. The Phillies had been the doormat of the National League for several years, having finished in eighth place in 1926, 1927 and 1928. The 1928 squad won 43 games and lost 109. But the Phillies rebounded in 1929 and finished fifth, behind the hitting of Lefty O'Doul, Chuck Klein, Don Hurst and others. They finished at 71–82 — 28 games better than the year before. Things were looking up.

One night after practice, Alex went to a bar in Leesburg and engaged a customer in conversation. The conversation soon became a heated disagreement with the man taking exception to some of Alexander's comments. The fellow picked up a bottle and was about to hit Alex with it when Cy Williams, a Phillies outfielder, stepped between the two and decked the man with one punch. Williams, who was no more than an occasional social drinker, had just stepped into the place when he spotted Ol' Pete about to get clobbered.

The National League's winningest pitcher was becoming an embarrassment to baseball. Those kinds of troubles did not end with the court appearances in Grand Island or the barroom in Florida. In fact, they had just begun.

• CHAPTER XII •

When the Cheering Stopped

"He was doing all right, asking no favors and taking the breaks — good and bad — as they came, until all of them turned bad."
— Sportswriter Harry Ferguson

Burt Shotton, Phillies manager and eternal optimist, thought his ballclub had a chance to be a pennant contender in 1930 despite its dismal finishes the past several years. In 1929, the Phillies made the quantum leap from eighth to fifth. Now, with the addition of Grover Cleveland Alexander to the pitching staff, why not dream the biggest of dreams? That's one of the magical things about spring training — everybody goes into it thinking they have a chance.

Philadelphia had terrific hitting. Chuck Klein and Lefty O'Doul hit .386 and .383 respectively. Third baseman Pinky Whitney hit .342. First baseman Don Hurst had a batting average of .327 and catcher Spud Davis .313. The lowest batting averages in the starting lineup came from shortstop and former Cardinal Tommy Thevenow, .286, second baseman Fresco Thompson, .282, and outfielder Denny Sothern, .280. Klein had 40 homers and 170 runs batted in. Combined with the .386 batting average, he would ordinarily have been a good candidate for the Triple Crown. But this was the year of the big bat. Chicago's Hack Wilson hit 56 home runs, drove in 190 (recently changed to 191), and the league as a whole hit .313. Many teams had hitting. Pitching was going to make the difference and, in the end, the Phillies didn't have it. Once again they finished eighth, winning only 52 and losing 102. One of the reasons was that the gamble on Alex didn't pay off, not so much for anything he did or didn't do. More than anything else, Father Time knocked him out of the box.

The Phillies opened their season with Les Sweetland throwing a shutout as Philadelphia beat the Brooklyn Robins at Ebbets Field. The following day, the Phillies were in New York, and Lou Koupal pitched a dandy but lost 3–2 to the Giants. The next day, 43-year-old Alex took the mound and, for the third time in his career, was matched up against Carl Hubbell. He lasted six innings but was in and out of trouble, walking four and giving up a solo homer to Mel Ott. The Giants won 2–1, saddling Alex with the loss. He didn't pitch again for eight days, when he faced the Boston Bees at Baker Bowl. Alex gave up runs in four straight innings before he was taken out. Philadelphia came back to win, 7–4, but Alex didn't get the decision. On May 7, the Phillies played the Cardinals at Sportsman's Park. It was Alex's first trip into St. Louis with his new team, and he got a rude welcoming. Having been demoted from the starting rotation, he came into the game in a relief role and got cuffed around in a game the Cardinals won 16–11. On May 11, the Phillies traveled to Cincinnati and Shotton decided to give Alex another shot in a starting role against the team he had the most wins against in his major league career. His teammates staked him to a 3–0 lead but Alex couldn't hold it. Cincinnati got to him for four runs in the fourth. The Reds won 5–4, but Alex was long gone and did not get the decision.

On May 28, the Phillies lost to the Bees 5–1 at Braves Field, burying the Phillies further into eighth place with an 11–20 record. Alex gave up two runs on two hits in relief and once again did not get the decision. The Philadelphia front office had made a decision. After the game, the Phillies announced they had given Alexander his unconditional release. For the man who had amassed 373 wins, 90 shutouts, 2,148 strikeouts, 5,190 innings pitched, a lifetime earned run average of 2.56 and had completed 437 of 599 career starts, the final line was not pretty:

W-L	Pct.	G	Starts	CG	IP	BB	SO	ERA
0–3	.000	9	3	0	21	6	6	9.14

The *Washington Post* told its readers, "Today Alexander takes the back trail that awaits all ballplayers when their steely arms turn to lead."

The *Chicago Daily Tribune,* the home paper for so many games in Alex's long career, was succinct: "Old Pete has petered out at last."

The *Los Angeles Times* was a little kinder: "Father Time has beckoned another former star out of the major leagues."

Alex tried to take it in stride, but he was realistic about his chances of getting another major league job. He told the press, "I'm just going to sit tight here for a few days and see what happens. I think I would like to play in the west. You know, I was raised in the west and I'm sort of used to it out there. I've been around the east for a long time now and I think I'm ready to try it in the other direction."

A reporter asked if he thought he could still win in the major leagues.

He said, "To tell the truth, I think I'm through as a big league pitcher. It's like the one-horse shay, you know. It doesn't last forever. Burt Shotton found it a hard job to tell me I was through. There are no hard feelings. I tried to win but I couldn't."

Aimee Alexander was in Lincoln, Nebraska, when Bill Maharg, a friend of Alex's, contacted her and begged her to go to Philadelphia to be with her ex-husband. Maharg had a brief major league career and was an assistant trainer on the Phillies teams that Alex was on 15 years earlier. Maharg was also said to be one of the go-betweens linking gamblers with the Chicago White Sox in the 1919 World Series. At Maharg's behest, Aimee went to Philadelphia. Years later, she recalled what she saw when the two were reunited. "Alex had been paid off for the season and when I entered his hotel room, he was in bed and all his money was stacked on top of the dresser. Bellboys who had been bringing him highballs took what they wanted from the poor guy," she said.[1]

Minor league club owners knew the potential Alex offered as a gate attraction but had to weigh that against the lifestyle that came with it if they took a chance on hiring him. Bob Tarleton, vice president of the Dallas Steers in the Texas League, decided to take the chance. He signed him to a contract calling for a salary of $1,500 a month — the most ever for a Texas League player — but it came with a stipulation: The old boy had to be ready to answer the call when it was his turn. Alex wanted Aimee to come with him. In all of his years of battling alcohol and sniffing ammonia to stave off epileptic seizures, she was the one stabilizing force in his life. But now they were divorced. It had been only six months since Ol' Pete had gotten himself into a jam for being a "love pirate" with another woman, a situation that had to sting Aimee, even though she and Alex were divorced. She had been on the road with him in St. Louis in 1926, and it had not been easy and certainly not fun. Aimee still loved Alex but had her own life now in Nebraska. She declined his invitation to go to Texas with him, a decision she later regretted.

On July 15, he was suspended for breaking training before he threw his first pitch for the Steers. Reporters found him in his Dallas hotel room looking, as one writer put it, "disheveled." Sitting on the edge of his bed, he said he didn't know what he was going to do with his life. "Maybe I've had enough," said Alex. "Ever since 1907 I've been tossing them up there. The old arm isn't what it used to be. I used to turn a ball loose and watch it flit by a batter. Now I watch it go up there and wonder what's holding it back." As he talked, he fingered a handsome ring on his finger, a gold ring with one diamond in it, the ring he earned as a member of the 1926 St. Louis Cardinal championship team.

"One thing I can say," said Alex in a rare moment in which he publicly felt sorry for himself. "I've given more to baseball than it's given me. I've never been a goody-goody boy but I stayed in there and pitched." He was asked if, despite his troubles, he still felt the urge to get out there and fire the ball past the hitters. He paused a moment and said, "Yeah, I do." Then he leaned down and buried his head in a pillow.[2]

Alex had been suspended, not released, and Tarleton made contact with him the next day. Alex repented and Tarleton, wanting to help the old fellow and also still wanting to cash in on his box office appeal, agreed to lift the suspension. "He told me he would buckle down and do the right thing if I gave him another chance. I am taking him at his word," he said.

Tarleton was frustrated by all of the circumstances involving Alexander. He had been scheduled to start in a home game that would have drawn the biggest crowd of the year for the Steers, but he wasn't ready to pitch — wasn't "in training" — so he missed that start and was suspended. Now, he promised to be ready to go, but his debut would be on the road, in the first game of a doubleheader at Wichita Falls on Sunday, July 20. The potential was there for a great crowd and big cash flow — and Tarleton — the man who made it happen — would get the visitors' share.

But Alex didn't start the first game. He was used in relief, and it was a disaster. The man the fans came to see threw three straight balls and walked off the mound to the bench, saying he had wrenched his knee. At the end of the game, Tarleton gave him his unconditional release, and that was not pretty either. Alex got the news from the press. "I don't consider myself released until Tarleton tells me," he said. "I can't say what my future plans are until he tells me I'm through. I have always heard baseball was a funny business and this proves it," he said.

"I am in good condition and wanted to start the first game. But they told me I would work the second. Instead they threw me as a relief in the first. The third time I wound up, I stepped into a hole about a foot deep and hurt my knee. Every pitch was agony after that and I was unable to start the second game. That hardly was my fault."

Alex went back to Chicago to ponder his fate and, he hoped, get another offer to pitch somewhere. Since being released by the Phillies, he was subject to mood swings, one day telling everyone he could still pitch somewhere, another day trying to cope with the thought that he might be through. One thing that never left him was the desire to go out and try. His challenge was to stay sober enough to do it when the opportunity presented itself. Also, at age 43, staying in shape was not easy, particularly for someone who had hardly given that notion a thought for many years.

One writer who showed no sympathy was the brusque Westbrook Pegler in the *Chicago Tribune*, who wrote:

XII—When the Cheering Stopped

Old Pete Alexander, the well-known horrible example, has just been released by the Dallas club of the Texas League and he is very sad about it, but do you suppose it ever occurred to Aleck to turn down his glass some time?

This thing has been done by some very good men in various walks of life but Alexander staggers through a blurry world feeling tremendously sorry for himself all the while and expecting a lot of people who have enjoyed less luck and prosperity to sit down with him somewhere on a park bench and bawl with him forever about the tragedy of it all."[3]

The Omaha Police Department called. It might find a job for him in the police department if he would be willing to pitch for the department's baseball team. That offer had some appeal because he would be back in his home state, not far from his native St. Paul and not far from the love of his life, Aimee, who was living near Lincoln. Another offer came from the Galesburg semi-pro baseball team in Illinois. Galesburg also held a special place in Alex's heart, for it was there he had gotten his start nearly 20 years ago. He still had friends in Galesburg. Plenty of people there still knew him, plenty more said they knew him, and most who didn't know him would love to get the opportunity. On July 25, he agreed to pitch one game in Galesburg in August as sort of a "job interview" with the team's manager, Harold Wicall. That was an indication of just how far Alex had fallen in a span of about two months. The winningest pitcher in the National League had to audition for a job on a semi-pro team in the countryside of western Illinois. The audition never took place because on July 29, Alex accepted an offer to pitch for the Toledo Mud Hens of the American Association. He was being given yet another chance to be back in professional baseball.

This one had some promise for Alex. The Mud Hens were managed by Charles Dillon "Casey" Stengel, who would later distinguish himself by winning 10 pennants in a 12-year span (1949–1960) with the New York Yankees. Stengel began his managerial career with Worcester in the Eastern League in 1925, the same year Joe McCarthy was piling up enough wins in Louisville to earn a promotion to the Chicago Cubs the following year. At one point in the season, one of Stengel's players mentioned that McCarthy was lucky. Stengel, frustrated with his team's lack of effort, replied "Yeah, and if we keep playing them, he'll be lucky until 1999." Stengel hooked on with Toledo in 1926 and managed the Mud Hens through 1931. His 1927 ballclub finished first, winning 101 games. In 1929, the Mud Hens slumped to eighth place, losing 100 games. In midseason, Stengel advised his players to invest in railroad stock. The way many of them were playing, said Casey, they would provide good business for the railroads because so many of them would be sent home on the trains.

But Casey knew Alex from their playing days in the big leagues. And he had a reputation in the minor leagues for spotting aging players who couldn't make it any more in the big leagues but who gave a minor league team a lift. There was a business side to it. If Casey could revive the major league talents in old ballplayers and sell them back to big league clubs, there was enormous profit possibilities. Grover Cleveland Alexander couldn't have been a better fit for the way Stengel handled a ballclub in 1930.

Or so it seemed. But this gamble, too, turned out to be a loser. For one thing, the day after Alex signed with the Mud Hens, it was announced that he had signed to pitch some games for the House of David, an independent ballclub originally affiliated with a religious organization that barnstormed through the Midwest. He was scheduled to make his first start with Toledo on Sunday, August 3. A crowd of 14,000 was expected, as well as a film crew ready to shoot newsreel footage. Alex didn't show up. The word was that he was in Chicago. Oscar Smith, president of the Mud Hens, was in Chicago at the time and learned Alex had sequestered himself in a hotel room. When Smith went to find out what was going on, a nurse standing outside the door prevented him from going in. She told him that Alexander was a "very sick man." She said she could say nothing else. "I suppose when there is anything to be said, Mr. Alexander will communicate with you," said the nurse.

Smith wanted to leave a message for Alex but the nurse refused to take it. So Smith went to the hotel lobby and wrote another message, this one a telegram he sent to Alex. It said, "The Toledo Baseball Co. hereby notifies you that the deal for your services is called off and the Toledo Baseball Co. does not desire your services." With that, Alex was released from his third team in two months.[4]

The next time he was heard from was a few days later when he was in New York and the press caught up with him. Alex told reporters he hadn't broken his contract with Toledo. He had become ill in Chicago and could not make the trip to Toledo. Alex didn't specify what ailed him but did say he called Mud Hen officials and notified them he was ill. Alexander was asked if he intended to observe "training rules" any better in the future. Ol' Pete responded, "I guess you mean my drinking, don't you? Well, I admit I drink. But I'm not the playboy you read about. I never have painted myself as an angel with one of those halo things, but it's physically impossible for any one man to hold all the liquor accredited to me."

He said it was his legs that were giving him trouble, not his arm. "Tricky things, legs. For the first three or four innings, everything will be rosy when all of a sudden your legs go dead," said Alex. "If I can get my legs in fairly good shape, I ought to be able to fool my share of batters next year."

XII—When the Cheering Stopped

The press was becoming weary of his behavior and excuses. An unsigned column in the *New York Times* on August 7, 1930, put it this way:

> Baseball has given Grover Cleveland Alexander a fair chance. It appears that he no longer feels he owes baseball or the public even partial return for the advantages and opportunities that it has proffered him.
>
> Once, twice, a third time he has disappointed the fans who have made it possible for him to enjoy adequate compensation for his employment for the display of his skill, and he has disappointed his friends and those who have tried to render him that kind of assistance which is good to a man when he needs it, as Alexander does.... No ballplayer in major league history ever had more chances.

In a syndicated column Alex wrote after his career was over, he offered advice to young pitchers just coming up.

Believe in yourself, he said. Study the hitters. Know their weaknesses. Practice putting the ball where you want it. Don't get discouraged.

"And one last word. Leave the liquor alone. It cannot help you and it may do you harm. If I was able to take it and still pitch good ball, that doesn't mean you can. Play safe and stay away from it."

On September 25, 1930, Alex was put in jail in Grand Island, Nebraska, pending a hearing on eight charges, most of them liquor violations, stemming from the "love pirate" auto accident earlier in the year. The next day he was fined and released.

• CHAPTER XIII •

The Long Road Downhill

"What happened to my World Series ring and the $700?"
— Grover Cleveland Alexander

The House of David was a religious sect whose principles were ancient and their morals questionable at times but whose ideas and works, in many ways, were far ahead of their times. It started out as a religious colony founded by Benjamin and Mary Purnell in Benton Harbor, Michigan, in 1903 with the purpose of gathering the 12 lost tribes of Israel together to await the millennium. Fending for themselves, members of the colony figured out how to do innovative things that it took years for the rest of the world to master. They learned how to preserve food in cold storage and built a whole cold-storage facility that was much more practical than an icebox in order to feed an entire colony. They not only made their own jellies; they developed the now common method of storing them in jars. Various accounts also credit the House of David with building its own amusement park, a bowling alley with the first automatic pinsetters and a vegetarian restaurant. They bottled water from their own springs, created their own hospital, had their own orchestra and jazz band and built an amphitheatre for their musicians to perform. While members of the House of David were certainly not part of the mainstream, they were not isolated either. They had their own logging operation and eventually a streetcar company. They were easy to spot as they went about their business. Men were not allowed to shave and were required to let their hair grow.[1]

In the latter part of the Roaring '20s, the House of David was under investigation by the state of Michigan for many alleged crimes and abuses. After Benjamin Purnell, the self-proclaimed king of this clan, died in 1927, there was turmoil and a struggle for power. The colony split into two factions, one led by Mary Purnell, the other by dissidents. It was into this mix of pseudo-utopian lifestyle, radical religious beliefs and erratic personal behavior that Grover Cleveland Alexander descended for one reason, and

XIII—The Long Road Downhill

one reason only. He needed a job. The House of David continued its baseball barnstorming, and Alex agreed to join the team on the condition that he didn't have to grow a beard. The House of David agreed to the terms, and why not? They were willing to forgo one of their religious principles in order to land one of the greatest pitchers in baseball history. As a publicity gimmick, the club announced that it added 35 cents a day to Alex's pay to cover the cost of razor blades. He served as player-manager of the team from 1931 to 1935.

Aimee Alexander said she learned of the deal shortly after Alex had blown his chances with the Dallas minor league club. Then he frittered away his opportunity in Toledo. Ray Doan, a friend of Alex's from Muscatine, Iowa, was running one of the House of David teams and approached Alex about it in Dallas. He would join the ballclub for the 1931 season.

Doan was a promoter, a man who knew how to take an idea, have a little fun with it and make a buck or two along the way. He was a short man with dark hair, white at the temples, and combed straight back. He could be seen along the circuit in a rumpled coat and pants, a tie that came down only about to the middle of his chest, and a white hat. He had the showmanship of P.T. Barnum, the promotional zany attitude of Bill Veeck, and the ability to put a team on a bus and travel from town to town and make a go of it, as Abe Saperstein did later in basketball with the Harlem Globetrotters. For people like Ray Doan, no matter how today went, there was always tomorrow, and people like Grover Cleveland Alexander could help get you there.

Ray Doan was a sports promoter who hired Alexander to manage and pitch for the House of David, a ballclub developed by a religious sect in which all the players wore beards except for Alex. Eventually, Alex's drinking became a problem for this club, just as it had in the big leagues. Doan worked tirelessly to try find a place for Alex to settle down (photograph courtesy of Muscatine, Iowa, Public Library).

He had other baseball ventures as well, including baseball schools for youngsters at places like Hot Springs, Arkansas, one of Alex's favorite places when he actually did train. Doan hired great ballplayers to spend a few days at the schools. The ballplayers made a few bucks. Doan made a killing and, like many showmen in sports, he got mixed reviews.

Bob Ray, writing in the *Los Angeles Times,* wrote about one venture:

> The Dean boys, Paul and Dizzy, didn't do badly on their barnstorming tour, but the gent who cleaned up was their manager, a Mr. Ray Doan. Mr. Doan is affiliated with such ventures as showing off the Dean boys, exploiting the athletic prowess of Babe Didrickson, and running a baseball school for boys who have enough money to pay for the course, but his chief source of income is a couple of House of David baseball clubs. He discovered that one House of David club wasn't enough so he organized another and, as soon as all the recruits had grown the required foliage, he sent one club east and one west so they could sweep the country, as it were, with their whiskers and baseball ability.
>
> But let us get out of the brush and back to the story of the daring Deans. It seems that last spring Mr. Doan signed up Dizzy and Paul, before he had any idea they'd be the World Series heroes, for a post-season barnstorming tour. He guaranteed Dizzy and Paul each $75 per game and was to pay all expenses. All Mr. Doan was to get was 50 percent of the gross receipts. But when Dizzy and Paul saw more than 10,000 fans out at their first exhibition at Oklahoma City, they demanded a recount and forced Doan to split his share 50–50 with them. So the astute Mr. Doan made as much as both the Dean boys, and even after paying all expenses, emerged with quite a chunk.[2]

A few years later, John Kiernan, venerable columnist for the *New York Times,* caught up with Doan in another venture at Hot Springs—an umpiring school. The professor, as Kiernan referred to Doan, had figured out that if the umpire school ran concurrently with the baseball training school, the umpires could get on-the-job training. Eventually, major league umpire George Barr bought the umpire school and Rogers Hornsby bought the baseball training school and, once again, Doan made a killing.

Kiernan reported on a typical day at Hot Springs: "There were 75 students in the umpirical school but Hot Springs was also swarming with rookies at the baseball school. There were ball games going on all around the town and there was no lack of practice for the umpires. After they officiated, they had to turn in a report of what they had done and seen, and what they had learned, if they had learned anything."[3]

Bob Considine in the *Washington Post,* related an incident about one of Doan's other hired hands—Babe Ruth. Doan told Considine the Babe was better than Alex or Hornsby or either of the Dean boys in working with kids, teaching them and having patience with them. Perhaps to the chagrin of Doan, Ruth never tried to talk a kid into coming back for another "semester" at the school — a $50 cost — if he knew the youngster would not make any progress. Ruth believed "if a boy could run fast and throw well, he could be taught to hit and field, and that if he couldn't run or throw, he was wasting his money."[4]

House of David players had two gimmicks that they performed at many of their games. One was the now familiar "pepper game," which modern day ballplayers often play to loosen up before a ball game and to have a little fun with the fans. The House of David players often played it between innings in the middle of the game. Three players would line up several feet apart from one another. A fourth player was the batter. He would hit a ground ball to one of the players, who would pick it up and do any number of things: He might toss it behind his back to another player or fake an overhand throw and then toss it underhand or roll it to another player, who would grab the ball and do the same kind of shenanigans. As they moved the ball from one player to another, they would go faster and faster, much to the delight of the fans. The other stunt was more bizarre. Doan instituted "donkey baseball," in which his players, at some point in the game, were required to perform while riding donkeys. Only pitchers and catchers were exempt. Hitters could bat in their normal stances, but once they hit the ball, they had to jump on a donkey and try to get to first base while fielders on donkeys tried to retrieve the ball.[5]

For Alex, this was a world a million miles away from the glory days of pitching to Babe Ruth and Rogers Hornsby and winning 30 games and throwing 16 shutouts in one major league season and striking out Tony Lazzeri with the World Series on the line. He thought it was a job an old drunk like himself could handle, but he knew he would need some help from the one person he knew he could count on.

Alex called Aimee, told her about the newest job offer, and promised to behave if she would come back and join him. By now, Ol' Pete realized the best way for him to stay out of trouble was to have her at his side. She rejoined him and eventually remarried him on June 2, 1931, in Rockford, Illinois As she explained years later, "Well, I still loved the guy. For six weeks, he was a lamb. We'd be sitting around the hotel room with some of the players and there'd be a bottle open, of course. Alex would play bartender but he wouldn't drink."

For the next three years, Aimee and Alex traveled separate from the rest of the team, with Aimee doing all the driving, averaging more than 50,000 miles a season. She said as long as she was nearby, Alex stayed on his good behavior. Then, as she told it:

But then there were nights like the one in Devil's Lake, South Dakota. We'd been on the go for a week or so and I just had to have my hair done. While I was in the beauty shop, some of the town sports got Alex in a room behind the barbershop and loaded him to the gills. At the ballpark that night, one of the town officials kept Alex primed with a jug he'd hidden behind the grandstand. Alex really got high. He tried to climb up the foul screen, picked a fight with an umpire and finally got thrown out of the game.

Two days later, while we were driving along the highway, he said to me, "Aimee, do you know what happened to my World Series ring and the $700 I had?" I told him I didn't. I let him sweat it out for a couple of days before I confessed that I had found his valuables in the room at Devil's Lake and had put them in my purse. He said, "I knew all the time you had 'em." That was Alex for you.[6]

The House of David teams, an East Coast one and a West Coast one, played 176 games in 1931 in a circuit that included not only Devil's Lake but Grand Junction, Colorado, Fargo, North Dakota, Spokane, Washington, Salt Lake City and any other towns where people like Doan felt they could draw a crowd. There is no record of it, so one can only guess what must have been going through Alex's mind on the night of September 22, 1931, when the House of David, with Alexander pitching a couple of innings, played the St. Louis Cardinals at Sportsman's Park, scene of so many heroics of Alexander the Great just a few short years before when he pitched for the Cardinals. On this night, he didn't last long, and neither did any other House of David pitcher as the Cardinals won 17–6.

A crowd of 9,000 showed up for the game, perhaps not just to see the bearded wonders but to experience the first night game at the major league park. This was accomplished by another innovation of the House of David, a portable lighting system that was hauled by truck from town to town. The system consisted of mammoth floodlights mounted on 50-foot poles that were set up on the ballfields. One of the trucks carried the "power plant"— a 100,000-watt generator with a 250-horsepower gasoline engine.[7]

Doan plucked other star athletes out of the big cities and put them onto the dusty trails, striving for good performances and big gate receipts and leaving the evangelizing to others. Chief Bender had a short tour of duty, and Satchel Paige's days on the circuit helped later make inroads with the best black athletes of the day so that the House of David played some of the great Negro League teams of the era. Cool Papa Bell, was one of the best ballplayers in the Negro Leagues— and certainly the fastest. Paige said Cool Papa was so fast that he could turn off the lights and be in bed before the room got dark. The first time he faced Alex, Cool Papa said, he took the first pitch for a strike just out of respect for the great old-timer. He then got a base hit and later scored a run. Another top performer who pitched for the House of David was the spectacular multi-sport woman athlete, Mildred "Babe" Didrickson, winner of two gold medals and a silver medal in the 1932 Olympics. In 1934 she pitched a few innings for the House of David, throwing in only the first two innings of the games in which she appeared. (Alex said he always hoped to be assigned to pitch the last two—and that the game would be called because of rain before then.) Doan later helped Didrickson form the Babe Didrickson All-American Basketball team, which he promoted.

The truth was that in the space of about a year, Alex had gone from being a major league pitcher to a carnival attraction complete with bearded ballplayers, donkeys and crowd-pleasing antics. He was an entertainer getting paid to show up and be seen, like a sword-swallower at a circus.

In that first season, on May 31, 1931, Alex worked the first three innings, striking out one, walking one and hitting one batter but giving up no runs as the House David defeated Duffy's Florals of the Chicago Semi-Pro league 2–1. On July 10, he made a ninth inning relief appearance, gave up a hit and struck out two in a 4–2 loss to Duffy's Florals. The next night, 7,000 fans showed up to see Ol' Pete start a game in Chicago, just as he had for nine years with the Cubs. This time, he pitched the first three innings, allowing three hits but no runs. The House of David lost to the Logan Squares, another Chicago Semi-Pro League team, 4–3. He finished out the season pitching here and there and in January signed on for another season.

He went to Catalina Island to play golf, fraternize and maybe give a hand to some of the Cubs' young pitchers. In an interview with the *New York Times,* he seemed resigned to his fate. "I have no plans," he said, "and I do not know the condition of my arm. Last season the House of David used me as an attraction and, as a rule, I pitched only one inning, and only once as many as five. So you see, I have no idea what my arm can do. When the boys arrive, I may get the fever and start throwing a few around." On February 26, he observed his 45th birthday. He managed to pitch some batting practice and that drew some crowds who marveled at how he could still hit the corners with a fair degree of consistency.

But when the time came, he rejoined the House of David and allowed himself to be a sure-fire gate attraction just by showing up. When it was announced he would pitch in both games of a doubleheader against the Florals on August 21, that was worth several paragraphs in the *Tribune,* and it was a banner day at the box office. He was still at it a year later. On May 22, 1933, he pitched four innings of shut-out ball as the House David beat Mills, a west-side Chicago team, 4–3. He was back in Chicago in September and worked the first two innings in a 2–1 win over a team called the Angel Juniors. By 1934, he was mostly a gate attraction in the same way a cigar store Indian is, and by the end of 1935 his career with the House of David was over.

Probably his most enjoyable time was in 1934 when the always-promoting Doan struck up an agreement with Satchel Paige, the great Negro League star who had recently left the Kansas City Monarchs for the Pittsburgh Crawfords. The Depression hit the Negro Leagues hard, and many of their games were eliminated to ease the travel expenses. So Doan latched on to Paige and the Crawfords and arranged a deal in which they would travel the rural roads of America with the House of David, stopping in towns and playing doubleheaders with the locals. The House of David would play one game with Alex pitching a couple of innings. The Crawfords would play the second game, with Paige pitching an inning or two. As with nearly everything else Doan touched, the gate receipts were fantastic.

Highlight of the season was the House of David's entry into the annual tournament sponsored by *The Denver Post* that drew the best semi-pro teams from all over the country. Doan took no chances. He hired Paige to pitch for the Davids. Alex would manage and coach and be available to pitch, although he was becoming more and more unreliable. As it turned out, he wasn't needed. Paige started and won three games, striking out 14, 17 and 12, and the House of David won the tournament.

Aimee made the trips with Alex for the first three years. When she decided she had had enough of the dusty roads, cheap motels, constant travel and sack lunches, she headed home and trusted Alex to stay on the straight and narrow. And once gain, he could not meet the challenge.

When his days with the club ended, Alex did not react with a sense of gratitude toward the people who gave him a job when he was unable to get or keep one anywhere else. "I was advertised like the elephant in the circus and had to pitch an inning or so every game. I always picked the eighth or ninth inning and prayed for rain," he said.

Eddie Deal, a catcher on the House of David from 1929 to 1942, was not an outstanding ballplayer, but he could hold his own against the caliber of competition he faced. And he was thrilled to have the opportunity to catch Grover Cleveland Alexander. This gave him something in common with Bill Killefer, Bob O'Farrell and other heroes of the major leagues.

But he had a different take on Alexander's career with the team than Alex did. He recalled that when Aimee was with him, she did the driving. When she left, she took the car. Alex traveled with the team but would often find his own way from the hotel to the ballpark. "Sometimes he couldn't get to the games because he was too drunk," said Deal. "Sometimes he was so lit up, you couldn't get him out of the dugout. He was a nice guy but we couldn't depend on him. He only had to pitch one inning and when he couldn't do that, we had to let him go."[8]

Doan was well aware of the problems Deal mentioned. Alex's drinking was out of control. Once one of the best-paid players in baseball, he now frittered away his meager paychecks on alcohol and was becoming a nuisance to those around him. Doan considered Alex a friend but saw that he could no longer help him. He took the bold step of telephoning Ford Frick, president of the National League, to see if major league baseball could be of any assistance to the superstar-turned-problem-child. Frick contacted Kenesaw Mountain Landis, a man who had restored the image of baseball after the Black Sox scandal of 1919 and vigorously protected that image. In a letter dated April 1, 1935, Frick wrote to the commissioner:

> My dear Mr. Commissioner:
> I had a telephone call this morning from Ray Doan in Hot Springs relative to Grover Cleveland Alexander who, it seems, has gone completely broke, is in terrible physical condition and is more or less making "a mess of himself" and consequently casting a none too good reflection on baseball. Doan was anxious to know whether or not we as a League could supply any monies toward Alexander's support.
> As you know, the National League at the moment has no funds available for that purpose. Following the All-Star game this summer, we will, of course, have $10,000 to be used in that way, but right now there seems nothing we can do.
> I understand that Alexander dropped his membership in the players association somewhere around 1928 or 1929 and therefore is technically not entitled to any help from that organization.
> However, it seems to me there should be some way we could get around that temporarily and until such time as the National League is in position to provide funds. Certainly, having the man running loose around the country, drinking, carousing, pawning his belongings at every opportunity, is not beneficial to the good name of baseball.
> I hold no brief [sic] whatsoever for Alexander. Doan tells me that even his own people refuse to have anything to do with him. But if we could find funds available to put him into an institution and perhaps give him the cure, it might help.
> I must admit to you frankly that my hands are tied on the thing and I would like a word of advice from you.

Frick signed the letter and added this postscript: "I think it is not a question of what we can do for Alexander, but is there anything we can do for him."

Frick did not know it, but Landis was also getting pressure from elsewhere. He had received a letter from Aimee Alexander, now living in Cincinnati, in which she said, "It is most pathetic that our Alex is unable to control this terrible thing and unable to be the very fine person we know he is capable of being. I have helped him all I can and even more than I have been able to, and the going hasn't altogether been an easy road, however, I am glad I can take care of myself." Aimee was particularly concerned, she said, because Doan had been picking up Alex's expenses out of his own pocket but was not going to do it any longer. He put a May 1 deadline on Alex or somebody else finding a way of supporting him.

Landis wrote back on April 11, telling Frick he had received a letter from Aimee expressing the hope, or as Landis put it, "the proposition to do something with him, to him or for him." With respect to advice for Frick, Landis wrote, "What is done in re: Alexander primarily should express the judgment of the National League in the first instance. What, if any, expenditure is made in that behalf prior to July (when the All-Star game was to be played), I suggest be advanced by your league and reimbursed to the league after the All-Star game."

It is clear from the tone of both letters that the days of musings about "old John Barleycorn" were over. Alex had become a problem to himself, his wife, his ex-employers and to the national pastime. And another factor was emerging. Dealing with the Alexander situation was becoming a public relations nightmare because of the perception that nothing was being done to help a man who many believed was a national icon who had simply fallen on hard times.

Sid Keener, a well-respected writer and columnist for the *St. Louis Star-Times,* wrote to Frick on April 12, suggesting that organized baseball give a hand to Alex.

> I have been informed that Alex is down and out — AGAIN. I hear they picked him up out of the gutter in Hot Springs several weeks ago without a quarter in his pockets. No place to go. They tell me he'd like to go back home, I think with relatives in Nebraska or some place up north, but he can't make it because he can't hitch-hike and he hasn't the necessary funds to get there.
>
> One party who heard the story suggested that the Players Fund for old-timers could take care of Alex. But it seems that Alex isn't a member of that organization, therefore, he is not entitled to financial assistance.
>
> Now I thought, Ford, that perhaps the National League could do a turn for Alex, rescue him from the poor man's home or some big place like it by rallying to his assistance. How does it strike you? I do not know his whereabouts at present but I imagine someone could put a finger on Alex.
>
> I thought the National League, secretly and without any great ballyhoo, could vote some financial assistance to the old boy, send him back home, give him a drawing account, or at least make some arrangements for his board and lodging for the remainder of his life. It wouldn't cost much, I believe.

Keener was obviously seeking humanitarian aid and was sympathetic toward Alex. He had no way of knowing Frick was simultaneously attempting to do the same thing for a much different reason. The baseball official was trying to rid himself of a headache.

XIII—The Long Road Downhill

BASEBALL

KENESAW M. LANDIS
COMMISSIONER
LESLIE M. O'CONNOR
SECRETARY-TREASURER

333 NORTH MICHIGAN AVENUE
CHICAGO

April 11, 1935

Mr. Ford Frick,
President, National League,
R.C.A. Building,
New York, N. Y.

Dear Mr. Frick:

    I enclose to you herewith letter from Mrs. G. C. Alexander, 255 McCormick Place, Cincinnati, Ohio, under date of April 9, concerning Grover Cleveland Alexander and the proposition to do something with him, to him or for him. I have wirtten to Mrs. Alexander that this letter has gone to you.

    Your letter of April 1 concerned this same matter, and in reply thereto I have this in mind: What is done in re Alexander primarily should express the judgment of the National League in the first instance. What, if any, expenditure is made in that behalf prior to July, I suggest be advanced by your league and reimbursed to the league after the All-Star game.

    I will discuss with you and President Harridge when we next get together the general process of operation with respect to league philantrophies, etc., in the light of the legislation adopted at the 1934 meeting.

With good wishes,

Very truly yours,

[signature]
Commissioner.

KML P

Commissioner Kenesaw Mountain Landis was interested in finding a stable situation for Alexander. As this letter to National League president Ford Frick shows, Landis had even corresponded with Alexander's wife about it. In this letter, the commissioner suggests that the National League donate money to Alexander and be reimbursed with All-Star game receipts (National Baseball Hall of Fame Library, Cooperstown, N.Y.).

Keener concluded his letter saying:

> Shucks, I think it's a shame that a grand old fellow like Alex should have this finish. We all know his trouble — drink, drink, drink some more. Nevertheless, I can't overlook the fact that he was a great guy when he was swinging that right arm out on the hill.
> I haven't told this story to Mr. Breadon. I know that Mr. Breadon has been more than generous to Alex. However, it is possible that you might be able to do something with the club owners or the surplus in the National League and have the owners vote some financial assistance to him. Alex wants to go back home ... back on the farm."

He closed his letter with a rather curious notation, considering the subject of the rest of his letter. He wrote, "Thanks for the little drinkee [sic] at Bradenton."

Frick, a former sportswriter, had known Keenan for years. Keenan assured him the letter was private and that he did not intend to write a column about it, making his ideas public. Frick typed a quick note back to him, saying he was well aware of the situation. "I think I can assure you that some sort of action will be taken," he wrote.

Frick knew that Breadon never forgot how Alex had helped bring the Cardinals' their first championship. That is why in 1929, when the good-hearted McKechnie felt the need to suspend Alex, Breadon sent him home for the rest of the season but with full pay. While Ol' Pete tried to hang on with the Phillies and then bounced from Dallas to Toledo to the backroads of America with the House of David, the Cardinals had come of age in the National League. With Gabby Street, Alex's old baby-sitter, at the helm, St. Louis won championships in 1930 and 1931 and won the pennant again in 1934 with Frank Frisch piloting the "Gas House Gang" that included the Dean brothers, Pepper Martin, Joe Medwick and Leo Durocher. Breadon was in a position financially to help but certainly was under no obligation to do so.

On April 16, a little more than two weeks after he had first contacted the commissioner about the problems with Alex, Frick dashed off two more letters, one to Judge Landis and one to Doan, who needed some kind of answer as to what would happen with Alex once the promoter stopped acting as unofficial guardian.

In the letter to Doan, he wrote:

> As you know, Aleck has been pretty well treated by baseball people everywhere and I frankly do not feel as much sympathy for him as I would for some others. On the other hand, I do appreciate the large part he has played in baseball and I do feel if it at all compatible with good judgment, we should try to aid him.
> I do not believe sending him money direct would have any value. What I

am willing to do, in case you will take the assignment, is to send you each month for the next few months the sum of $50, you to use and spend this money for his benefit as it is needed. I don't think you can turn over cash to him. I don't believe it would be wise to send the money direct to him but with your cooperation perhaps we can be helpful to Alec.

His letter to the commissioner advised Landis of what he had in mind. He was even more direct with the judge than he had been with Doan. "Sending the check direct to Aleck would, of course, be nonsensical or permitting him to get his hands on the cash at all would be equally foolish."

Frick realized Alexander's standing in the history of baseball but had obviously lost patience with a former ballplayer turned town drunk who was occupying way too much of his time and attention.

"I personally have very little sympathy with Aleck," he wrote. "I feel that baseball has been very kind to him and that he has been given every opportunity to make good. On the other hand, I do feel that having him running loose on the country, so to speak, is a very bad advertisement and it would probably be worth $50 per month to us to prevent that occurrence."

He concluded the letter by asking the commissioner if he had anybody in mind who could manage the money for Alex. The only person Frick had in mind was Doan, the very person who was tired of the responsibility.

Landis too was obviously tired of fooling with the Alex problem. His reply to Frick was a terse two sentences dated April 18, 1935: "Acknowledging your letter of April 16, I have nothing in mind as to how the Alexander matter should be handled. Whatever you decide upon in that regard will be agreeable to me, of course."

By May 16, Breadon felt the need to check in with Frick. By this time, he not only was well aware of Alexander's embarrassing behavior but most likely had been approached by Keener and others about helping his former employee. Breadon wrote to Frick, "I have just been thinking of the All-Star game, and it came to my mind that old Alexander has done more for baseball than anyone connected with the Players Association. Why can't they take care of Alex?" Frick responded by letting Breadon know that since Alex had dropped out of the association, he wasn't eligible for its funds.[9]

Meanwhile, Doan continued to be Alex's caretaker. Frick let him know in August that funds were now available and that he was anxious to know how Doan thought the situation should be handled. He asked Doan for "whatever other information you may have concerning him" and to "please give me as much of the story as you know."

That was an invitation for the perplexed promoter to unload about his difficulties with Alex, and unload he did in a letter to Frick dated August 12, 1935.

"He has been with my Western House of David Club all season and has been a constant source of trouble. It appears that Alex has lost all ability to control his appetite, and while in other years I have had trouble with him, this year has been the worst of all. Only the fact that I have agreed with you that I would take care of him during the summer has prevented me from discharging him and abandoning any effort to do any more for him. I expect to close my season about September 18th or 20th, and while I will do the best I can to keep him until that date, it will only be over the protest of my manager and other players."

Doan said it wouldn't do any good to provide Alex with money for the winter because he would just blow it. Doan thought the only solution would be to find someone who would agree to keep him and provide that person with his room and board money and some cash to give him from time to time for tobacco and incidentals.

In the winter of 1934, Doan said, he found Alex a rooming house and paid his room and board. Alex got drunk and set a bed on fire. Doan paid for the damage. It was no wonder he wanted to rid himself of the responsibility of Alex's well-being. Doan said in the spring of 1935 he tried unsuccessfully "to send him to his people," including his wife, but they all declined.

As upset as Doan was with Alex's conduct, he ended his letter with the same type of conclusion that Landis, Frick, Breadon and Keener had all expressed.

"I do not feel like I am under any further obligation to Alex," he wrote, "but I dislike to see a man that has meant so much in the past to organized baseball to become a public charge which he will be if someone does not look after him."

But Doan made one more offer and Frick quickly took him up on it. He said he would look around to see if he could find someone who would put up Alex for the winter — and put up with him — and what the cost would be. It was an offer Frick could not refuse.

Doan thought Catalina Island might be a possibility. Maybe the Wrigley family would be gracious enough to give Alexander a resting place in familiar territory where he could enjoy the company of the ballplayers when spring training began. Another possibility was back in his roots. Doan was planning a trip to Denver when the season ended. He decided to go through St. Paul, Nebraska, the little town where Alex grew up and where he still had family and friends. Maybe there, Doan thought, he could find shelter for Ol' Pete. But the question was fast becoming: If not there, where?

On September 23, nearly six months after the search had begun for a place for Alex, Doan wrote to Frick with some good news. L.B. Conklin,

XIII—The Long Road Downhill

secretary of the Community Club of St. Paul, told Doan that a man by the name of J.C. Toman would provide a place for Alex to stay. Doan's letter indicated that the reputation of the one-time hometown hero had made its way to St. Paul. "As everyone knows his habits in regard to drinking, this Mr. Toman knows Alex, he lives on a farm about three miles from St. Paul, there is good hunting and fishing to take up his time there, and I believe this will be an ideal place for him," Doan wrote. "Mr. Toman knows of his habits and will do all that he can to control his drinking. They will take him for $40 a month board and room."

Frick jumped at the opportunity. On September 16, he dashed off letters to both Doan and Toman confirming the deal, asking Doan for one more favor—to deliver Alex to the Toman farm. On October 7, Alexander arrived. Toman scrawled a note to Frick confirming his arrival, saying "I think this will be a good place for Alex if I can just keep him here."

Alexander was back in the place where he grew up, the area where he learned to throw stones side-armed and hit whatever he was aiming at, the place where he developed great arm muscles doing farm chores for his father and where, in 1926, just nine years earlier, he was the object of adulation and affection in a great celebration after his masterful work in the World Series against the Yankees. On November 7, Harvey Traband, secretary of the National League, sent a check for $40 to J.C. Toman to pay the first month's room and board for the vagrant he had taken in named Grover Cleveland Alexander.

• CHAPTER XIV •

Brother, Can You Spare Me a Dime?

"I wake up in the morning wondering what town I'm in."
— Grover Cleveland Alexander

At about the time Doan and Frick were frantically trying to find a winter roosting place for Alex, he was now occupying a place on the roster of Doan's House of David eastern squad. Newspaper columnist Frank Graham found him in the lobby of a dingy hotel and renewed acquaintance with him. Alex told him:

> We see plenty of country. I come from a little old town in Nebraska called St. Paul, and after I got in the big leagues and saw places like New York and Chicago and Philadelphia, I began to think that maybe St. Paul wasn't much of a town after all. But since I've been with this outfit, I've seen towns that make St. Paul seem like Paris. We don't miss many towns. The team I was with the first half of this season went up through Oregon and Washington into Canada — we played away up in Prince Albert, which is pretty far north — and then swung down through the west and middle west. I joined this team in Berlin, New Hampshire, a couple of weeks ago and we came down through New England, hitting towns like New Bedford, New London and New Haven. From here, we go to Philadelphia, play around there for a few days and then go west. We'll wind up somewhere around St. Louis about the end of the month.
> I don't keep track of the places I go, although some of these fellows do. Sometimes I can't even tell you where I was the day before. Lots of times I wake up in the morning wondering what town I'm in — but even when I recall the name of it, it usually doesn't make much difference. All I see of any of them is the hotel and the ballpark.

Alex made no mention of his personal demons — of the reason he was traveling with a bunch of bearded ballplayers, the reason he sometimes couldn't remember where he was or where he had been, the reason Doan and Frick were trying to find someone who would put up with him. Alex dealt with his drinking problem in one of two ways. He either didn't acknowledge that it existed or apologized for it but said it never affected his performance. If he was aware at all that he had become a public nuisance, he showed no signs of it. Rather, he wore the persona of someone who deserved more than he was receiving from the game of baseball.

"It's a grind and it isn't the best job in the world," he told Graham. "But it's a job and it pays well. It pays better than any minor league job I could get, and there are no worries attached to it. You don't have to worry about whether your team is going to win the pennant or whether you are going to win enough games to get a contract for the next season."

Graham was in the press box that day in October of 1926 when Alexander provided one of the greatest moments in baseball history. Now, almost 10 years later, in a shabbier part of the same city, the writer said he couldn't resist having Alex tell the story one more time.

"About the time I struck Lazzeri out in the last game of the World Series in 1926 — right? I knew it," said Alex. "Somebody asks me about that everywhere I go. Funny, isn't it? I pitched for 20 years in the National League and that's the one thing they remember best about me." And he retold the story, beginning with the night before, insisting, as he always had, that he was stone sober and not hung over when Hornsby summoned him to relieve Jess Haines in the seventh inning.[1]

Two weeks after Graham talked with Alex, Doan and Frick made the final arrangement to put Alex on a train to St. Paul. Alex stayed on the J.C. Toman farm, surrounded by the fields and roadsides and sights and sounds and smells he had been familiar with since his boyhood. He hunted and fished as weather permitted and continued to drink rain or shine. The National League dutifully sent a check each month to the gentleman farmer for providing the space for his famous tenant. All was well until early February 1936, when the league office received word from Toman that Alex was gone.

"Mr. Alexander has left for Louisville, Kentucky, in regard to a position offered him by a broadcasting station," Toman said in a letter requesting Alex's rent for January. "If Mr. Alexander does not qualify for the position, he will return to make his home with us again."

It is not known whether Alexander told Toman he would return and the kindly man believed him, or whether Alex ever intended to return or if it was just wishful thinking from either or both of them. Whatever the case, when Alex took off for Louisville, he never set foot on the Toman farm again. The Louisville job was one of many he would accept over the next several years in which he allowed his name and his fame to be a commodity that someone else could use for their own profit. Any income Alex received was just a necessary expense of the user, the purchase price for the commodity. And he would never again have anyone personally look out for his welfare as he had when Ray Doan took him under his wing and when J.C. Toman boarded him for those three months in the winter of 1935–36.

The deal in Louisville was simple and naïve. A local businesswoman, Mrs. E.H. Hussey, made and sold cosmetics for women. She sponsored a show in which Alex would come on and talk about baseball and give tips to boys on how to play the game. The inane marketing idea was that the boys would be so enthralled with what Alex was telling them that they'd take their allowance and run out and buy Mrs. Hussey's cosmetics. Alex got no salary from the radio station. Mrs. Hussey agreed to split the profits from the cosmetics sales with him. As if the deal weren't shaky enough from the outset, it crumbled completely when the radio station canceled the show after six weeks. Unfazed, Mrs. Hussey moved her business to Evansville, Indiana, and Alexander, having no money and nowhere else to go, followed his newfound friend. His arrival in Evansville was greeted with hoopla from the local media, but things went sour when Mrs. Hussey bounced some checks and was put in jail. Alex, a long way from the big leagues or the House of David or the comfort of J.C. Toman's farm, was left to fend for himself.

He associated himself with a semi-pro team in Evansville that was happy to have him because of his ability to draw fans and the knowledge that he might pass on to younger players. He declined an offer to pitch the first inning of a game because he knew his arm strength wasn't up to par — he hadn't been "training" after all — and he didn't want to give up a home run and put the home team behind just for the sake of a publicity stunt. He did agree to manage the team for a while. The ballclub was to enter a tournament similar to *The Denver Post* semi-pro tournament, and there was bonus money available for the winners. Alex needed any kind of money he could get.

In the early morning hours of August 2, 1936, Alex was walking alone on the streets of Evansville when he was knocked unconscious and nearly killed. Passersby found him lying in the street with a deep cut on his head. They thought he had been struck by a hit-and-run vehicle. Police were notified and he was rushed to an Evansville hospital, where he remained unconscious for several hours. He was listed in critical condition with a possible skull fracture and was at first thought to be dying.

Had he been hit by a car? Had he suffered an epileptic seizure that caused him to fall? Had he been beaten and robbed? Nobody knew for sure. By the next afternoon, the *Washington Post* described his condition unsympathetically as "a slight concussion and a big hangover." The newspaper reported Alex telling police detectives, "I was drinking beer at a tavern and then I started downtown about 12:30. After that, it's all a blank. Wow, how my head hurts." On August 9, he was released from the hospital, the police now saying they were unable to determine whether he fell or was slugged by somebody.[2]

By now, most people who followed baseball realized that Ol' Pete had become a pathetic figure, virtually unable to help himself. But there was great disagreement or misunderstanding about what, if anything, should be done to help him. Commissioner Landis, National League President Frick, House of David promoter Doan and others had worked feverishly behind the scenes for 18 months to put some controls on Alex because he could no longer control himself. In an effort to spare Alexander and major league baseball any further embarrassment, their efforts on behalf of Alex were made outside the glare of national publicity. The result was that many fans thought baseball was still unwilling to help a helpless man who once had meant so much to the game.

While Alex was recovering from his concussion in Evansville, Frick received a letter from a baseball fan, W.J. Sherman, Jr., of Dayton, Ohio:

> I am writing to you of the pitiable condition of Grover Alexander, a newspaper article describing which, I am enclosing.
> All my life I have been a rabid National League fan, as partisan I suppose as any politician and it grieves me greatly to realize the misery of this former great National League star. I am well aware that he is himself responsible for his present plight. However, the fact should not be lost site [sic] of that many men once down do not have the strength to pull themselves back up.
> I feel the National League should do something for Alex. No other player, with the exception of Mathewson, ever brought more glory to the old National League. Why couldn't a benefit be held for him or possibly he could be given a job that would require him to go straight? Could he umpire? Any money accumulated in a benefit could be invested in a small farm for him. The title could be held in trust for him by the league.
> A benefit held for him in, say September, including say stars of 15 years ago like Maranville, Kelly, Traynor, Hornsby, Grimes, Lajoie, Rousch, Groh, Casey, Bancroft, etc., would draw an immense crowd. After all, what greater pleasure is there than helping such as him? In conclusion, I wish to say no one feels the plight of "Old Alex" more than I do and I sincerely hope the National League won't forget him.[3]

Frick responded by letter and told Sherman frankly how the league had tried to help Alex on several occasions, including the arrangement on the Nebraska farm the previous winter where all his expenses were paid. He assured the fan that the league would continue to try to help Alex. "Unfortunately, however, he is a very hard man to help," said Frick.

```
                                                   1228 A
Charge to the account of____NATIONAL BASEBALL LEAGUE    $_____

         WESTERN
         UNION
```

> Sam Breadon, Pres.   JAN 25 1937
> StLouis National Ball Club
> 3623 Dodier St., St.Louis, Mo.
>
> Is there anything we can do about Alexander
>
>   FORD FRICK

National League President Ford Frick appealed to many people as he tried to control the antics of Grover Cleveland Alexander. Here is a one-sentence plea sent to Sam Breadon, owner of the St. Louis Cardinals (National Baseball Hall of Fame Library, Cooperstown, N.Y.).

    On September 1, Alex made it back to St. Louis for a 10-year reunion of the 1926 championship team, the last time he ever appeared in uniform in a major league ballpark. Breadon picked up the tab for travel expenses, hotel bills and meals for 19 members of the '26 ballclub who made it back. Free travel, food and lodging were sure-fire ways of bringing Ol' Pete to the surface. He showed up and was the starting pitcher for the 1926 squad. The team played a three-inning game against the 1936 team, in which manager Frank Frisch had a lineup loaded with second-stringers. The old-timers went down scoreless in the top of the first. When they took the field — Bottomley at first, Hornsby at second, Bell at third, Toporcer at short, Hafey, Douthit and Wattie Holm in left, center and right, O'Farrell behind the

XIV—Brother, Can You Spare Me a Dime?

plate, and Alexander on the mound — the crowd at Sportsman's Park went wild. Sid Keener, covering the event for the *St. Louis Post-Dispatch,* said the reception the old-timers received was on a par with any ever given a Cardinals ballclub.

Forty-nine-year-old Alexander had trouble finding the strike zone with his first few pitches. The '36 Cardinals nicked him for a bunt single, followed by a throwing error by Toporcer on what appeared to be a double play ball, allowing the runner to score all the way from first. It was the only run of the game. Keener pointed out it was the last inning Alexander would ever pitch for the Cardinals, and he allowed but one infield hit and an unearned run.

While Alex was in town, he met with Breadon. On October 9, the Cardinals owner wrote to Frick, briefing him on their meeting. Alex told

Sam Breadon, owner of the St. Louis Cardinals, was always indebted to Grover Cleveland Alexander for helping the Cardinals win their first World Series in 1926. Years later, when Alexander's antics were seen as an embarrassment to baseball, Breadon became one of his benefactors (National Baseball Hall of Fame Library, Cooperstown, N.Y.).

Breadon he did not want to go back to the Toman farm in Nebraska and would prefer to go to live with his brother, William, and his family in Grand Island, Nebraska Not long after that, Breadon said he got a letter from William Alexander's daughter — Alex's niece — asking if Breadon or the Cardinals knew Alex's whereabouts. Apparently, Alex returned to Evansville to pick up his bonus check for working with the semi-pro ballclub. Alex expected the check to be about $800, he told Breadon. "Whether he received the check or not, I do not know, and I don't suppose we will hear from him until he has spent it," Breadon wrote.

Frick's reply, dated October 22, was brief and terse: "I guess nothing can be done in the case of Aleck but wait for him to settle down somewhere and stand by ready to help when and if the occasion arises."

Alex took his bonus money and made his way to Springfield, Illinois, where Johnny Connor, a sports promoter agreed to let him live in a hotel Connor owned in Springfield. Frick, Breadon and Alexander's relatives in Nebraska did not know where he was until they opened their newspapers on January 16, 1937, to learn that Alex was hospitalized once again, this time at St. John's Hospital in Springfield. He was reported to be in serious condition with complications of a leg injury suffered in an auto accident several weeks before. Dr. Paul Levis, the attending physician, said Alex's leg was badly infected but was being treated with hot packs and was improving. It was not clear when the auto accident had occurred. By this time, the Evansville incident in August was being regarded as a mugging. In any case, it was a different time and a different place, but Alex was in the headlines again.

John P. Carmichael, sports editor and columnist for the *Chicago Daily News*, paid a visit to Ol' Pete in his hospital room and found him giving a nurse a hard time when she came in and offered him a slice of pineapple. At first he objected and then smiled and told her, "After all, I'm a guest here and shouldn't complain about the food." Carmichael talked a little baseball with Alex and, as it always did, the strikeout of Lazzeri came up. Carmichael asked him if, given the chance, he'd like to start all over again. "Not if I knew what I know now," he said. "If I knew I'd strike out Tony Lazzeri with the bases full that day, there wouldn't be any kick to it."

In Carmichael's "The Barber Shop" column in the *Daily News,* he recounted a story Alex told him that had to do with his pinpoint control on the mound. "For the last 10 years, I wasn't so fast," he said. "I got by on control. I was pretty handy with the ball. One day Carl Mays was pitching against us and he nicked Gabby Hartnett on the neck. When I went out to pitch, Mays was the hitter and I was kinda sore [at him]. So I said to him, 'Carl, I haven't decided which eye I'm going to hit you in, but you know dang well I can call it, don't you?' He pleaded that he'd hit Gabby accidentally. I told him not to have another accident. He didn't, either."[4]

While Alex was lying in a hospital bed spinning baseball tales for a sportswriter, Frick was frantic, losing patience, and knowing he was in danger of losing public support and understanding. He had turned to Commissioner Landis and Ray Doan and Sam Breadon. He had paid rent for three months to a Nebraska farmer whom he had never met. On January 25, 1937, he fired off a one-sentence telegram to Breadon that had a sense of urgency. It asked: "Is there anything we can do about Alexander?" Breadon reiterated that the best bet was to hook Alex up with his brother's family in Grand Island. Beyond that, he was out of ideas for the moment.

Meanwhile, Branch Rickey, general manager of the Cardinals, a proud, pious man who did not drink and who once managed the Cardinals, had had enough of bad publicity the Cardinals and the National League were receiving from writers who thought baseball was ignoring its fallen prince.

Rickey wrote a lengthy memo to Ed Staples, the Cardinals publicity director. Staples sent it to Frick, saying he hoped it would be given "wide circulation over the country" so as to end the bad press that had been leveled against the National League because of its alleged treatment of Alexander.

In the memo, dated March 13, 1937, Rickey wrote:

> The National League has been under considerable fire from time to time in editorial comment on the sports pages of many of our papers because of its lack of attention to player Grover Cleveland Alexander. One of the New York papers gave a leading editorial to it very recently — a bitter, caustic criticism of the National League, comparing it to the American League at the time that Alexander was having some of his notorious reverses in the press.
>
> The National League has from time to time taken care of Alexander. It pensioned him, placed him in the care of certain people in Nebraska and gave him ample funds per month. He ran out on this program and the National League was unable to locate him for several weeks. Then he turned up in some escapade or other down south. Then followed a series of episodes, none of them very complimentary to Alexander. The National League was concerned all this time and during this time Mr. Breadon took care of Mr. Alexander in one way or another — medical attention, loans of money, redemption of his clothes or his ring, and only recently I sent $55 to a pawn shop in Atlanta to redeem his World Series ring and also sent $78 and some odd cents to a hotel to get back his clothes and his personal belongings.
>
> I wrote Alexander to find out about his whereabouts and I indicated to him that I had a job for him and told him I would like to have him come and see me. I had no reply for some time and then came a brief word saying that he would come to see me at some time or other. But he did not

come. I got in touch with him again and found him in Springfield, Illinois, working in a saloon. The glad-hander, he called himself. After several days of insistence by telegraph and telephone, I found that he simply would not pick up a ticket which I provided for him at the railroad offices, and then I got in touch with his so-called employer. Finally, I succeeded in having this employer drive Alexander to my office where I had an extended interview.

I offered Alexander $100 per month, his board and room and all traveling expenses, laundry, etc. I offered to put him in the care of three men, all exemplary policemen, and there was some guarantee about it, of course, that Alexander would be able to live a comparative sober life for the next six months. At the expiration of that time, I felt that he might have a new grip upon himself and I told him I would continue his pay for the next six months. Then I told him that while this was a salary that was merely intended to keep him in possession of his necessities, yet it was not the salary that was calculated to give him security for the future, and that if he wished to continue this employment with us, providing such employment was satisfactory, he would be able fairly to write his own ticket in any future arrangements he might make with us. I also told him that if this proposition was not satisfactory, I thought I would be very willing to accept whatever proposition he cared to make to me.

Alexander expressed appreciation of the offer, told me that he had tentative offers from colleges for coaching work and that as soon as he had definite information regarding these offers, he would in turn give me a definite answer to my proposition. This interview occurred on Wednesday, February 24. I have not heard from him since and it is probable that I will not hear from him. On Friday morning March 12, I wired Alexander asking him for an answer to my proposition. I have received no reply to that wire.

As a result of these various experiences and negotiations, I am under the impression that Alexander does not care to be helped by the National League or any club in it and is beyond help, personal or otherwise, in so far as the offer of a job is concerned. This club on behalf of Alexander and on behalf of the National League has done all that it knows how to do to show its appreciation and gratitude for the past services of this player. I think it may be that Mr. Frick and perhaps the other presidents of the National League should know the offers that we have made.

It should be kept in mind that this matter has been discussed at various league meetings and at the meeting recently held in New York in early February, the writer of this letter indicated to the gentlemen of the National League the interest and effort the Cardinal club had manifested and was at that time manifesting. And the League seemed to feel that it could trust the St. Louis club to make such overtures to Alexander as seemed to fit the circumstances.

In a manner, this is a sort of report to Mr. Frick and the gentlemen of the National League and I wish you would in turn see that they get the gist of it so that they can properly defend the National League against criticisms that may come from time to time from the press.

In thinking over what I have said, I recall my reference to policemen.

These policemen are simply boys who will do summer camp work for us, and these three men, composed of Pat Crawford, Wid Mathews and probably Joseph Schultz, former big league players and men of fine character, who would take a very genuine personal interest in seeing to it that Alexander enjoyed his work and kept his job.

I have to leave within a few minutes for Florida and I have dictated this general survey of the Alexander situation very rapidly, and I am sorry not to have the opportunity to talk the case over with you thoroughly before leaving.

Rickey's memorandum, on file at the Hall of Fame, provides historical record on the efforts made by the St. Louis Cardinals to help Alexander. But at the time, it did not get the widespread publicity Rickey envisioned. Frick thought the tone and substance put the National League on the defensive. He wrote back to Rickey, thanking him for the update, but said he didn't think it would be wise go public with it. Instead, he said, he would continue with what he had been doing, talking with sportswriters off the record as often as he could, explaining the league's efforts to help Alexander.

"I do feel that if we could make a statement to the effect that a job had been offered Alexander and that a job was still waiting for him any time he dared to meet the conditions, it might be a proper type statement," said Frick.

Alexander stayed in Springfield, living in Connor's hotel and working in his saloon, as Rickey referred to it, and also agreed to manage the promoter's baseball team. His name would show up in print again on the sports pages occasionally as it did on May 10, 1937, when the Empire team of Springfield played the season opener for the semi-pro season against Spencer's Coals in Chicago. Alex, at age 50, started for the Empires but left the mound with a sore arm after throwing only five pitches.

At about this time, The *Los Angeles Times* happened to get a photograph of Cy Young and publish it side by side with Alex's picture. Young was shown on the front porch of his farm in Dover, Ohio, looking relaxed and dapper in retirement as he smoked a pipe and smiled for the camera. Alexander was shown on the pitching mound in Chicago, hat cocked to one side as it had been for 30 years, and a stern look on a face in which crow's feet were starting to wrinkle their way down from his eyes to his cheeks. The contrast was striking between the two old ballplayers, one a man at ease, the other a man very much ill at ease.

• CHAPTER XV •

The Last Hurrah

"It is a sad picture for those inclined to be sentimental over the ex-heroes with which the field of sports is strewn."
— Al Laney

When Frick wasn't dashing off letters trying to figure out what to do with Grover Cleveland Alexander, he was doing other league business, including working on a unique plan to promote major league baseball. The idea sprang from the discovery of an old, tattered baseball in the attic of the late Abner Graves in Cooperstown, New York. Graves' niche in baseball history is that in 1907, he responded to a search committee that had been formed to determine the origins of baseball. Graves wrote to the committee that he had seen a man named Abner Doubleday play a game called "town ball" with youngsters in Cooperstown in 1839. The committee took Graves' account as the gospel truth and credited Doubleday with inventing baseball and Cooperstown as being the birthplace. Several scholarly works have since disputed the Graves story. Doubleday was a cadet at West Point in 1839. He went on to be a prolific writer but never mentioned baseball in any of his writings, and his obituary in the *New York Times* in 1893 does not mention baseball. But in 1932, the Doubleday baseball creation was taken as fact. When some people found the old baseball in the Cooperstown attic, a businessman named Stephen Clark bought it for $5 and put it on display, with other baseball relics he could find, in the Cooperstown Social Club. The display was a big hit. People came from all over to view it. So Clark and a friend, Alexander Cleland, decided to expand and to create a national baseball museum. What better place than Cooperstown, given the history associated with the town. The two men approached Frick, who enthusiastically supported them. He in turn sold Commissioner Landis and Will Harridge, president of the American League, on the idea.

Baseball officials had begun making plans to celebrate baseball's centennial in 1939 — again a date predicated on Graves' account of seeing

Doubleday playing "town ball" a century earlier. Frick came up with the idea of creating a Hall of Fame to honor the game's greatest ballplayers and to have the Hall of Fame in the museum. Early in 1936, as plans for a grand museum were in the talking stages, and a few months before Frick started the frantic back-and-forth letter writing trying to figure out what to do with Alexander, baseball's biggest embarrassment, the Baseball Writers Association voted on the first members of the hallowed Hall of Fame. To be included, winners had to receive 75 percent approval of those voting. Alexander, the winningest pitcher in the National League and third winningest in the history of baseball, did not make the cut. Alex learned about the results while he was drying out on the Toman farm in western Nebraska.

The leading vote-getter in 1936 was Ty Cobb, who held most of the major league batting records that Babe Ruth didn't hold. Chief among them were his .367 lifetime batting average and his 4,190 career hits. Cobb also held the lifetime stolen base record of 896. In years to come, the base-stealing record has been surpassed by many, and Pete Rose overtook him in the all-time hit parade, but his .367 career average remains baseball's best. Ruth, whose single-season home run total of 60 in 1927 and 714 career homers were tops in the big leagues for many years, and Honus Wagner, the great Pirate infielder, were tied for second. Christy Mathewson and Walter Johnson, often mentioned with Alex as the three greatest pitchers, finished third and fourth respectively in the balloting. No one else received enough votes to qualify. What is striking about the balloting is that 14 players got more votes than Alex. Cobb and Ruth were both men of questionable character during their playing days, Cobb for his fiery temper and win-at-all-costs behavior, and Ruth for his bawdiness and, to borrow and expression often used to describe Alex, his lack of attention to "training." Yet, they were in and Alex was out.

Particularly striking was the voting for the pitchers. Alex received 150 fewer votes than Mathewson and 134 fewer than Johnson. Why would Mathewson and Johnson receive the ultimate adulation and honor from the men who covered their careers and Alexander be virtually ignored? Donald K. McKim suggests that Ol' Pete's off-the-field behavior caught up with him — again. "If Christy Mathewson was the ideal American hero of baseball, his counterpart, Grover Cleveland Alexander was the flawed hero. Spoken in the same breath, along with Walter Johnson, as the premier trio of pitchers, Alexander matched Matty in pitching prowess and stature yet did not capture a nation's attention for his virtues."[1]

Baseball historian Donald Honig goes further. "Equal in glory with Mathewson and Johnson, he outdid them in drama and tragedy. His is the most poignant superstar story in all of baseball, a story that began with matchless talent and beguiling innocence and kept going through an ever-deepening and darkening abyss of horror, illness and self-degradation. We, who prefer our heroes to be luminous with purity, cannot condemn the fall from grace of the one known inevitably as Alexander the Great because he became suddenly a prototypical victim of a world and a time he never made and was utterly unprepared for.[2]

So when the roll was called for the first inductees into the Hall of Fame, Alex was not among them. With 226 votes cast and 170 needed for induction, the totals were:

Cobb	222	Matthewson	205
Ruth	215	Johnson	189
Wagner	215		

Also receiving votes:

Lajoie	146	Sisler	77
Speaker	133	E. Collins	60
Young	111	J. Collins	58
Hornsby	105	Alexander	55
Cochrane	80		

Alex received just 24.3 percent of the total vote. There is no question that politics and personalities got in the way of the voting, and not just in the case of Alexander. Consider that four writers failed to vote for Cobb, 11 for Ruth and Wagner, 21 for Mathewson and 37 for Johnson.

The next year, tales of Alex's escapades in Louisville and Evansville had been in the news, and he was in the Springfield hospital when baseball writers were casting their second ballots for the Hall of Fame. The vote was closer but the result was the same. Alex was once again denied a place with the game's elite. Napoleon Lajoie and Tris Speaker, two of the game's greatest hitters, and Cy Young, still baseball's winningest pitcher with 511 career victories, were the 1937 inductees. Of 201 ballots cast, Alex received 125 votes, 62.9 percent. The 1937 totals were:

Lajoie	168	E. Collins	115
Speaker	165	Sisler	106
Young	153	Delahanty	70
Alexander	125	Waddell	67
Keeler	115	J. Collins	66

By the time of the 1938 balloting, there was only one glaring omission among the game's greatest pitchers in the Hall of Fame. Cy Young, whom Alex faced as a rookie in 1911 in one of Young's last starts, was looked on as an elder statesman as he lived in quiet retirement on his farm in Ohio. Walter Johnson, with more than 400 wins and more than 100 shutouts, had gone on to be a big league manager whose biggest fault in managing was said to be that he was too nice a guy.[3]

Christy Mathewson was regarded as a model ballplayer and model citizen in the way he conducted himself on and off the field. The baseball world grieved when he died of tuberculosis on October 7, 1925, at the age of 45. And then there was Ol' Pete, who was suspended from two of the last three major league teams he played for, then spent four years with a bearded brand of barnstormers and spent his off hours in bars, flophouses and with people who were paid by others to give him shelter. His moment of post-career glory finally arrived in January of 1938 when the Baseball Writers of America rated performance above character, as they had in the past with Cobb and others, and elected Grover Cleveland Alexander to the Hall of Fame. Alex got 212 votes, 81 percent of the total votes cast and was the only player elected that year. The totals were:

Alexander	212	Chance	133
Sisler	179	Delahanty	132
Keeler	177	Walsh	110
E. Collins	175	Evers	91
Waddell	148	J. Collins	79

The Associated Press, in reporting Alex's election, paid homage to his career but did not ignore his reputation:

"Old Pete, who ended a brilliantly colorful but somewhat checkered career in 1930 after nearly 20 years in the National League, was the only star to qualify for the all-time galaxy in the third annual vote of the Baseball Writers Association of America." The story cites Alexander's remarkable accomplishments: 28 wins in his first year, still a record for rookies; 30 or more wins three years in a row; 90 career shutouts, including 16 in 1916 and four one-hitters that year; most National League games pitched, 696; most wins, 373; 1.22 earned run average in 1915, the lowest for any pitcher with 250 or more innings; and 90 career shutouts, a National League record.[4]

The story concludes, like most stories about Alexander's career do, with an account of his heroics in the 1926 World Series.

> Legend persists that Old Pete, who had pitched and won the sixth game to tie the count at 3-all, was dozing when summoned unexpectedly in the seventh inning to face Tony Lazzeri, with two out, the bases filled, and the Cardinals fighting to hold a 3-2 lead.
>
> Astonishment gave way to dramatic excitement as Alexander trudged to the box, calmly surveyed the situation and struck out Lazzeri on three pitched balls. The balance of the game was an anti-climax as Old Pete finished his job in businesslike fashion. It is worthy of note that the Yankees have not lost a World Series since then.[5]

George Kirksey of United Press remembered the Alexander of old in telling his readers, "There'll soon be hung on the wall of the baseball museum at Cooperstown, N.Y., a bronze plaque depicting the image of a leather-necked, freckle-faced, auburn-haired baseball player, the latest addition to the Hall of Fame." Kirksey then gave a long synopsis of Alex's career, from Galesburg to Indianapolis to Philadelphia to Chicago to St. Louis and back to Philadelphia. It was a tribute to a great career with little mention of the troubles along the way.

Sports columnist Bill Corum tried to give Alex his due. But even in his tribute, he couldn't ignore how Alex had handled himself the past few years. For as Corum wrote his words in January 1938, many in the sports world had no idea where Alex was or what he was doing. So Corum wrote an open letter to "Mr. Grover Cleveland Alexander" and addressed it to "Somewhere in America."

"Dear Pete. The writer hasn't had anything to say about the latest choice of a name for the Baseball Hall of Fame at Cooperstown, N.Y. We had a vote to cast, and cast it. But a vote is a personal thing so we needn't go into that. However, we have just read a headline in a paper which reads, 'Hall of Fame Niche for Alex.' That must be you, Pete. Congratulations! In a small way, that makes us even."

Then Corum did what almost every writer did in those days. He didn't mention Alex's 373 wins or three straight seasons of 30-plus wins or his 90 shutouts or his 1916 season of 16 shutouts and four one-hitters. Instead, he devoted the rest of the column to Ol' Pete striking out Lazzeri in the 1926 World Series and, of course, gave his take on it.

Corum said he talked with one of the Cardinal coaches, Buzzy Wares, who said he was dispatched by Hornsby to find Alex when Alex didn't make it down from his hotel room to catch the team bus that was headed for Yankee Stadium for the seventh game of the World Series. In Wares' account, as told by Corum, the coach got a passkey, opened Alex's hotel room door, and found him sleeping. Wares got him out of bed and told him he had to get to the game, even though he had pitched yesterday. "No rest for the wicked curve," is the way Corum put it. Wares said as Alex was getting dressed, he kept making treks to the bathroom. Wares went in the bathroom and found an open bottle of whiskey hidden under some towels. Wares said Alex finally was ready and they took a cab to the ballpark, but the kindly coach had the cabbie stop along the way so that Wares could buy his pitcher a ham sandwich.

Corum then described Alex coming in from the bullpen in the seventh inning to face Lazzeri. "You practically came in by way of China to that pitching ridge," he wrote, and after striking out Lazzeri, "I can see you yet tossing that glove away as you walked toward the bench as if to say: Get me another soft touch like that."

Corum concluded: "That Hall of Fame's all right now, Pete. It's got Alexander the Great — and no more worlds to conquer. Take care of yourself and the high hard one, partner. Always your friend. Bill."[6]

So even in his ultimate moment of baseball glory, in receiving baseball's highest award for achievement, his checkered past and mysterious present circumstances surrounded the event like storm clouds on this, the sunniest occasion of his life. For his part, Alex continued to be a moving target, this time taking up residence in St. Louis, still looking for something he could call permanent work. His recent resume worked against him. He took a job as the host in a tavern operated by a man named Frank Langley who was willing to take a chance on Alex, putting him within arm's length every day of the demon that plagued him. A St. Louis reporter who spotted him said Alex was "sober in the midst of temptation."

Alex found a way to pick up some more pocket money when he wrote a piece for the June 1938 American Legion magazine (most likely ghostwritten for a price) titled "King Baseball" in which he reflected on his Hall of Fame election, as well as many aspects of his long career. He obviously knew who was paying him. A sidebar story in boldface type and in a box offered this about Alex: "An ex-service man, Old Pete says that the greatest influence for sportsmanship in baseball during the last decade is the American Legion Junior Baseball program."

In the main article, Alexander said, "When the pleasant news recently arrived that I was placed in the baseball Hall of Fame by an almost unanimous vote, I was interested in noting the comments of my old friends, the sportswriters. They were generous to the extreme in their appraisal of my baseball accomplishments. They recited the records I had made. Some of them expressed the opinion that my record of 90 shut-out games — games in which my team's opponents failed to get a score — will likely stand for all time."

Alex gave readers some insights into his career that he had never before revealed to the press. Among them:

- For five years straight, he won every game he pitched against the Cincinnati Reds. "No reflection on the Reds. Just the breaks of the game."
- Rabbit Maranville was the only player to leave him with a scar. "I've been hit black and blue by batted balls. One of Rabbit's wicked drives raised a bad place on my leg that will always be there."
- The most satisfying of his 90 shutouts was the one he threw for the Cardinals against the Cubs in his first start in a Cardinals uniform — against

the Cubs. "I confess I felt a trifle chesty as I walked off the field, thumbing my nose good-naturedly at Manager Joe McCarthy of the Cubs."
- Most satisfying strikeout in the regular season — any time he struck out Honus Wagner. "During a game, he had two strikes and he swung at another of my curves, which sailed by the end of his bat. He passed me as I went to the dugout. 'You darned freckle-faced farmer,' he grinned."

Alex might have been able to have magazine articles ghostwritten for him but he couldn't have anyone lead the rest of his life for him. As was his habit, his stay in St. Louis was short-lived. Early in 1939, he managed to come up with train fare for New York, where he must have thought his chances for a better life were better. Maybe he had a job offer — Alex had a history of chasing any job that was dangled in front of him, from Louisville and Evansville with Mrs. Hussey and her cosmetics, to Springfield and Johnny Connors' hotel and bar to St. Louis and Langley with his hotel and bar. He had found a life as a huckster, and in New York, "Hubert's Dime Museum and Flea Circus" found him.

Located on the edge of Times Square, Hubert's was a penny arcade with pinball machines and other games at Seventh Avenue and West 42nd Street. It was a place with a dirty linoleum floor where, for a quarter and the turn of a crank, many a boy with raging hormones could put his eyes up to a set of peep-holes and watch a 10-second film of a gal taking off her blouse. In the back, there was a turnstile, where, for another nickel, a patron could proceed through and go down a winding, rickety wooden staircase to the basement, a dimly lit, dank and dark cavern that had a perpetually musky odor. In one corner of the basement, the Hecklers, William and sons Leslie and LeRoy, operated a flea circus featuring trained fleas. The family operated the flea circus in that spot for 30 years until LeRoy finally gave it up because of the changing culture and how "nude shows were giving my fleas a bad name." Eventually Hubert's gave way to Peepland.

In 1939, 42nd Street had seen its better days but was still bustling with mostly cheap entertainment. It was still a part of Times Square and had been given its due by songwriter George M. Cohan, in "Give My Regards to Broadway." In January 1939, Alex was a regular on 42nd Street, pitching not a baseball but old story after old story in the basement at Hubert's. It was a simple means to a simple end — a way to make a few bucks.

It wasn't long before sportswriters like Al Laney of the *New York Herald-Tribune* discovered his latest place of employment. He wrote:

> A year ago yesterday, every paper in the country carried the news that Grover Cleveland Alexander had been elected to the Baseball Hall of Fame. Yesterday, on the first anniversary of that date, Alex the Great came back

to New York and went to work in a flea circus, a minor attraction among freaks in a sideshow in the midst of the tawdry glitter of West Forty-Second Street, a thoroughfare which, like Old Pete himself, has come far down the scale from past glories."[7]

Laney said that, all things considered, Alex looked good. "Alex looks well, a good deal better than he did a few years back. He is well dressed and, considering the places he has been and the things he has seen and done, he shows few traces of wear and tear. His face is deeply lined and a little too red around the membranes of the eyes, but otherwise he is the Alex of old and there is not a trace of gray in his dark red hair."[8]

A carnival barker type of fellow introduced Alex in typical sideshow fashion, on the order of "Ladies and gentlemen, step right up and hear the stories of one of baseball's all-time greats." Then Alex stood on a small stage and spoke slowly and in a voice that those in back had to strain to hear. He talked about his early baseball days and told the crowd about some of the great players he had played with and against. And of course he recounted the strike out of Lazzeri in the 1926 World Series. By the time he was done with his little talk and had answered questions, he had gone far beyond the 10 minutes he was advertised to do. He had just enough time to catch his breath and get ready for the next show.

When Tom Meany of the *New York Times* caught his act, someone asked Alex to name his all-time team. Ol' Pete had Hal Chase at first base, Rogers Hornsby at second, Harry Steinfeldt at third, Honus Wagner at short. His outfield was Zach Wheat and Frank Schulte ("for their hitting," he said) and Max Carey for his defense and base running. Alex's top catcher was Gabby Hartnett, whom he said he picked over his old buddy Bill Killefer because of Gabby's hitting ability. His pitcher was Christy Mathewson, but he unsheepishly told his audience he would also put himself on that team. His manager, he said, would be Pat Moran, his mentor at Philadelphia. He told his audience he was picking only from the National League because that's where he played his entire career.

Meany mentioned that a head cold apparently affected Alex's hearing and he had to ask several people to repeat their questions. In truth, Alex had been hard of hearing in one ear since experiencing the booming sounds of explosions in Germany in World War I, and his hearing was getting steadily worse. Laney said Alex seemed to accept his fate, and the writer perhaps stumbled into the reason Old Pete left the saloons of the Midwest for the freak show in New York. "He does not consider his lot such a hard one," wrote Laney, "but there is one thing he wants very much to do. He wants to go to Cooperstown, N.Y., where they erected a plaque for him in the Hall of Fame just a year ago yesterday. He would like to be there on

June 12 when they celebrate the centennial of baseball. He should be there of course. No one has a better right. But Old Pete thinks it will be a little hard under the circumstances and he is a little sad about that."[9]

There is no clear record as to how Alex made it to Cooperstown, but it is likely he found a donor somewhere, because he showed up for the festivities in June looking none the worse for wear and sporting a coat, tie and vest. Among the dignitaries there were Commissioner Landis and National League president Frick, the two men who for years had been trying to figure out what to do with Alex so he would quit embarrassing major league baseball. Perhaps it was because of their presence that Alex had the presence of mind to stay on his good behavior.

Eleven living members of the Hall of Fame were honored. Ty Cobb arrived late and missed some of the activities. The ten other members posed for a photograph that is most likely the greatest assembly of baseball talent ever captured in one picture. In the front row, there was Eddie Collins, the great infielder, sitting solemnly in a business suit with hands clasped in his lap. Next to him was "the Babe," Babe Ruth, as colorful as ever in checkered suit, sport shirt and no tie. To Ruth's left was Connie Mack, sitting as he always did, straight as an arrow, looking stiff, yet prim and proper like a preacher about ready to spring up and deliver a sermon. Next to Mack was Cy Young, the winningest pitcher in baseball history, who slouched back in his chair and looked much more relaxed than many of his counterparts. Standing behind them was Honus Wagner, smiling and looking as if he were about to let loose with one of his old baseball yarns. Alex was next in his three-piece suit, staring straight at the camera, his full head of reddish brown hair a little ruffled at the front, as if the wind had caught it. On Alex's left was Tris Speaker, the great center fielder, standing at attention as he stood directly behind the Babe. Next was Nap Lajoie, so popular in Cleveland that the ballclub was called the Naps for a while, now standing behind Mack and looking a bit rigid. Filling out the row were George Sisler, whose 257 hits in one season remained the major league record for 80 years, and Walter Johnson, the "Big Train" who pitched 406 games for the Washington Senators.

The front door of the Hall of Fame museum was decorated with red, white and blue ribbons. Theodore Lettis, chairman of the Baseball Centennial Committee, handed a pair of shears to Frick, who cut the red ribbon. Will Harridge, president of the American League, cut the white ribbon. The blue ribbon was snipped by William Bramham, president of the organization of minor leagues.

When the Hall of Fame players gathered on a platform and were introduced individually to the crowd that had gathered, Ruth, Johnson and Alex

XV—The Last Hurrah

got the biggest ovations. Indeed, the other ballplayers on the platform stood as the three were introduced. After the ceremonies, a "pick-up" game featuring current major league ballplayers was held, with 10,000 fans watching. A highlight for the fans was Ruth making an appearance as pinch hitter, with nobody caring much when he popped up weakly to the catcher Arndt Jurgens.

When the game was over, when the cheering had stopped, when the thousands of people left Cooperstown to resume their everyday lives, Alex went back to New York City, to 42nd Street, to the flea circus where he earned his keep. And his off-the-field reputation continued to dog him, to haunt him, in large part because he did nothing to try to counteract it.

And so it was that in December of 1939, after Lou Gehrig was voted into the Hall of Fame by special election after he was forced to retire because of illness, Bob Considine of the *Washington Post*, wrote a parody on Gehrig's entrance into the Hall that included a stinging reference to Alex.

In Considine's piece, Gehrig enters the Hall and hears from the plaques of those who are already there:

The newcomer swallows. He says, "Gee fellas ..." and then he stops and he looks around to a vacant spot on the wall. "Somebody's missing," he says. "Old Pete's not here. There's his name plate — Grover Cleveland Alexander — but his plaque's not here." Babe coughs uncomfortably. "Now listen, Lou, you're going to be here a long time so you better learn the first rule of our club. Pete never gets in before 6 A.M. He made them promise to do that before he'd join the joint."[10]

Chapter XVI

Coming Home

"All of these illnesses ... would defeat most of us, wouldn't they?"
— Aimee Alexander

On July 20, 1939, about a month after the Hall of Fame celebration, the Associated Press reported that Alex had accepted an offer to manage a House of David team for the remainder of the 1939 season, but there is no documentation that he ever showed up. What is known is that he went back to the flea circus on 42nd Street and continued to spin his baseball tales to those who made their way past the peep shows and the legless swimmer to his little stage.

Alex still dreamed of getting back into baseball. In May of 1940, he placed an ad in *The Sporting News* letting it be known that he was available for work. At about the same time, Bill White of the Associated Press wrote a sympathetic piece about him, pointing out that his job at the nickelodeon, which was supposed to last three weeks, had now gone on for more than a year. White took in Alex's show and reported that he was neatly dressed, clear-eyed and not looking as if he were in need of any tear-jerking stories about him. White obviously caught Ol' Pete on one of his good days, because it was Pete himself who often tried to generate most of the sob stories about him.

White imparted the flavor of the surroundings at the arcade when he reported "the floor jarred occasionally as the neighborly lady sword swallower bounced iron cutlasses on the floor" to show that they weren't fake.

Alex told White, "I'd like to get back into baseball if there's a place for me. But I don't feel that the game owes me a living. They paid me well when I was up there. I'm working for a nice guy here. He lets me off to see the games and they treat me well. I've made a lot of mistakes, I guess, but who hasn't? And that idea of me being sick is out. I never spent a day in a hospital in my life." He apparently was forgetting or ignoring the mugging in Evansville and the aftermath of the accident in Springfield, where the writer John P. Carmichael had interviewed him in his hospital room.

XVI—Coming Home

Alex said the toughest part of his job now was sitting around between shows and answering what he called "fool questions" from the audience such as "Is Hubbell going to win 20 games?" or "Is Feller better than you were?"

White pointed out to Alex that critics said the Hall of Famer was now living off fleas. "It's better than having them live off you," he replied.[1]

In late May, Alex got a job offer from and old teammate he hadn't seen in 30 years. Clarence Lehr and Alex were rookies and roommates on the 1911 Philadelphia Phillies. Alex won 28 games that year and went on to have a Hall of Fame career in the big leagues. Lehr, a utility infielder and outfielder, appeared in 23 games and got four hits in 27 at bats for a .148 batting average. He never played in the majors again and went on to be a successful lawyer. In 1940, Lehr was president of the Detroit Racing Association. He offered his old roommate a job as gatekeeper at the Detroit race track and Alex accepted it without hesitation. "He seemed tickled to get it," said Lehr, who saw Alex's ad in *The Sporting News.*

He went to work for Lehr in May, but by July, he was in Cleveland, where he was a ticket-taker at Thistle Down race track. "I never cared much for the races," he said. "When I get home now and my wife asks me who won, I couldn't begin to tell her." Aimee Alexander was once again trying to hang in there with her husband, who still clung to a dream that wasn't to be. "I'd like to get back into baseball," he once again told the press.

Within a year he was back in New York, where he was admitted to a veterans hospital and stayed three weeks for treatment of undisclosed illnesses and ailments. United Press writer Harry Ferguson was among those who thought Alex needed and deserved some help. Ferguson wrote that Ol' Pete didn't have the price of a bleacher seat in his pocket and that his worldly assets amounted to his Hall of Fame plaque and the clothes on his back. Ferguson acknowledged that Alex brought on most of his troubles because he was a man who couldn't say no when someone suggested "just one more round." Ferguson said Alex was now out of the hospital but unable to go back to work (at the flea circus) and unable to pay his bills. He concluded his piece by writing, "Old Pete didn't ask me to do anything about it and I'm not urging you to do anything about it, but if a dime or dollar is burning a hole in your pocket …" He then gave details on a benefit for Alex in which tickets were $2.50 or $5 and checks should be made payable to Grover Cleveland Alexander.[2]

John Kieran of the *New York Times* and Billy Cunningham of *The Boston Record* had been hearing stories about Alexander for years from Frick. It had been four years since Branch Rickey wrote to Frick, telling him detail-by-detail how the Cardinals and other had tried to help Ol' Pete and how he had blown it every time. Rickey had wanted Frick to go public with it because of all the bad press the Cardinals, the National League and organized baseball were getting. Frick chose to play it close to the vest. He told some of his sportwriting cronies and figured the word would get around without embarrassing Alex or baseball. But when Ferguson and other writers went to bat for Alex to try to get him some help, those in the know thought it was time to set the record straight.

Kieran, in his "Sports of the Times" column, told readers how Sam Breadon and Rickey had a standing job offer for Alex "if he cared to take it. He didn't care." He told of how the National League was sending monthly checks to a Nebraska farm until Alex ambled off to Louisville. "The point is, it's hard to help a fellow like that," he wrote. He reported that Alex earned $200,000 during his major league career and had blown it all. But, wrote Kieran, organized baseball had a pension plan to help down-and-out players, and all other retired players for that matter. For $10 a year, a player could join and get the benefits later. Alex, one of the highest paid players in his day, had never joined.[3]

Cunningham, in his column, told readers he had the difficult chore of trying to provide facts without intentionally hurting someone who was obviously already down and out. "The picture being unconsciously painted for the fan who reads at or on the gallop is that baseball hungrily wrung dry this great star of another time then flung him aside when the good was all flung out of his arm and isn't in the slightest concerned about whether he lives or dies. That isn't the way it was or is," wrote Cunningham. He then told pretty much the same story Kieran had. As for Alex trying to get a job in baseball, Cunningham wrote bluntly, "There are good jobs in baseball and clean veterans get them." He concluded the column with this, regarding other writers' pleas for donations for Alex: "Here's hoping Old Pete will be generously taken care of but that the record will be kept straight as to what the situation consists of." The column was published with two pictures of Alex, one taken in 1928 looking sleek and proud in his St. Louis Cardinals uniform, the other 10 years later with Alex wearing a coat and tie, pot belly hanging over the top of his pants and a lit cigarette between the thumb and forefinger of his right hand.[4]

Two years after being inducted into baseball's Hall of Fame, Alex was alone, broke, deaf in one ear and experiencing great pain in it, battling periodic epileptic seizures that were often mistaken for drunken stumblings and either unwilling or unable to hold a steady job, depending on the day and the circumstances. He seemed perplexed that baseball wouldn't hire him and oblivious to how perplexed baseball was with him.

On July 26, 1941, Lefty Grove of the Philadelphia A's became the first

XVI—Coming Home

pitcher to win 300 big league games since Alex had accomplished that feat 17 years earlier. Also on that day, Dan Parker, sports editor of the *New York Daily Mirror*, received some money in the mail that was part of a fund drive he had started for Alexander. Fans had contributed more than $2,500, which was given to Alex in weekly allotments. Parker called Alexander and told him to stop by the office to pick up the stray contributions that had come in.

"He was asleep when I called but he said he'd be by. He looked in excellent condition when he came by later and some of the boys in the city room remarked how well he looked," said Parker. "He didn't have any fat on him and he had the carriage of a soldier. He was in good spirits when he left me."

Several hours later, about 12:30 A.M. on July 27, a taxicab driver discovered Alex lying on a sidewalk and delirious with cuts over his left eye and bruises on his scalp. The cabbie summoned a cop driving by, Patrolman Peter Dunn, who called an ambulance. Alex was taken to Bellevue Hospital, where he was listed in critical condition. It was not known whether he had fallen in an epileptic seizure or had been mugged — or had spent the charity money in a saloon and had just passed out. The police blotter that night noted that Alex was a known alcoholic. First reports were that he had a possible skull fracture, but that did not turn out to be true. Aimee came to the hospital, but no other visitors were allowed. News of Alex's latest setback made headlines in sports pages across the country. United Press reported it was the third time in five years that Alex had been found on a street in bad condition, citing the incident in August 1936 in Evansville, Indiana, and in January 1937 in Springfield, Illinois He was released from the hospital on August 1. Doctors told Aimee that Alex had suffered a brain hemorrhage that he would recover from but that he required prolonged rest. She drove him home to the little apartment they could afford.

No one knows what goes on in the private conversations between a man and his wife, but not long after Alex recovered from his latest incident of his head hitting pavement, Aimee divorced him for a second time. She went her way, he went his, and she lost track of his whereabouts for about three years.

In 1942, Alex was back living in Nebraska, with his niece in Grand Island, in another arrangement set up and paid for by the National League. On July 19, he made the news in an unusual way back east. Parker, the New York sports editor who had been collecting money for him the year before, revealed in a column that an imposter had hit the streets claiming to be Alexander. The guy didn't have much of a routine. He just got drunk, told people he was Grover Cleveland Alexander and asked for money. One regular passer-by, a stockbroker, not only gave the man beer money—he bought him a suit of clothes. The broker became suspicious when one day a kid asked the man for an autograph and the fellow misspelled "Cleveland." The broker contacted Parker and asked for a description of Alex. Parker told him that one distinguishing feature was that Alex had a part of his right ear missing, about the size of nickel, because of a growth he had removed. When the broker went back and discovered that the man on the street was fully eared, he had him arrested.

About a week later, Parker received a letter from Alex with a postmark of Grand Island, Nebraska "Thanks a lot for your article of July 19, exposing that phony who was impersonating me. For once, it wasn't Old Pete. It has happened before. I have been out here since last March and am living with my niece and family. While we are not on a farm, it is not far to several of them. I have not stirred up anything to do although I have tried everything. Did have hopes of some semi-pro baseball job but war restrictions knocked that out. I will just stay in there and keep pitching, hoping for the best. Once this summer, the wire services carried a story that I was to appear in Philadelphia in an old-timers game. I never even heard of it until I read it in the papers. I did not think that was very fair to me but what could I do about it?"

The best Alex could do for employment in the immediate future was odd jobs here and there—a cashier in a Broadway billiard parlor, a pitchman for a museum in another part of the city, a handyman in Chicago, where he was arrested for disorderly conduct in January 1943. The next month, a day after his 56th birthday, Alex talked with reporters in Ironwood, Michigan, where he mused about the possibility of pitching in the big leagues again because of all the pitchers who were in the service and dispatched overseas. Ever the optimist and short on facing reality, Old Pete told the writers, "When I was up there before, I got by the final 10 years without much on the ball simply because I could put them where I wanted to. I can still do that."

By April, he had gone to Cincinnati looking for wartime work in any plant that would hire him. Alex took in a ballgame and watched Johnny Vander Meer shut out the Cardinals 1–0 at Crosley Field. His attitude about pitching had changed radically in two months, perhaps because reality had set in where blind optimism once abounded. "Of course I wouldn't even dream of playing again," he told the press. "There's a little too much rubber in the old legs for that. But I'd like to have a go as a coach for some team. I think I could teach these young pitchers a thing or two.

"Right now, I'm looking for a job. Of course I'd like to hook up with some team as a coach, but if I can't land that, I want to get in war work. I've tried several places around Cincinnati, but my age is against me."

XVI — Coming Home

Alex received another jolt he didn't expect when baseball took away from him the one possession he would have never traded or sold for beer money — his distinction of being the sole winningest pitcher in the National League. Baseball researchers, scouring back records, discovered that Christy Mathewson should have been credited with one more win in the 1902 baseball season, that his won-loss record for the year should have been 14–17 rather than 13–18. Though Joe Reichler, a writer and later a staffer in the commissioner's office, is thought to be the person who officially changed the record, another researcher, Leonard Gettelson, is probably the one who actually made the discovery.

In 1942, *The Sporting News* issued a publication titled *The Dope Book* compiled by Gettelson. It listed batting, fielding and pitching records for an inning, game, season, career, etc., and showed Alexander and Mathewson as co-holders of the record for most career victories (373) in the National League. (The publication later was renamed *One for the Book* and is now *The Sporting News Complete Record Book*.) The first baseball records book of this type that was published annually was the *Little Red Book of Baseball,* which dated back to the mid–1920s, when Alex was still playing. The Elias Bureau, official statistician for the National League, took over the *Little Red Book* (now called *The Book of Baseball Records*) in 1938. Up through its 1943 edition, it listed only Alexander as the National League career leader in wins with 373. In 1944, two years after the Gettelson/*Sporting News* publication, it added Mathewson, thereby officially giving him a win and tying him with Alexander. Reichler worked for the Elias Bureau in 1943 and 1944 before joining the Associated Press and is likely to have made the change in the *Little Red Book* after seeing Gettelson's listing in his publication. Whoever made the discovery, the result was the same. Alexander had to share a record that could have easily been his alone had he not been suspended for the last six weeks of the 1929 baseball season — had he not celebrated his 373rd win so bawdily that he botched his chance to win not only many more but, as it turned out, any more.[4]

Toward the end of 1943, Alex managed to get a job as a security guard at Wright Aeronautical, a plant that manufactured airplane engine parts and was located in Lockland, just outside Cincinnati. If he couldn't get a job in baseball, Ol' Pete had said repeatedly, then he wanted to work in a war plant, helping the war effort. Though his job at the plant was peripheral, it appeared to be a good fit. It was steady work, he was not being taken advantage of because of his famous name, and it wasn't a freak show. But like everything else in his recent history, it didn't last. Grover Cleveland Alexander and steady work were just not a good match.

"I walked all day out there at Wright's and stood an hour on a street car to get there, an hour to get back. Pushed and shoved around by a bunch of hillbillies. I couldn't stand it longer than five months," he said. He then tried his hand at being a host in a diner, but he said that too was too hard on his legs.

Alex told a reporter that he was worried that he might get kicked out the hotel where he was living. The writer asked him why he didn't stay in Nebraska, where the National League was willing to pay his room and board. Alex bristled. He said the arrangement to live with his niece didn't work out. "Frick put up $35 a month. Why, I didn't have money to buy a package of cigarettes," he said.

His health was becoming steadily worse. He went back to the St. Louis area and got a room in East St. Louis, Illinois, living off the small pension arranged by Breadon and Frick, donations from fans who thought the National League was ignoring him and whatever handouts he could get. On September 6, 1944, he was admitted to St. Mary's Hospital in St. Louis, where he was treated for what was described as a nervous condition. It might have been related to his epilepsy or was just a result of his deteriorating body.

In addition to all his other ailments, it had been determined that Alex had cancer. That is what was causing so much pain in his ear. The pain had plagued him for years. His hearing had never been right since he came back from Germany in 1919 suffering from shell shock. Ballplayers and others around him recognized that he was hard of hearing, as in the incident 15 years earlier when fireworks went off at a ballpark, startling the players around him but not affecting Alex at all, as if he didn't hear them. He had been treated for infection in the ear, as noted by sportswriter Parker when he told the stockbroker that one of Ol' Pete's distinguishing characteristics was a hole in his ear. But the infection turned out to be cancer.

In 1946, Alex was living at the Broadview Hotel in East St. Louis when the Cardinals won the National League championship. Alex took advantage of his pass and his connections and attended the seventh game of the World Series between the Cardinals and the Boston Red Sox on October 15 at Sportsman's Park. It was a thrilling game in which Boston got a run in the first inning off Harry "The Cat" Brecheen. The Cardinals tied it in the second and then put two across in the fifth inning to take a 3–1 lead. The Red Sox came back to tie it with two runs in the eighth. In the bottom of the eighth, Enos Slaughter was on first when Harry Walker got a base hit that was fielded in the outfield and thrown to second baseman Johnny Pesky, the relay man. Pesky turned and cocked his arm and hesitated momentarily. Slaughter, running at full speed, was into third easily, and when Pesky hesitated, he dashed safely home with what turned out to be the winning

XVI—Coming Home

run. Slaughter scoring from first on a single became a part of World Series lore, much like Alex's strikeout of Tony Lazzeri 20 years earlier.

As Alexander left the ballpark after the game, he became ill with chest pains. Friends took him back to his hotel room in East St. Louis. United Press reported that night that Alex had suffered a heart attack and was resting comfortably.

A month later, he was in Barnard Hospital in St. Louis. The cancerous ear had to be removed to keep the cancer from spreading. In his file at the Hall of Fame in Cooperstown is a set of instructions he received from a Miss MacDonald with the Social Service Department at the hospital. The instructions said:

> Before you leave the hospital, be sure that you have an appointment slip showing when you are supposed to return to the clinic. It is very important that you come back at the times suggested by your doctor in order that he may watch you carefully and help you to avoid future trouble. If you have difficulty in arranging to come back, communicate with the Social Service Department. An appointment has been made for you to enter the Barnard Free Skin and Cancer Hospital on November 18, 1946. We would like to have you come to the clinic at 1 P.M. on that date prepared to stay at the hospital. If your relatives desire information about your condition, they may call Jefferson 3621. If you wish, they may come to the hospital on the morning of your operation and wait in the reception room downstairs for a report of your condition which may be obtained from the front office.

By this time, Alex and Aimee had reconnected to the extent that she knew where he was and he had called her. Their on-again, off-again relationship was on again, thanks in large part to radio announcer Bill Stern. "I'd heard scraps of news about Alex from time to time but never anything definite," said Aimee. "Finally, I appealed to Mr. Stern. He put out the word on his radio broadcast and within an hour, telegrams came in from all over the country, sent by people who said they'd seen Alex here and there. Finally, Alex himself called me from St. Louis." Since their divorce, Aimee had been working for a New York publishing company that required a lot of travel. She sent him money from time to time, and Sam Breadon was sending him $100 a month. He was also getting government assistance of about $60 a month.

For all the trouble Alex had caused Aimee over the years—his excessive drinking, the epilepsy, the wanderings, the blowing of money, the muggings and stumblings and hospital stays—she remained loyal and tried to be understanding to the man she loved but could not live with anymore. "All of these illnesses—epilepsy, cancer, deafness and alcoholism—would defeat most of us, wouldn't they?" she told a reporter for *The Sporting News*.

On February 26, 1947, a few months after the cancer surgery, Alex celebrated his 60th birthday at a quiet dinner with a few friends in Wood River, Illinois, not far from St. Louis. He was well enough to give a brief radio interview, and again he made a pitch for getting back into organized baseball in some capacity. The Associated Press said Alex's birthday dinner was one the happiest observances he had experienced in many years.

In September, Arthur Daley had a piece in the *New York Times* in which Billy Southworth, a teammate of Alex's on the 1926 pennant winner, reminisced about Ol' Pete's appearance in the seventh game of the World Series. Twenty-one years had passed and, while Alex's version of what happened remained consistent over the years, some of the other accounts either stretched the truth or were victims of faulty memories. Southworth told Daley that after Lazzeri hit the long foul into the left field stands on the second pitch, Alex curved him outside on the next pitch and umpire George Hildebrand called it a ball by inches. According to Southworth, Alex told the umpire that if it was that close, he should have given him the benefit of the doubt. In truth, Alex fanned Lazzeri on three pitches. By most all other accounts, including Alex's, the exchange between him and the umpire came after he walked Babe Ruth with two out in the ninth inning. Southworth rightfully contended that when Alex came on in the seventh inning, he had figured out if he got everyone else out, Ruth would be the last batter of the game and could not win it with one swing of the bat.[5]

In May of 1948, Alex traveled to Albuquerque at the invitation of Dr. Chester F. Bebber, an old Army buddy from World War I. On the night of May 12, after visiting Bebber and his family, Alex returned to his hotel and fell hard on a stairway, possibly the result of a seizure. He was taken to a hospital where it was determined he had broken a vertebra in his neck Despite the pain and a cast on his shoulder and neck area, Ol' Pete signed himself out of the hospital the next day and headed for southern California. It was there, on October 31, 1949, that he collapsed in a Hollywood drugstore where he had gone to have breakfast. An ambulance took him to Hollywood Receiving Hospital, where it was determined he had suffered a slight stroke. He was treated at the hospital for a couple of hours and then went home to the apartment he was now renting near Los Angeles. Aimee had moved to the West Coast, and Alex's meanderings had put him close to her geographically, a situation neither of them resisted. The attending physician at the hospital, Dr. Kearney Sauer, had been a medical student in St. Louis when Alex was pitching for the Cardinals and had seen him pitch several times in the 1926 pennant-winning season. The doctor said the two of them talked as much about baseball as they did about his latest ailment.

XVI — Coming Home

The drugstore fall may have been the result of a stroke, but doctors also noticed that it was remarkably similar to the fall he had taken in Albuquerque a year earlier. Both falls could have been triggered by epileptic seizures. Aimee told his doctors the seizures were probably brought on by the incident 40 years earlier when he was hit in the head by a thrown ball while he was trying to break up a double play in Galesburg. Aimee said that over the years he had tried to stave off the attacks and had been successful most of the time on the ballfield. But when he came back from the war, she said, he was worse. She recalled a time when they were in bed and she was awakened by the noise of his teeth chattering during a seizure.

A little more than a month after the drugstore fall, in the early morning hours of Christmas Eve 1949, Alex was found lying in an alley, unconscious, near his apartment. He was taken to Los Angeles County General Hospital, where he was kept for several days and then released. Wire services reported to the nation that Ol' Pete was seriously ill with cancer and that he had been hospitalized twice in the last six weeks after collapsing from the effects of epilepsy or alcoholism or both.

The Associated Press sent a reporter to the hospital who was taken aback by how seriously ill Alex seemed to be. Cancer had taken one ear, and he couldn't hear well out of the other, so the interviewer wrote out questions on a pad of paper and Alex responded in a voice the reporter described as "halting." Aimee was at his side, serving as his ears and voice. She said Alexander's cancer was the result of sun irritation on his fair skin during his long playing career.

What he talked about hadn't changed much in 20 years. He wanted to get back in baseball — work with kids if he could — which was a little different than his usual prattle about getting back into professional baseball. The unidentified AP writer was sympathetic, noting that after he left the majors, "he wasn't even offered a minor league manager's job."

His first big thrill was beating the Red Sox in the 1915 World Series, but his greatest thrill was the Lazzeri strikeout in 1926. He said his first salary was $1,500 and his highest salary was $10,000 — good money during the era in which he played — but Alex told the reporter something everyone knew by now. The money was gone. As if to show that at one time he could manage his own finances, he said, "I did own my own home once."

In early 1950, Alex experienced two bits of good news. One was the public response to his latest set of problems. He spent his 63rd birthday, February 26, signing 400 autographs and sending them to fans who had sent him get-well cards. But the big news was that the American Legion Baseball program in Nebraska offered him a job working with youngsters as an advisor to their junior baseball program. He was to tour the state and teach kids sportsmanship as well as providing tips on how to play better baseball. Alex was showing his years now. He was battling cancer, epilepsy and alcoholism, had had a mild heart attack and suffered a slight stroke in recent years. But this was the break Ol' Pete had been seeking for years — a paying job in baseball, albeit a far cry from professional baseball. Aimee, who had been living in Long Beach, was set to relocate in Omaha so she, who was his closest friend, would be nearby. Alex arranged to move back to St. Paul — back to his roots — and got a room in a boardinghouse run by a widow named Jo Nevrivy.

Before leaving California, Alex gave a luncheon speech for an organization called the Helms Hall of Fame and, for a couple of hours at least, it was vintage Alexander the Great. He almost always wore a business suit and a dress hat on occasions such as this and, just as in the days he wore a uniform, the suit was a little rumpled and the hat, cocked to one side, looked a size too small on the top of his head. He enjoyed the attention he got and gave an interview to Pat Conger, sports editor of the *Los Angeles Mirror*.

"I'm not much on talking," he said. "Didn't do much on the farm in Nebraska and then when I got into baseball, I couldn't say anything or the umpires would throw me out. I've never had much call to say anything since."

Alex then proceeded to list the three toughest hitters he ever faced — Rogers Hornsby, Babe Ruth and Honus Wagner, in that order. Conger asked Alex about his relationship with Joe McCarthy, who got rid of Alex in his first year as manager of the Cubs and then went on to become the legendary manager of the New York Yankees and, at the end of his career, the Boston Red Sox.

Alex told about a game he was pitching against the Giants. "Joe McCarthy was our new manager. I've got the bases full with Long George Kelly up. McCarthy comes out and says, 'pitch high to him.' I say, 'he's a high-ball hitter.' McCarthy says 'never mind that.' I pitch him high, and a man in the left field bleachers has a souvenir. I walk to the dugout, hand McCarthy my glove and tell him, 'here, you know how to pitch to them.' He tells me, 'I just want you to know who the manager is.' Next morning I read in the paper where I belong to St. Louis."[6]

Alex went back to St. Paul to begin his new job. In anticipation, city fathers declared May 24, 1950, as Grover Cleveland Alexander Day, envisioning a parade and barbecue that would remind many in town of the bash they threw 24 years before when Alex came home the hero of the World Series against the Cardinals. This time, it was not to be. The turnout was poor for the parade, baseball game and banquet. The *St. Paul Phonograph*, the newspaper that had chronicled Alex's ball playing from his sandlot days almost a half-century earlier, noted that the 1950 celebration "would have been a much bigger one if more folks had bothered to attend and pay respect to a man who has brought fame and recognition to their hometown, even though he HAS had 'ups and downs.'" Alex soon learned after arriving in town that St. Paul was a place where bartenders refused to serve a guy just one more drink, even if the guy's name was Grover Cleveland Alexander — nay, especially when the guy's name was Grover Cleveland Alexander.

• CHAPTER XVII •

Bottom of the Ninth

"If there is another Hell in this world, I don't want to ever get there. St. Paul is enough."
— Grover Cleveland Alexander

The 1950 pennant race was a classic one in which the schedule had the two top teams, the Brooklyn Dodgers and Philadelphia Phillies, playing each other in the final series of the season with the pennant on the line. The Phillies had a seven-game lead going into September, but Curt Simmons, their left-handed ace, was drafted into the Army on September 10. Right-hander Bob Miller hurt his arm a couple of days later, and Bubba Church, another pitcher, was sidelined when he was struck in the face by a line drive on September 15. The Phillies found themselves struggling to put a pitching rotation together. Still, on September 23, they maintained their seven-game lead, and even most pessimists didn't think they could blow it in nine days. The Dodgers edged closer when they swept a two-game series from the Phillies on September 23–24. Philadelphia then went to Boston and won two out of three.

Disaster struck at the Polo Grounds. With the pitching staff depleted, the Phillies lost doubleheaders to the Giants on successive days but remained three games ahead with three to play. When the Dodgers won both games of a doubleheader from the Braves while the Phillies were idle, the lead was shaved to two games as the Phillies headed to Ebbets Field. Brooklyn, behind Erv Palica beat Philadelphia 7–3 in the first game of the series to move within one game of the top with one game left to play. On October 1, Don Newcombe took the mound for Brooklyn against Robin Roberts for the Phillies, each gunning for their 20th win. The game was knotted at 1–1 in the bottom of the ninth when Roberts walked Cal Abrams and gave up a base hit to PeeWee Reese, moving Abrams to second. Duke Snider then singled to center and Abrams rounded third and took off for home with the game-winning run. But Richie Ashburn, playing a shallow center field, nailed Abrams at the plate. Roberts retired the next two batters to get out of the inning.

Dick Sisler hit a three-run homer for the Phillies in the 10th inning as Philadelphia won 4–1, capturing their first pennant since 1915 — when Alexander put together the first of his three consecutive 30-plus win seasons.

Alex was living in St. Paul, at a rooming house run by Jo Nevrivy, a widow. It was a brick house at Sixth and Elm streets, one of the oldest houses in St. Paul. Mrs. Nevrivy lived there with her son Ed who had recently come home from the service and was working in a clothing store. Alex Johnson, who also worked at the clothing store, lived there too, as did Ted Wild, a mail carrier. Another Nevrivy son, who suffered from polio, had a room in the basement. He worked in a watch repair shop that was one of Alex's hangouts. Ed Nevrivy said he thinks Alex found out about the rooming house through his association with the crippled Nevrivy boy at the watch shop.

Alex had a room on the second floor and kept pretty much to himself. In the afternoons, he would come downstairs and sit on a swing on the front porch. He was often there when Ed Nivrivy came home for lunch from the clothing store. Nevrivy, who was 30 at the time, didn't have much interest in baseball and had only an hour for lunch. "He would tell me all sorts of old baseball stories— how many guys he struck out and that sort of thing. Sometimes he'd talk so much I had a heck of a time getting away from him," said Nevrivy.[1]

He said even at age 63, Alex had a full head of reddish-brown hair and a ruddy complexion — "a blotchy face from years in the sun, I suppose," said Nevrivy, "and one ear."

Friends and fans recognized the part Ol' Pete played 35 years earlier and tried to come up with a way of financing a trip to the World Series for him. At first, a New York newspaper offered to finance the trip but backed out at the last minute. So two friends, Quentin Lynch, a jeweler in St. Paul, and Bill Graunke, who operated a flying service, raised enough money for Graunke to fly him to Chicago where radio personality Tommy Bartlett, host of "Welcome Travelers" radio program, offered to pay for the rest of the trip.[2]

The plane from Chicago encountered mechanical problems and was grounded in Cleveland. Alex, frail and tired, had to be put to bed to get some rest. By the time he reached the East Coast, the Phillies had lost the first two games in Philadelphia and were headed to Yankee Stadium for the next two. Alex tried to listen to the games on the radio but had difficulty hearing because of increasing deafness.

When he finally got to the ballpark, he wandered aimlessly, like a lost soul, before finding a place to stand in a walkway between sections of the grandstand. Tall and gaunt, with hat cocked to one side, hands gripping the iron rail in front of him, Alex tried to get his bearings, something that used to come naturally to him in a ballpark. More than 64,000 screaming fans around him either didn't recognize him or chose not to stand near a wobbly man with one ear and wrinkles chiseled into his face.

Sportswriters Fred Lieb and Billy Cunningham recognized him and found a place for him in the press box. There Alex regaled them with stories from his past — all the old stories that rolled off his tongue so easily. As usual, the Lazzeri strikeout entered the conversation. Alex's account hadn't changed in 24 years. He said he wasn't drunk when he struck out Lazzeri, that he walked slowly in from the bullpen to make Tony sweat a bit, and that if the pitch Tony hit foul into the left field stands had straightened out, Alex would have been the goat and not the hero. He said the toughest hitter he ever faced was Hornsby but that Wagner was a helluva hitter too, and that being in the Hall of Fame was nice, but you can't eat a plaque. It was a disarming conversation for Lieb, who had covered Alexander in his prime and remembered him as a superb athlete and competitor. On this day, Lieb described the man in the press box with him as "pathetic."

The Phillies lost two in a row to the Yankees at Yankee Stadium as New York completed the four-game sweep. Alex didn't like what he saw. He told the press afterwards he didn't see how the Phillies made it to the World Series in the first place. On his way back to Nebraska, he stopped in Chicago to do an interview with Bartlett on the radio—fulfilling a part of the deal that allowed him to go to the series. "I broke in to the National League with the Philadelphia team and I had hoped to see them do a little winning. Of course I was disappointed when they didn't," he said.

In another interview, Ol' Pete was asked how he would have pitched to Joe DiMaggio if he had faced him in his prime. He said he didn't know about DiMaggio but that he had faced Babe Ruth 13 times in the World Series. "All he got was a single," said Alex. He apparently forgot that in the 1928 World Series, when the Babe hit three home runs in one game, the third one came off of Alexander.

He told reporters the eighth inning of the third game of this World Series reminded him of the seventh inning of the seventh game of the 1926 series. In each case, the Yankees had loaded the bases with the game on the line. One difference in this series was that Philly hurler Ken Heintzelman had walked three men in a row, something Alex said he never did any time in his career. Then he once again launched into a pitch-by-pitch dissertation on how he struck out Lazzeri.

When he got back to Nebraska, all of his troubles seemed to surround him again and started to crush him. He was seriously ill and virtually broke, and there wasn't a bartender in town who would serve him. He did what he always did when he hit rock bottom. He confided in Aimee. Though they were no longer married, Aimee said, "I don't think he ever considered we were divorced. He was that way."

He wrote to her almost every day from the day he returned from the World Series. Sometimes he wrote in pen, sometimes in pencil, sometimes banging out the notes on a manual typewriter in the little room on the second floor of Mrs. Nevrivy's rooming house. He had a premonition of his death that he referred to constantly in his letters. He also expressed contempt for St. Paul, the town that had adopted him as its native son and then wouldn't even serve him a drink when he was down and out.

In a letter dated October 11, he wrote:

"Aimee dear:

"I finally arrived back from the Series. It did not take my fancy and I found three letters here from you ... being in this town is one of the worst things I ever did. I feel the finish is not far away but I do not want it to come to me here."

Later in the same letter, his mood swung and he remembered a good time the two of them had together when they went to a dance in Burwell, Nebraska, earlier that year. It also indicated that Alex might have had a few drinks that night under the watchful eye of Aimee.

"You and I, and the things you say I did, will always remember our one spell of pleasure in Burwell. It made me think I was young and I will never think so again. Did sure enjoy the picture that you sent and it will be carried next to my heart and if I had it on my Series trip I could of showed it with pride. I did not get any money out of the trip but I did find that I still have friends and have many promises for what little time I feel is still left for me, and when I do leave here I do not know just where I will be going. You know I did not get much from this trip and am only as sorry that I did not have it to go to you and wish I had it now. Do hope to see and talk to you in the near future."[3]

Alex was obviously hoping to gain financially from his trip to the World Series, but that did not work out. His reputation for blowing money and being a public embarrassment was well known from coast to coast. He was living off a $60 a month Army pension and a $100 a month stipend from the estate of Sam Breadon, who died May 10, 1949, but even in death looked after his old pitcher. Alex was too ill to do the American Legion work that brought him back to Nebraska.

In a letter dated October 14, three days after the first one, Alex made reference to "Grover Cleveland Alexander Day" in St. Paul on May 23, 1950, an event that was pretty much a bust in terms of public participation, when Nebraska Gov. Val Peterson appointed him as an "admiral" in the Nebraska Navy:

"If I had only thought, I would have been in Lincoln today. The Gov. made me an Admiral in the Nebr. Navy and I do want to have a talk with him. One thing I will ask is just who is running this Navy around here and what I have did that I am no longer an American Citizen as I am treated here where you and I once did enjoy life and some of the people. Say, you remember the days of Prohibition. We never went places but what we did find at least some home brew.... Shooting has turned strong today so look for the shooters to get at least some birds. I will not be one of them as my legs would most likely refuse to carry me out to a sand bar or blind."[4]

Alex apparently mailed that rambling letter and then went down to the local American Legion post to try to get a drink and was refused. He wrote another letter to Aimee that afternoon, saying:

"Just a little more I can't figure out, why I was such a fool to come here and be treated as I am, and that, after the days when I had been heard of. Wasn't I elected to the Legion after the 1st War?"[5]

The next day, Sunday, October 15, Ol' Pete sat down at the little table in his room and wrote yet another letter to his beloved Aimee:

"This letter will probably not amount to much. The day has sure been one of those you hear about. It was rain and was cold until after noon as did not have any breakfast and then the flies were real pesty and just what I ate is a mystery.... Amy [sic] I must say that I am as near the finish as I ever was.... I do wish in some way you get in touch with Gov. Peterson ... don't think I won't have plenty to say to him if I get a chance and it will be of St. Paul and its people. Duck season opened yesterday and 5 fellows got a total of 20 teals. What they did today I did not find out and don't expect to get at myself."[6]

The very next day, he wrote to Aimee again. Scarcely two weeks after attending baseball's grandest event, Alex was sinking deeper and deeper into depression. His ex-wife was the lifeline to which he clung. "Well, it is not much of a day," he wrote. "No mail at all this morning and it is a cold, rainy day so just what H--- is there to pass away the time? Too cold to stay in my room and the swine and their young ones keep every other place filled."[7]

That same week, Alex's brother Nick died. On October 17, as Alex prepared to go to the funeral, he wrote Aimee again, his sixth letter in six days, a long, rambling note, some of which doesn't appear to make sense. But thoughts of his own death are clear.

"Yes, that was my brother Nick who died and his funeral is today so will be a sad day for me as I am going. I will not know those I see but will do my best and can't hear so will not learn anything.... It looks as though I will be here next week so will be just another week or so of Hell.... Only have a short time but still want to say this. The places that are here to go and eat, well they make me feel young in a few ways. It makes me remember when I used to slop hogs and really do feel better about my hearing being bad ... but guess I will just have to go hungry or, Oh well, what the Hell, I am not to be here for long."[8]

The day after the funeral, Alex was in a reflective mood about his life, not an unusual reaction from anyone soon after a loved one has died. In a letter to Aimee on October 18, he wrote:

"Well, in a way yesterday was a sad day and just who all I did meet I don't know. I could tell by their looks they were some relatives.... If this had been the same sort of world when I was growing up, I would have never went where I did or have ever saw my name in print unless I had of done something that as yet has not happened. It looks like I am here for another week at least. Did get out of a few bad innings in my baseball time so still have hopes."[9]

The next day he seemed to be in a better mood. Once again, he was dreaming the impossible dream of getting back into baseball. His letter of October 19 said, "As you said in your letter, if we had only staid [sic] out of Nebr. Why, there was Hollywood, making pictures and other things. Maybe the World Series would of got in somewhere. There is so much going on in baseball deals that I am still waiting for the promised word from many of them....

"Am afraid to go out in the country for as you know they all feed their hogs and someone might think I needed a big feed so as to get me in shape for the winter market. If I was able I would go back to husking corn. They are paying 12 cents a bushel now and I used to get as much as 1½ or two cents and then had it to shovel off the wagon. Oh well, here's a hope for something better for you and I, that at least we will meet again sometime in the not to [sic] far distant future."[10]

On October 19 or October 20, Alex received a letter from Aimee in which she had found a way for Alex to take a trip back to California as a traveling companion with people he did not know. But Alex didn't care as long as it got him out of St. Paul. "Just had the short note of Thursday from you about the chance to ride to California," he wrote on October 20. "I sure would be glad of the chance but as of yet my check has not come in so paid another week's room rent.... Say, just where I might be dropped off (in California) would be like a big game for me, and it would not be St. Paul."[11]

On October 24, he made no mention of a possible trip to California. Instead, he was thinking of past mistakes and also apparently had the idea that his rank as "admiral" in the Nebraska Navy had some real status to it. "Am still sorry we made the trip back to Nebr. and I guess we are both the loosers [sic]," he wrote to Aimee. "I did drop Gov. Peterson a few lines and told him as an Admiral of the Nebraska Navy I was a failure. I won't say that you were at fault in anything and do just recall what I had when Prohibition was a law. I sometimes did not know what the brand was but it always had a kick. I only wish I still had the kick."[12]

By the next day, Alex was back to expressing his hatred for St. Paul, the town that wouldn't give him a drink. "Yes, the day is gone and I am in my room. I have this to say. If there is another Hell in this world, I don't want to ever get there. St. Paul is enough. At least for my finishing time. Worse than some of the game of Baseball that I went through.

"I had a thought today. I guess you can remember what a talker Johnny Evers was in his time. I would just like to have him as a partner in this herd of swine that I run into quite often. I guess you remember Oscar Dugey (a teammate in Philadelphia) and how that he held a big league job on finding out just what the other fellow was trying to do. What a team he and Johnny could be and then I might find out what all was going on or at least being talked about. But of course without a good arm I would still be helpless to do anything. Amy, I have not quit as yet and will be only too glad when I can get out."[13]

On October 26, his note was brief. He told Aimee there had been no mail that day, "not even an autograph request."

The following day, Sunday, October 27, he expounded again. "Well, here it is Sunday again and you know what a great day that is here. I got a little to eat but had to go down on the High W (a nearby highway) and my legs are tired from the walk. I saw a lot of pheasant hunters in through here yesterday but I did not see any today so I suppose they staid [sic] for the day. They were from all over and were going to all parts of the state. Four fellows from in town only got one and they said they are hard to find and I guess it's a good thing I am not out with such legs as I have everything would be safe from me."[14]

On October 30, Alex got a check in the mail and was anxious to use it to help him leave town. But he still had no idea where he was going. He seemed excited when he wrote, "Your little note of Sat. came and my check, which had been sent to St. Paul, Minn., also came in, but I am up on my room rent until Friday and my other check will show before then, so I will not be leaving for a day or so. I do not know where to go. Omaha will be vacant without you.

XVII—Bottom of the Ninth

"I did have a note from the Gov. saying I should call on him when I was in Lincoln, but what I am looking for (his other check) don't show so I guess I will just stay the week out and keep looking for something. The weather is nice here so that was a little help.... do hope you had a nice Sunday."[15]

On October 31, Ol' Pete had his checks and he had a game plan. He was going to Lincoln to call on the governor and then he was going to try to get to Kansas City, where Aimee had gone for a few days. Alex never gave up hope that the connections he thought he had, in baseball, and now in the Nebraska governor's mansion, would land him a job and, perhaps more important, a feeling of security that he had been without for more than 20 years. He wrote, "I wrote the Gov. a letter saying I would be in Lincoln Thursday so have made arrangements to go to Gd (Grand Island, Nebraska) Thursday morning and then on to Lincoln. What it will amt. to I do not know but I am going to take a chance on it just to see. Your time is up Sunday (in Kansas City) so I will try to be there by that time. I sure hope I will be lucky."[16]

The thought of seeing Aimee seemed to give Alex some pep. On Nov 1, he received two letters from her in the mail. Hearing from her always brightened his day. He wrote back, "Well, I just got up town and had my coffee and also your letters.... Well, I don't know just what to do. The Gov. wrote that he would be glad to see me and someone in the east wrote B. Jensen (a clothing salesman in St. Paul) that they had a suit and topcoat for any order so he took my measure and sent them in. It can't be here until next week so I don't know whether I go to Lincoln until after election or not, for when I do go, it is going to be a long trip.... My Gov. check should show this week so it looks like I am here for another week and won't even get into Omaha before you leave Sunday. Guess I am just getting too old to be moving so much. I do wish I had never came to Nebr. I will be writing you again in the morning and I really do hope for the best all the way through."[17]

Years later, Aimee explained that she and Alex had hoped to meet in Omaha before she left for Kansas City. When he learned an anonymous benefactor was going to send him a suit and a topcoat, he decided to wait for those to arrive, because his plan was to leave St. Paul and never come back. In his next letter, like a youngster in love, he tried to plan a rendezvous with the woman he adored. It was dated Friday, November 3, and he wrote it knowing she would not receive it until she returned from Kansas City.

"Well, this will be waiting for you. It is not much but will do until later. Last night I planned on Omaha today but the mail of the morning put that all off until I can hear more from you as I was told this morning that my clothes should be here around election time (the following Tuesday) and my other mail should be showing about that time as all I will need to do is pack and go to wherever it is going to be and I know it will be better than this, so all you need to do is name the spot.

"I cannot tell just exactly what my new outfit is going to look like, but from what I see all around, I guess I don't need to worry. I do wish there was something I could do for you and I feel there will be something come out of the trip I made East (the World Series) but BB (baseball) deals are a little out of season so I guess one will just have to pass away the time.... It is cold here today and we had rain all day yesterday. So it looks like just stay in and think of the past. Anyhow, a lot of luck to you and all that goes with it."[18]

But the next day, Saturday, November 4, Alex had a saddening mood swing. Just 24 hours earlier, he was telling his sweetheart to "name the spot." Now, he wrote, "Well, it's still Sat. morning and the mail is not out yet so I don't know if I got any or not so will wait for it and try to finish this when and if I do get any. I am still sorry that the start of the trip did not take place (meeting Aimee in Omaha). I could of at least been in some other spot away from here. Just what it is going to be, the rest of my time here, I have no way of knowing and then where I am to go is something to wait and find out. Time for the mail and will try to finish if there is any."

When the mail came, it did not include his checks or his new clothes. So Alex sat down and finished his letter to Aimee. "Well this on top of what I wrote this morning will no doubt be something. Honest Amy, I am worse off than I ever was in my game and I always got through somehow so am going to try once more. I am not rich but I have a few $ left and am still looking for a few more. Just how I will go through it all I don't know. Still have some more mail due so will finish this when it comes. Am still sorry that I did not get to Omaha, but more later. Love, Alex."[19]

He left his room and walked down to the post office a few blocks away to mail his letter. Passers-by who didn't know him would have thought he was 83, not 63. His tired legs allowed him to only shuffle along, so even a short walk tired him. He mailed his letter and returned to his room at Mrs. Nevrivy's boarding house. At about lunchtime, Jo Nevrivy mentioned to her son Ed that she had not heard any sounds of movement in Alex's room and that he was usually up and about. She asked Ed to check on him.

"I proceeded up there, and when I got to his room, I knocked," said Ed Nevrivy. He didn't answer. I knocked again. No answer. I opened the door and there he was. He had rolled off the bed and must have had a heart attack. He was face down on the floor and he must have hit his head when he fell because there was blood. I think he chipped some teeth."[20]

XVII—Bottom of the Ninth

It was Alex's final fall. The death certificate filed with the Nebraska Department of Health described the cause of death as "very likely cardiac failure. Found dead on the floor of his room, face downward. No signs of a struggle."

Aimee Alexander heard the news on the radio in Omaha that afternoon. She said she was certain he had had an epileptic seizure that caused the fall. She speculated that he might have suffocated as a result of the seizure. She said his bag was packed because he still held out hope of meeting her in Kansas City.

Alex was buried next to his parents in Memorial Cemetery just outside St. Paul. The St. Louis Cardinals paid for the funeral.

Branch Rickey, the straightlaced Cardinal general manager who didn't drink and had to put up with a great pitcher who did, expressed sadness at Alex's death but also at the tragic life that Alex could not shake himself away from. Rickey, who 13 years earlier wrote the letter blowing the whistle on Alex's shortcomings and how he had refused or ignored most of the help offered to him, told Arthur Daley of the *New York Times*, "I doubt that I ever felt sorrier for any man who ever worked for me than I did for Alexander. He was a perfectly wonderful fellow and his only enemy was himself. I had many a long talk with him. 'I don't want to drink,' he told me, and I believed him. 'Once I take that first sip, I'm lost.'"[21]

Aimee believed it all started to fall apart for Alex as far back as 1909 when he was hit in the temple with the baseball and was unconscious for parts of two days. That injury is what triggered the epilepsy that plagued him later in his life, she said. The turning point, though, was World War I. Aimee said when he came home from the war, the epilepsy had taken hold and he had also turned from a social drinker to an alcoholic.

One time in Chicago, in the early 1920s, the Alexanders played host to some of Alex's Army buddies. One of them asked Alex what was the cause of the "spell" he'd experienced in France. Aimee said that was the first she knew of any seizures, but of course she witnessed them herself later during the course of their marriage.

In 1952, Aimee served as an adviser for the movie *The Winning Team*, Alex's life story in which Ronald Reagan played Ol' Pete. It got a lot of advance publicity, but critics called it "a foul ball."[22]

After his death, the American Legion post in St. Paul updated its records with a handwritten note from Ed G. Paulsen, secretary of Post 82 in St. Paul. A 3 × 5 card in the file had a typewritten entry mentioning that the post had presented Alexander with a beautiful Masonic watch charm during his homecoming celebration in February 1927 when he came home after the 1926 World Series championship. The card mentioned the celebration with

15,000 in the streets. Paulsen's handwritten addendum cites the facts that Alexander was elected on December 21, 1922, initiated on December 28, 1922, passed some sort of requirement on January 15, 1923, was "raised" on February 8, 1923, was suspended on March 20, 1930, and died November 4, 1950.

That bit of record-keeping completed, Paulsen wrote the following: "He is buried in Elmwood Cemetery, St. Paul, Neb. I was very well acquainted with Alec as we called him and considered him a fine gentleman with one exception and you named it on the reverse side of this page. (The word "it" is circled, and Paulsen drew a line to the margin where he wrote the word "booze.") "They did have a fine celebration for him but I don't know of the Masonic watch charm. I have only the card from our card index which states as above written. Alec was subject to spasms of some kind but not from drink as I have seen him go into a rigid spell stone sober." Paulsen's scribblings, part of the official lodge records, was just another indication that Alex's alcoholism and epilepsy overshadowed his baseball career in the view of many, including those who knew him best in his hometown.

Aimee defended Alex until the day she died in 1979 at the age of 87. She often said Alex never really considered himself divorced from her. There is ample evidence to suggest she felt the same way. In 1974, Jim Murray, a syndicated sports columnist whose home newspaper was the *Los Angeles Times*, wrote a column about Ferguson Jenkins, then a star pitcher for the Chicago Cubs who was known for his pinpoint control. Murray wrote that Jenkins was the most effective pitcher in Cub history. The day the column was published, said Murray, he got a phone call from an elderly woman with whom he had conversed in the past. She wasn't angry. She was polite. She made reference to Murray's assertion about Jenkins being the best Cub pitcher ever.

"Aren't you forgetting someone?" asked Aimee Alexander.[23]

"There's no rest for the wicked curve," Bill Corum had written long ago, recounting Grover Cleveland Alexander's triumphant march into the 1926 World Series but also creating a metaphor for Alex's life.

Only a wicked curve could afflict a man with alcoholism, epilepsy, deafness, cancer, poverty and loneliness after his having achieved unparalleled success in his chosen profession earlier in his life.

Only a wicked curve could take a man's greatest moment — the striking out of Tony Lazzeri in that 1926 World Series — and couple it in conversation and in print with alcoholism so that most of the time, both are mentioned in the same breath.

Only a wicked curve could provide a man with his proudest achievement — being the sole all-time leader in wins in the National League — and then take it away from him with the stroke of typewriter key in an office somewhere more than a decade after he retired.

And perhaps the ultimate wicked curve: The man died in a town he grew to hate, where, in his last days, he referred to the townspeople as swine.

Today, that town, St. Paul, Nebraska, holds an annual three-day festival each summer full of fun and games and laughter. They call it "Grover Cleveland Alexander Days."

Appendix: Lifetime Statistics

Grover Cleveland Alexander

Born in Elba, Nebraska, February 26, 1887; died in St. Paul, Nebraska, November 4, 1950; height 6 feet, 1 inch; weight 185 lbs.; bats right; throws right

Minor League Record

Year	Team	G	IP	W-L	Pct.	H	BB	SO	ERA
1909	Galesburg	24	219	15–8	.652	124	42	198	2.53
1910	Syracuse	43	245	29–14	.674	215	67	204	2.20

Major League Record

Year	Team	G	GS	CG	IP*	W-L	Pct.	ShO	BB	SO	ERA
1911	Phil (N)	48	37	31	367	28–13	.683	7	129	227	2.57
1912	Phil (N)	46	34	25	310	19–17	.528	3	105	195	2.81
1913	Phil (N)	47	36	33	306	22–8	.733	9	75	159	2.79
1914	Phil (N)	46	39	32	355	27–15	.643	6	76	214	2.38
1915	Phil (N)	49	42	36	376	31–10	.756	12	64	241	1.22
1916	Phil (N)	48	45	38	389	33–12	.738	16	50	167	1.55
1917	Phil (N)	45	44	34	388	30–13	.698	8	56	200	1.83
1918	Chi (N)	3	3	3	26	2–1	.667	0	3	15	1.73
1919	Chi (N)	30	27	20	235	16–11	.593	9	38	121	1.72
1920	Chi (N)	46	40	33	363	27–14	.659	7	69	173	1.91
1921	Chi (N)	31	29	21	252	15–13	.536	3	33	77	3.39
1922	Chi (N)	33	31	20	245	16–13	.552	1	34	48	3.63
1923	Chi (N)	39	36	26	305	22–12	.647	3	30	72	3.19
1924	Chi (N)	21	20	12	169	12–5	.706	0	25	33	3.03
1925	Chi (N)	32	30	20	236	15–11	.577	1	29	63	3.39
1926	Chi (N)	7	7	4	52	3–3	.500	0	7	12	3.46
1926	StL (N)	23	16	11	148	9–7	.563	2	24	35	2.91
1927	StL (N)	37	30	22	268	21–10	.677	2	38	48	2.52
1928	StL (N)	34	31	18	243	16–9	.640	1	37	59	3.36
1929	StL (N)	22	19	8	132	9–8	.529	0	23	33	3.89
1930	Phil (N)	9	3	0	21	0–3	.000	0	6	6	9.14
20 years		696	599	437	5,190	373–208	.642	90	951	2,148	2.56

World Series

Year	Team	G	GS	CG	IP	W–L	Pct.	ShO	BB	SO	ERA
1915	Phil (N)	2	2	2	18	1–1	.500	0	4	10	1.53
1926	StL (N)	3	2	2	21	2–0	1.000	0	4	17	0.89
1928	StL (N)	2	1	0	5	0–1	.000	0	4	2	19.80
3 years		7	5	4	44	3–2	**.600**	0	12	29	3.35

*Fractions of innings pitched are rounded off.

Notes

Chapter I

1. Lieb, Fred, *Baseball As I Have Known It* (Lincoln: University of Nebraska, 1977) 185–186. As a sportswriter, Lieb had covered Alexander in his glory days, so his observations of the former great pitcher are especially poignant.
2. Kavanagh, Jack, *Ol' Pete: The Grover Cleveland Alexander Story* (South Bend, Ind.: Diamond Communications, 1996) 169. Kavanagh's biography includes many first-person accounts of Alexander's problems with alcohol, either through his own admissions or the observances of players, managers and even his ex-wife.
3. Lieb, *Baseball As I Have Known It*, 186. In his conversation with Lieb that day, Alexander tried to explain his problems with liquor, telling Lieb he was a third-generation drinker.
4. Effrat, Louis, "Old Pete Standee; Alexander, Unrecognized by Fans, Finally Gets Seat, Recalls Days as Phil," *New York Times*, Oct. 7, 1950. Effrat's account in the *New York Times* is significant because it confirms Lieb's recollections of Alexander's appearance in the press box at Yankee Stadium.
5. Meany, Tom, *New York World Telegram*, Jan. 20, 1939. Meany wrote, "It was a busy day for Alex yesterday when he made his debut at the dime show. He was hauled hither and yon by photographers, posed with models and magicians and along side bill posters depicting his 1926 World Series performances. He submitted gracefully and with a sort of simple dignity."
6. McKim, Donald K., "Matty and Ol' Pete: Divergent American Heroes," an essay included in *The Faith of Fifty Million*, by Christopher H. Evans and William Herzog II (Louisville: Westminster John Knox, 2002) 76–77. McKim's work compares the lives of Alexander and Christy Mathewson, who remain tied for the most wins in the National League, whose lives, reputations and legacies are so different, particularly in how they behaved off the field.
7. McKim, "Matty and Ol' Pete: Divergent American Heroes," 77.
8. Cunningham, Bill, "Facts Behind Plight of Pete Alexander," *Washington Post*, May 15, 1941. The column was published with two photos of Alexander, one as a slim, trim member of the St. Louis Cardinals in 1928, the other, taken 10 years later, showing a pot-bellied Alexander with cigar in hand, looking more like a bar fly than a Hall of Fame ballplayer.
9. Robin Roberts has told this story many times. This account is from Bob Broeg's foreword to Kavanagh's *Ol' Pete: The Grover Cleveland Alexander Story*.
10. Alexander's niece, Elma O'Neil and Ed Nevrivy, whose mother ran the rooming house where Alexander died, reminisced about Alexander's last days in an interview for the Nebraska Historical Society in 2000. A transcript of their interviews provided the information included here. Nevrivy discovered Alexander's body when he went to check on his welfare.

Chapter II

1. Kavanagh, *Ol' Pete: The Grover Cleveland Alexander Story*, 3.
2. Nebraska Historical Society transcript.

3. *Ibid.*

4. "Alexander Tells Life Story," North American Newspaper Alliance. In 1930, Alexander struck a deal with the North American Newspaper Alliance in which his life story was reported in a series of articles and published in newspapers that had membership in the alliance. Recollection of his boyhood days is taken from an article that was part of that series, published with Alexander's byline, on June 15, 1930, in the *Los Angeles Times* and other newspapers.

5. *Ibid.*

6. A writer named F.C. Lane chronicled Alexander's early life, based in large part on interviews with Alex's father and other family members, for the January 1916 issue of *Baseball Magazine.*

7. Woodruff, Harvey, "Young Players Who Are Making Good in the Major Leagues," *Chicago Daily Tribune*, July 30, 1911. Woodruff liked this story so well he reported it again in almost the same words in a story published Aug. 3, 1913, in the *Tribune*. Kavanagh tells the story a little differently. In his biography of Alexander, he also reports that he threw three perfect innings, and that Alexander's team made a remarkable comeback, but in Kavanagh's version, Alex's team lost 16–15. Alex himself recalls the incident in the June 15, 1930, story he wrote for the North American Newspaper Alliance. Contrary to what Woodruff reported — twice — Alexander said he was brought in from the outfield to pitch (not second base) but confirms that he retired every batter he faced. Alexander does not tell the final score in his account. All agree that from that day on, he was a pitcher.

8. Alexander told the story of how he was signed in a story he wrote for the North American Newspaper Alliance. Other accounts, including Kavanagh's biography, report that Jap Wagner was manager of the Galesburg team, rather than the shortstop on the Oklahoma team, as Alexander had said. No one disputes that it was Wagner who gave Alexander his first professional contract. A third detailed account is found in the previously cited story by F.C. Lane in *Baseball Magazine.*

9. Lieb, Frederick G. and Baumgartner, Stan, *The Philadelphia Phillies* (New York, Van Rees, 1953) 91. This is a significant passage because it implies Alexander may have had the start of a drinking problem at an early age. Equally significant is the fact that the authors knew Alexander and may have had special insight because of that. Lieb was a highly respected sportswriter for several New York newspapers and *The Sporting News* in a career that spanned 50 years. Baumgartner was a pitcher for the Philadelphia Phillies (and a teammate of Alexander's) who later became a *Philadelphia Inquirer* sportswriter. Writers in Alexander's era used various euphemisms for his drinking problems. In this passage, Lieb and Baumgartner refer to Alec's fondness for a "certain corn by-product." Other writers, including sportswriter Bill Cunningham and baseball historian/author Donald Honig, call the by-product "John Barleycorn." Those are terms that make fun of the substance and, by inference, the drinker. Today's society does not use such "nicknames" and considers alcoholism either as an illness or a form of substance abuse, neither of which is a laughing matter.

10. Kavanagh, *Ol' Pete: The Grover Cleveland Alexander Story,* 9.

11. Lane's article, while full of rich background and history on Alexander and his family, is nonetheless a piece that casts Alex in a decidedly favorable light. To say that "it goes perhaps without saying that Alexander is free from the vice of drink" perhaps should have gone without saying. One thing is certain: It was not prophetic.

12. Lieb and Baumgartner, *The Philadelphia Phillies,* 82–86.

13. *Ibid.*, 92–93. Obviously, neither Lieb nor Baumgartner was present to hear the conversation. Lieb is reporting either what someone told him about the conversation or is guessing at what might have been said, an acceptable journalism practice at the time but one that is frowned on today.

14. Jennings recounts the story of how the Tigers passed on Alexander in "Rounding Third," a newspaper column published in the *Los Angeles Times,* Feb. 11. 1926.

15. Kavanagh, *Ol' Pete: The Grover Cleveland Alexander Story,* 47. Pat Moran has the distinction of winning pennants in his first year as manager of two teams, the 1915 Phillies and the 1919 Cincinnati Reds, who beat the White Sox in the scandal-ridden World Series. Kavanagh describes Moran as a "whiskey-drinking Irishman" whom

Alexander loved and who did not discourage his players from hitting the barrooms after ballgames.

Chapter III

1. Society for American Baseball Research, *Deadball Stars of the National League* (Washington: Brassey's, 2004) 189.
2. *Ibid.*, 213. Sportswriter Fred Lieb, who witnessed the catch, called it "an epic in big league baseball" and one of the three best catches he'd seen in his career, which spanned 42 years at the time he was writing about it. For as famous a catch as it was, there is uncertainty as to who was batting. In The *Philadelphia Phillies*, by Lieb and Baumgartner, they say Fred Merkle hit the ball. In *Deadball Stars of the National League*, David Jones, writing for the Society for American Baseball Research, says it was Fred Snodgrass.
3. *Ibid.*, 192.
4. "Alexander Tells Life Story," North American Newspaper Alliance, published in the *Los Angeles Times*, June 22, 1930.
5. *Ibid.*
6. "Credit Due Catchers: Good Batterymate Does Much Good Toward Pitcher's Success," *Washington Post*, Aug. 27, 1911. The writer's point is a valid one, of course, but in the case of Alexander, the ironies are worth pointing out. The article says it was Dooin who put Alexander on a pedestal, when in fact it was Dooin who was about to cut Alexander in spring training until Pat Moran convinced him otherwise. The writer also wonders how Alexander will do with Moran, and not Dooin, catching him. Again, it was Moran who had confidence in Alexander from the beginning.
7. "Alexander Tells Life Story," *Los Angeles Times*, June 22, 1930.
8. Frisch, Frank and Stockton, J. Roy, *Frank Frisch: The Fordham Flash* (Garden City, NY: Doubleday, 1962) 111.
9. Ritter, Lawrence, *The Glory of Their Times* (New York: Vintage, 1985) 194.
10. Lieb and Baumgartner, *The Philadelphia Phillies*, 98.
11. Kavanagh, *Ol' Pete: The Grover Cleveland Alexander Story*, 21.
12. "Fate Plays Queer Tricks with the Young Pitchers," *Washington Post*, Jan. 5, 1913. The column carried no byline.
13. "Fogel Will Be Given a Trial," *Washington Post*, Oct. 18, 1912.
14. "Fogel Barred Out of Baseball Councils," *New York Times*, Nov. 28, 1912.
15. Kavanagh, *Ol' Pete, The Grover Cleveland Alexander Story*, 35.
16. Kavanagh, *Ol' Pete: The Grover Cleveland Alexander Story*, 71. Kavanagh calls Lobert's story "concocted," told well after Alexander's later problems with epilepsy were known. Kavanagh says the Cubs would have questioned Alexander's health before accepting a trade for him and wonders why he would have been deemed suitable for military service had he suffered from epilepsy at that time in his life. Also, contends Kavanaugh, Alexander came from a small town where news would have spread quickly among townspeople if their favorite son was ill.

Chapter IV

1. "Alex Reviews 1915 Campaign," *Los Angeles Times*, July 12, 1930.
2. Authors Lieb and Kavanagh report that Magee was traded for Whitted and the others. Some baseball record books list them as separate transactions.
3. "Alex Reviews 1915 Campaign," *Los Angeles Times*, July 12, 1930. Alex's memory failed him in one respect. He mentions Humphries as one of the pitchers the Phillies could put up against their opponents. Bert Humphries pitched for the Phillies in Alexander's rookie year of 1911 but did not play for the team after that. Alexander may have been thinking of Al Demaree, who won 14 games for the Phillies that year but whom Alex fails to mention in this article.
4. Lieb and Baumgartner, *The Philadelphia Phillies*, 116–119. Baumgartner pitched for the Phillies in 1915, so the observations about spring training are from personal experience.
5. "Moran Clinches National Flag," the *Los Angeles Times*, Sept. 30, 1915.
6. *Ibid.*
7. "Can Phillies Win with Two Pitchers?" *New York Times*, Oct. 6, 1915.
8. "Mighty Alexander Is Beaten by the Red Sox," the *Los Angeles Times*, Oct. 12, 1915.
9. Devaney, John and Goldblatt, Burt,

The World Series: A Complete Pictorial History (New York: Rand McNally, 1972), 67.
   10. Honig, *Baseball America*, 88.
   11. "Stray Items of Sport from Various Sources," *Washington Post*, Oct. 20, 1915.

Chapter V

1. The first reference is to manager Pat Moran signing a three-year contract with the Phillies. The second reference is to the demise of the Federal League after two seasons.
   2. This is most likely the hunting trip in which Alexander fell off a buckboard and into some murky peat moss—one of the theories for how he came to be known as "Ol' Pete." Newspapers continued to refer to him as "Alex," "Alec" and "Alexander the Great" with no mention of "Ol' Pete" until later in his career, giving credence to the theory that Alexander's fondness for Prohibition liquor—"sneaky Pete" as it was called—is how the "Ol' Pete" nickname really came to be.
   3. Alexander's letter was published in the *Washington Post* on Jan. 10, 1916.
   4. The 1982 *Baseball Research Journal* and *National Pastime* (1992), both publications of the Society for American Baseball Research, provide in-depth reports on Alexander's numbers for the 1916 season.
   5. At the end of the 1965 baseball season, Drysdale and Koufax, both future Hall of Famers, refused to sign contracts with Dodger owner Walter O'Malley unless each received the raises they sought. This was in the days before agents and free agents, a time when ballplayers negotiated for themselves. Drysdale and Koufax eventually signed and O'Malley's wallet was a little lighter.

Chapter VI

1. Quoted from the *Washington Star*, July 21, 1918.
   2. The story, under the headline "Alex the Great Joins Cub Squad to Settle Terms," was published in the *Chicago Tribune* on March 14, 1918, and is not sympathetic or complimentary to Alexander. The headline itself could be a play on words, with "Alex the Great" as both his nickname and a sarcastic reference to his sense of self-worth. Crusinberry refers to him twice as a "prima donna," which is not a welcoming sentiment for someone just joining a ball club and who has not yet thrown his first pitch in a Cub uniform.
   3. Published in the *Washington Post* on April 14, 1918.
   4. Alex's farewell message was published in the *Chicago Tribune* on April 27, 1918, next to a big photo of Alexander in his pitching motion and under a headline that said, "Good-By, Aleck! Good Luck!"
   5. Kavanagh, *Ol' Pete: The Grover Cleveland Alexander Story*, 70. Reports of the marriage differ in several details. Kavanagh says Alex and Amy met on a blind date. The *Chicago Tribune* refers to the bride as Aimee and says the two were childhood sweethearts. The *Tribune* identifies the judge as E.E. Morris, whereas the *New York Times* identifies him as G.E. Morris and says Alex and Amy were childhood playmates and later attended the same college.
   6. The battles in which the 89th Division participated are well documented in many resources dealing with World War I. Details about the 342nd Field Artillery are not as specific so it is difficult to trace Alexander's day-to-day participation on the battlefront.
   7. Soldiers who served with Alex recalled some of their experiences in articles for *American Legion* magazine in 1926.
   8. As told by Dan Parker in the *New York Daily Mirror*, July 19, 1942.
   9. "Alex Tells of Army Life," the North American Newspaper Alliance, published in the *Los Angeles Times* on July 27, 1930.
   10. Honig, *Baseball America*, 93, 156.
   11. Dickey, Glenn, *The History of the National League Since 1876* (New York: Stein and Day, 1982) 105.

Chapter VII

1. "Alexander the Great Back from War Service in France," *Chicago Tribune*, April 15, 1919.
   2. The exploits of Shufflin' Phil Douglas are well-documented in baseball annals. An excellent account of his relationship with John McGraw and his eventual downfall can be found in Charles C. Alexander's *John McGraw*, 239–243.

3. Widely quoted.
4. Lieb and Baumgardner, *The Philadelphia Phillies*, 145. Cravath's comment was first published in the *Philadelphia Evening Bulletin* and quoted by Lieb in his book.
5. Society for American Baseball Research, *Deadball Stars of the National League*, 224.
6. Kavanagh reports the Attleboro games taking place after the 1920 season. A *Boston Globe* story published June 2, 1929, recounts the events as having taken place in 1922. George Anderson, curator of the North Attleboro Museum, in an article for *Monthly Baseball* magazine, says the year was 1920. In fact, Anderson states, "By 1922, the teams consisted mostly of local talent. Fans stayed away but in 1923 money induced some Major Leaguers to once again get involved in the games. By 1924, the money had run out, fan interest had waned, national attention was gone and the series petered out."
7. In 1989, David Strickler, husband of Reese's granddaughter, self-published a biography of Reese titled *Child of Moriah: A Biography of John D. Bonesetter Reese*. In it, Strickler lists an all-star team of Reese's patients. Pitchers: Cy Young, Christy Mathewson, Walter Johnson, Ed Walsh, Grover Cleveland Alexander, Addie Joss, Chief Bender and Stan Coveleski. Catchers: Gabby Hartnett and Roger Bresnahan. First basemen: George Sisler and Frank Chance. Second basemen: Eddie Collins, Rogers Hornsby and Napoleon Lajoie. Third basemen: Frank "Home Run" Baker and Jimmy Collins. Shortstops: Honus Wagner and Donie Bush. Outfielders: Ty Cobb, Shoeless Joe Jackson, Tris Speaker, Edd Roush and Max Carey. Manager: John McGraw.
8. Bob Broeg, "Spunky Aimee Still Loyal to Alexander the Great," *St. Louis Post-Dispatch*, Feb. 6, 1977.
9. Ibid.
10. The *New York Times* of Sept. 21, 1924, published a story with a headline and three deck heads, never mentioning Alexander's 300th win. The headline was "GIANTS ARE BEATEN IN THE 12TH, 7–3." The next headline said "Cubs' 4-Run Rally Overwhelms Champions After They Tie Score in Ninth." Then, "ALEXANDER IN TOP FORM." And finally, "Grantham's Error Alone Sends Game Into Extra Innings; Frisch Hurt in 11th." There is no mention in the accompanying story of Alexander's milestone victory.
11. Grimm, Charlie, and Prell, Edward, *Baseball, I Love You: Jolly Cholly's Story* (Chicago: Henry Regnery, 1968) 27.
12. Kavanagh, *Ol' Pete: The Grover Cleveland Alexander Story*, 89.

Chapter VIII

1. Maranville, Walter, *Run, Rabbit, Run* (Cleveland: Society for American Baseball Research, 1991) 56–57. A year before he died in 1954, Maranville started writing down memories of his baseball career for an autobiography he intended to write. After his death, the notes were found and the book was published 37 years later. In editor John Holway's introduction, he mentions that "Rabbit's memory played tricks on him" and that the record was corrected whenever errors were found. There are some discrepancies in Rabbit's account of his firing. He says Alexander became ill in New York and didn't pitch. When the ballclub went to Philadelphia for a five-game series, according to his recollection, Alexander volunteered to pitch twice. He pitched and won one game and didn't show up for the next, which led to Maranville's firing on Sept. 1. The record shows that on the Cubs' road trip prior to that, Alexander *did* pitch in New York and lost a 7–6 decision on Aug. 19. The Cubs then went to Brooklyn, where they played three doubleheaders in a row, Aug 22–24, splitting each of them. Alexander was the starting pitcher in a 9–7 win on Aug. 23. Then the ballclub went to Philadelphia but played three games, not five games, as Maranville had said, and Alexander didn't appear in any of them.
2. Kavanagh, *Ol' Pete: The Grover Cleveland Alexander Story*, 95.
3. Ibid., 96.

Chapter IX

1. Lieb, *The St. Louis Cardinals*, 119–120. Sportswriter Lieb was in the locker room after the game and overheard the exchange.
2. Honig, *Baseball America*, 156.
3. Vidmer, Richard, "Yank Sluggers

Tamed by Veteran Pitcher," *New York Times*, Oct. 4, 1926.

4. Finch, Fred, "Sober When He Whiffed Lazzeri, *The Sporting News*, May 2, 1951.

5. Carmichael, John P., *My Greatest Day in Baseball* (New York: Grosset & Dunlap, 1945) 2–3.

6. Kavanagh, *Ol' Pete: The Grover Cleveland Alexander Story*, 104–105.

7. *Ibid.*, 105.

8. Harrison, James, "Alexander Again the Hero," *New York Times*, Oct. 11, 1926. Harrison also points out how fate prevented Hoyt from being the hero. Had Koenig not muffed a ball at shortstop, and if Meusel had caught the fly ball that he could not come up with, Hoyt would probably have thrown a shutout to beat the Cardinals.

9. Carmichael, *My Greatest Day in Baseball*, 2.

10. The *Look* magazine article is included in Charles Einstein's anthology, *The Fireside Book of Baseball*, published by Simon and Shuster in 1956.

11. Bell, Les and Honig, Donald, "Yesterday," *Sports Illustrated*, Oct. 9, 1978.

12. Toporcer, George, "The Greatest Pitcher of All Time," *Blue Book*, July 9, 1952.

13. Devaney, John and Goldblatt, Burt, *The World Series: A Complete Pictorial History* (New York: Rand McNally, 1981) 113.

Chapter X

1. Broeg, Bob, "Spunky Aimee Still Loyal to Alexander the Great," *St. Louis Post-Dispatch*, Feb. 6, 1977.

2. Toporcer, George, "The Greatest Pitcher of All Time," *Blue Book*, July 9, 1952.

3. "Alex Advises Against Own Example," *Washington Post*, Oct. 14, 1926.

4. Honig tells the Pipgras anecdote in his book, *Baseball When the Grass Was Real*.

Chapter XI

1. Kavanagh, *Ol' Pete: The Grover Cleveland Alexander Story*, 124.

2. "Alex Hopes for Reconciliation," *Omaha World-Herald*, Jan. 31, 1929.

3. McKechnie told the story many times. Accounts included here come from Arthur Daley's "Sports of the Times" column published Nov. 6, 1950, and from an article in *The Sporting News* on Nov. 13, 1965.

4. "Cardinals Give Alexander Rest for Season at Full Salary," *Washington Post*, Aug. 22, 1929.

5. Pegler, Westbrook, "St. Louis Folk Sit Brooding As Their Team Whips A's, 2–1," *Chicago Daily Tribune*, Aug. 21, 1929.

Chapter XII

1. Finch, Fred, "Sober When He Whiffed Lazzeri," *The Sporting News*, May 2, 1951.

2. "Alexander, Once the Great, Waits Decision on Fate," *Chicago Daily Tribune*, July 17, 1930.

3. Pegler, Westbrook, "Speaking Out on Sports, *Chicago Tribune*, July 1930.

4. The account of Alex's short-lived employment with the Toledo Mud Hens is found in a *Washington Post* story published Aug. 7, 1930, under the headline, "Alex Released by Toledo President."

Chapter XIII

1. Hawkins, Joel and Bertolino, Terry, *The House of David Baseball Team* (Chicago, Arcadia, 2000) 7.

2. "Manager of Dean Boys Cleaned Up," *Los Angeles Times*, Nov. 4, 1934.

3. "Sports of the Times," *New York Times*, Nov. 17, 1938.

4. "On the Line with Considine," *Washington Post*, March 11, 1941.

5. Hawkins, Joel and Bertolino, Terry, *The House of David Baseball Team*, 37.

6. Finch Fred, "Sober When He Fanned Lazzeri," *The Sporting News*, May 2, 1951.

7. Hawkins, Joel and Bertolino, Terry, *The House of David Baseball Team*, 37.

8. *Ibid.*, 41.

9. The All-Star baseball game was the idea of *Chicago Tribune* sports editor Arch Ward to promote baseball, entertain the fans and provide funds for the Players Association. The first All-Star game was played at Comiskey Park in Chicago on July 6, 1933, with the American League winning 4–2. Fittingly, Babe Ruth hit the first home run in All-Star history. On July 10, 1934, the second All-Star game was played at the Polo Grounds. The American League won this

one, too, 9–7. It was in this game that Carl Hubbell struck out Ruth, Lou Gehrig, Al Simmons, Jimmy Foxx and Joe Cronin in succession. By 1935, the game was established as an American institution with guaranteed big gate receipts. It was played in Cleveland on July 8, and the American League won its third straight, 4–1.

Chapter XIV

1. Graham, Frank, "Setting the Pace," *New York Times,* Sept. 12, 1935.
2. "Alexander Found in Daze; Not Dying," *Washington Post,* Aug. 2, 1936. The story was picked up by the Associated Press and published and broadcast throughout the country.
3. Mr. Sherman's letter is part of the Grover Cleveland Alexander file in the library of the National Baseball Hall of Fame in Cooperstown. It is included here because it is an indication of the passion of baseball fans for the game and its stars and the feeling by many that Alexander was not getting the assistance he needed or deserved.
4. Carmichael recalled his visit with Alexander in the Springfield hospital in a column published in the *Chicago Daily News* in November 1950, not long after Alexander's death.

Chapter XV

1. "Matty and Ol' Pete: Divergent American Heroes," an essay by Donald A. McKim in *The Faith of 50 Million,* edited by Christopher H. Evans and William R. Herzog II (Louisville: Westminster John Knox, 2002) 60.
2. Honig, Donald, *Baseball America,* as quoted in *The Faith of 50 Million,* 60.
3. Walter Johnson was a hard-throwing, hard-nosed pitcher in his playing days. Off the field he was known as a gentleman, and as a manager was sometimes criticized for it. In 1935, the year before the first Hall of Fame balloting, Johnson was managing Cleveland and Indians management decided to fire him and replace him with Steve O'Neill. Ever the gentleman, "The Big Train" pointed out to his bosses that the Indians were about to go on a rugged road trip in which they weren't likely to win many games. Why not delay the firing until the club came back home, he said, giving O'Neill a better chance to get off to a good start. The club agreed and delayed the firing.
4. In 1968, Bob Gibson of the St. Louis Cardinals had a 1.12 earned run average in 304⅔ innings pitched, topping Alexander's record. In 1943, official National League records were changed to give Christy Mathewson credit for one more win, his 373rd, tying him with Alexander for most wins. And the advent of everyday relief pitchers has caused Alexander's record of 696 pitched games to be buried in the record books. At the start of the 2004 season, Jesse Orosco held the major league record with 1,252 appearances. Alexander was in 70th place.
5. The Associated Press mentions that the Yankees had not lost a World Series since then (1926). They didn't lose another one until 1942 when once again the Cardinals beat them.
6. Bill Corum worked for the *New York Times* from 1920 to 1925 and then moved to the New York Journal where he worked until 1935. He then joined the staff of the *Detroit Evening Tribune.* Later in his career he was named president of Churchill Downs race track in Louisville, Ky., the home of the Kentucky Derby. A master with words, Corum's reference to "no rest for the wicked curve" was a classic description of what he perceived to be Alexander's fate in the seventh game of the 1926 World Series. He is credited with coining the phrase, "Run for the Roses" to describe the Kentucky Derby.
7. Laney, Al, "Alexander Spiels in Flea Circus Year After Joining Hall of Fame," *New York Herald-Tribune,* Jan. 20, 1939.
8. *Ibid.*
9. *Ibid.*
10. Considine, Bob, "On the Line with Considine," *Washington Post,* Dec. 12, 1939.

Chapter XVI

1. Alexander told White that his bosses at Hubert's allowed him time off occasionally to go to ballgames. It is obvious from his lifestyle that Alex wouldn't have had the money to go to games. He was able to do it because the National League had given him a lifetime pass to any ballpark in the league.

2. Ferguson's story was picked up by newspapers across the country that subscribed to the United Press service.

3. Kieran was a well-respected journalist and intellect who was a regular on the popular "Information, Please" radio program for 10 years. He began his newspaper career in 1915 and his column, "Sports of the Times," was the first bylined sports column in the *New York Times*. He died in 1981 at the age of 99. Cunningham was a brash Boston sportswriter from 1922 until his death in 1960 who was also a popular radio commentator and after-dinner speaker throughout New England. Ted Williams once referred to him as "one of the five bad apples" in Boston.

4. There is no clear account as to who was responsible for changing the record. Gettelson was involved in the initial research. Reichler worked for the Elias Bureau at the time the change was made. The author is indebted to Cliff Kachline for his assistance in researching how this occurred.

5. Daley, Arthur, "Sports of the Times," *New York Times,* Sept. 2, 1928. Daley was a sports reporter and columnist for the *Times* for nearly 50 years and in 1973 became the first sports columnist to win a Pulitzer Prize. The Lazzeri strikeout, like Babe Ruth's "called shot," was dramatic enough that it didn't need exaggeration. There are stories that Alex was drunk in the bullpen that day and other stories that he was hung over and asleep. There are various accounts of what he said when he reached the mound after coming in from the bullpen. But there is no question that he struck out Lazzeri on three pitches, not four, and Southworth was the only one who said Alex's conversation with the umpire took place in the Lazzeri at bat. In point of fact, it couldn't have if Alex fanned him on three pitches, which he did.

6. Conger, Pat, "From the Fanstand," *Los Angeles Mirror,* April 19, 1950. The Helms Hall of Fame was an honor established by a Los Angeles baker named Paul Helms in 1936 that focused primarily on Olympic athletes. Alexander wasn't a member nor an inductee, just a guest speaker.

Chapter XVII

1. Ed Nevrivy recalled his experiences with Alex in an interview with the author on Jan. 25, 2005. Nevrivy worked in a clothing store in St. Paul, a store that he later owned. One of his fond memories of his times with Alex was "outfitting him" in new clothes for his trip to the 1950 World Series. Alex died a month later. Nevrivy said he didn't have a close association with Alex because he didn't have much of an interest in baseball. But the two of them lived in the same house and were pleasant to one another. Nevrivy said he knew of Alex's reputation but never saw him drunk.

2. Tommy Bartlett is more famous for something he discovered from one of the segments of his "travel show" on the radio. He was introduced to the sport of water skiing and loved it so much that he produced extravagant events of water entertainment, beginning in Wisconsin Dells, Wis., known around the country as "Tommy Bartlett's Water Shows."

3. Mrs. Alexander shared the letters with Frank Finch of *The Sporting News,* who included excerpts in a long retrospective of Alex's life published on May 2, 1951, about seven months after he died.

4. Ibid. Aimee had informed Alex that she was taking a trip to Kansas City and invited him to meet her there. Alex held out hopes of meeting her there but needed his pension checks to arrive.

5. Ibid.
6. Ibid.
7. *Ibid.* It is not clear to whom Alex is referring when he makes reference to "swine and their young ones."
8. Ibid.
9. Ibid.
10. Ibid.
11. Ibid.
12. Ibid.
13. Ibid.
14. Ibid.
15. Ibid.
16. Ibid.
17. Ibid.
18. Ibid.
19. Ibid.
20. Nevrivy recalled the day Alex died in an interview with the author.
21. Arthur Daley wrote several columns in his career about Alex. He quotes Branch Rickey in a column published in the *New York Times* on Nov. 7, 1950, three days after Alex's death.

22. A *Los Angeles Times* review of the movie is headlined, "The Winning Team Fouls Out on Facts." The review, published June 21, 1952, points out many factual errors in the movie, including a scene from the 1926 World Series when Cardinal manager Rogers Hornsby picks up a dugout telephone and calls for Alexander to come in to pitch. In actuality, Hornsby was playing second base at the time. The movie also shows Alex's days with the House of David as if they occurred in the middle of his major league career instead of when it was over.

23. Ferguson Jenkins started his career with the Philadelphia Phillies in 1965. He pitched for the Cubs from 1967 through 1973 and in 1982–83. In between he hurled for Texas and Boston. He won 20 games or more six straight years for the Cubs, 1967–1972. He retired after the 1983 season with 284 wins, 226 losses. He was 161–114 with the Cubs. Jim Murray's column was published in the *Los Angeles Times* May 21, 1974.

Bibliography

"About Broken Down Ball Players." *New York Times,* Marcy 29, 1941.

"Aleck Marries His Sweetheart of Boyhood Days." *Chicago Daily Tribune,* June 1, 1918.

"Aleck at Hot Springs Getting in Shape; Bonus Talk Later?" *Chicago Daily Tribune,* Feb. 20, 1918.

"Alex Advises Against Own Example; Always Drank, Does Not Recommend It." *Washington Post,* Oct. 14, 1926.

"Alex Crashes New York—This Time as Museum Freak." *Chicago Daily Tribune,* Jan. 18, 1939.

"Alex Getting Ready; Takes Up Bowling." *Chicago Daily Tribune,* Jan. 11, 1926.

"Alex Gets Offer of $1,000 a Week to Join Circus." *Chicago Daily Tribune,* Feb. 20, 1917.

"Alex Grows Reminiscent." *Los Angeles Times,* Dec. 22, 1929.

"Alex in First Draft Class; Cubs Up in Air." *Chicago Daily Tribune,* Jan. 16, 1918.

"Alex Lives Up to Old Praise." *Los Angeles Times,* Oct. 17, 1926.

"Alex Named Pilot of House of David." *Washington Post,* April 5, 1931.

"Alex Refuses to Take Part in Cub Drill." *Chicago Daily Tribune,* March 17, 1918.

"Alex Released by Phillies." *New York Times,* June 2, 1930.

"Alex Reviews 1915 Campaign." *Los Angeles Times,* July 10, 1930.

"Alex Tells How He Struck Out Lazzeri in 1926 World Series." *New York World-Telegram,* June 17, 1930.

"Alex Tells of Army Life." *Los Angeles Times,* July 27, 1930.

"Alex Tells of Eventful Life." *Los Angeles Times,* June 29, 1930.

"Alex the Great to Don Uniform." *New York Times,* April 14, 1918.

"Alex Wins to Equal Record Set by Matty." *Los Angeles Times,* Aug. 2, 1929.

"Alexander and Ex-Wife Marry Again." *Chicago Daily Tribune,* Nov. 3, 1931.

"Alexander Asserts Arm is OK and That It Only Needed Rest." *Washington Post,* Jan. 10, 1916.

"Alexander Badly Hurt." *New York Times,* Aug 2, 1936.

"Alexander Back on Broadway." *New York World-Telegram,* Jan. 21, 1939.

"Alexander Breaks Pitchers' Records." *New York Times,* Oct. 3, 1915.

"Alexander Career Finished After Deacon Punished Him." *The Sporting News,* Nov. 13, 1965.

"Alexander Completed 437 of 600 Games He Began." Albany *Knickerbocker News,* Jan. 4, 1951.

"Alexander Equals Mathewson's Feat." *New York Times,* Aug. 2, 1929.

"Alexander, Ex-Pitcher, Suffers Heart Attack." *New York Herald Tribune,* Oct. 18, 1946.

"Alexander Found in Bronx Hospital After Job Appeal." *Washington Post,* March 21, 1941.

"Alexander Found in Daze; All Is a Blank to Ex-Hurler." *Washington Post,* Aug. 2, 1936.

"Alexander Found the Needle's Eye." *Christian Science Monitor,* Jan. 13, 1973.

"Alexander Gets Release." *Los Angeles Times,* July 22, 1930.

"Alexander Going Strong in His 18th Year of Big League Ball." *Boston Globe*, June 10, 1928.

"Alexander Got $1500 First Year, Won 28." *Los Angeles Times*, Feb. 26, 1950.

"Alexander Has Broken Wrist; May Not Pitch Again This Year." *New York Times*, July 15, 1924.

"Alexander Hurls for '26 Cards Against 1936 Redbirds." *St. Louis Post-Dispatch*, Sept. 1, 1936.

"Alexander Ills Did What No Man Could." *Los Angeles Times*, April 28, 1974.

"Alexander Is Dead; Noted Pitcher 63." *New York Times*, Nov. 5, 1950.

"Alexander Is Discharged: Former Hurler, Treated for Head Injuries, Leaves Bellvue." *New York Times*, Aug. 1, 1941.

"Alexander Is Given Release." *Los Angeles Times*, June 4, 1930.

"Alexander Is Sued as Love Pirate." *Omaha World-Herald*, Jan. 18, 1930.

"Alexander Is Voted Place in Baseball Hall of Fame." *Chicago Daily Tribune*, Jan. 19, 1938.

"Alexander Joins Immortals in Cardinals' Series Triumph." *New York Times*, Oct. 14, 1926.

"Alexander Now Improved." *New York Times*, Jan. 17, 1937.

"Alexander, Once the Great, Waits Decision on Fate." *Chicago Daily Tribune*, July 17, 1930.

"Alexander Released by Toledo President." *Washington Post*, Aug. 7, 1930.

"Alexander Seeking Job: Wants to Return to Baseball as Coach." *New York Times*, April 22, 1943.

"Alexander Sent Home for Breaking Rules." *Los Angeles Times*, Aug. 20, 1929.

"Alexander Sent to Jail on Many Liquor Counts." *Washington Post*, Sept. 25, 1930.

"Alexander Seriously Ill — May Have Cancer." *Washington Post*, Dec. 28, 1949.

"Alexander Showing Courage in New York Nickelodeon." *Jackson (Miss.) Daily News*, Jan. 3, 1940.

"Alexander Shows He's Great as Ever But Reds Beat Him." *Chicago Daily Tribune*, May 10, 1919.

"Alexander Signed to Pitch for Dallas." *New York Times*, June 20, 1930.

"Alexanders Silent on Divorce Case." *New York Times*, Jan. 31, 1929.

"Alexander Slated to Start Home from Germany Today." *Chicago Daily Tribune*, March 16, 1919.

"Alexander Spiels in Flea Circus Year After Joining Hall of Fame." *New York World-Telegram*, Jan. 20, 1939.

"Alexander Surprises by Terms He Makes." *Washington Post*, Feb. 23, 1917.

"Alexander Suspended." *Los Angeles Times*, July 16, 1930.

"Alexander Suspended for Breaking Rules." *New York Times*, June 17, 1926.

"Alexander Suspension to Stick." *Los Angeles Times*, June 17, 1926.

"Alexander Tells Life Story." *Los Angeles Times*, June 22, 1930.

"Alexander the Great." *New York Times*, May 21, 1953.

"Alexander to Rejoin Team." *New York Times*, July 13, 1929.

"Alexander Traded to the Phillies." *New York Times*, Dec. 12, 1929.

"Alexander Turns 60 and Finds He Is Not Forgotten." *New York Herald Tribune*, Feb. 27, 1947.

"Alexander Turns Twirler on Just a Minute's Notice." *Washington Post*, Aug. 13, 1913.

"Alexander Victor, Sets League Mark." *New York Times*, Aug. 11, 1929.

"Alexander Voted to Baseball's Hall of Fame." *New York Times*, Jan. 19. 1938.

"Alexander Was Sobering Sight to Would-Be Hitters." *St. Louis Post-Dispatch*, June 2, 1975.

"Alex's Appearance Here Recalls Hectic Moments of World Series of 1926." *Rochester (N.Y.) Times Union*, July 14, 1936.

"Alex's First Season Came Near Being Last." *New York Times*, Dec. 9, 1926.

"Alex's Off Resin Bag, He Says as Cubs Roll West." *Chicago Daily Tribune*, Feb. 12, 1926.

"Along the Sports Rialto," *Youngstown Daily Vindicator*, July 1, 1941.

"Ancient Aleck Shows Cubs' Mistakes." *Washington Post*, Oct. 10, 1926.

Bibliography

"And No More Worlds to Conquer." *Detroit Evening Tribune*, Jan. 19, 1938.

"Auto Injuries Send Alexander to a Hospital." *Chicago Daily Tribune*, Jan. 16, 1937.

"Ball Team Keeps Beard Monopoly." *New York Times*, May 24, 1934.

"The Barber Shop." *Chicago Daily News*, Nov. 6 1950.

"Barry Saves Red Sox from Defeat." *New York Times*, Oct. 12, 1915.

Baseball Research Journal 1982. Cooperstown, N.Y.: Society for American Baseball Research, 1982.

Baseball Research Journal 1983. Cooperstown, N.Y.: Society for American Baseball Research, 1983.

Baseball Research Journal 2001. Cleveland: Society for American Baseball Research, 2001.

"Baseball's Alexander Taken to Hospital Again. *Los Angeles Times*, Dec. 25, 1949.

"Baseball's Highest Salaried Pitcher." *Boston Globe*, June 2, 1929.

"Bewhiskered Nine to Play Here Tonight." *Los Angeles Times*, Sept. 13, 1933.

"Bid to Babe: House of David Promoter Offers Him $35,000." *Washington Post*, Nov. 2, 1934.

"Big League Stars Bring 100 Years of Baseball Up to Date." *New York Times*, June 13, 1939.

"Bill Wrigley Spends Quarter Million on New Talent." *Los Angeles Times*, Jan. 22, 1932.

"Bob Addie's Column." *Washington Post*, Aug. 20, 1956.

Brown, Gene. *The Complete Book of Baseball: A New York Times Scrapbook History*. New York: New York Times, 1980.

Brown, Warren. *The Chicago Cubs*. New York: Putnam's, 1946.

"Can Phillies Win With Two Pitchers?" *New York Times*, Oct. 6, 1915.

"Cards Beat Yanks and Capture World Series." *New York Times*, Oct. 11, 1926.

"Cards Give Alexander Rest for Season at Full Salary." *Washington Post*, Aug. 22, 1929.

"Cards New Champions; World Series to St. Louis." *Los Angeles Times*, Oct. 11, 1926.

"Cards of '26 Display Old Pennant Enthusiasm." *St. Louis Post-Dispatch*, Sept. 1, 1936.

Carmichael, John P. *My Greatest Day in Baseball*. New York: Grossett and Dunlap, 1951.

"Cooperstown Has Big Day." *Los Angeles Times*, June 13, 1939.

Creamer, Robert. *Stengel: His Life and Times*. New York: Dell, 1984.

"Credit Due Catchers." *Washington Post*, Aug. 27, 1911.

"Cub Prexy Hurries West to See Alex; Worried About Star." *Chicago Daily Tribune*, Jan. 24, 1918.

"Cubs Beaten by Cardinals, 3–2; Old Mates held to 4 Hits by Alex." *Chicago Daily Tribune*, June 28, 1926.

"Cubs Buy Battery of Alexander and Killefer." *Chicago Daily Tribune*, Dec. 12, 1917.

"Cubs Favor Plan Urged by Fogel." *Chicago Daily Tribune*, Sept. 23, 1912.

"Cubs Send Alexander to Cards for Waiver Price." *Los Angeles Times*, June 23, 1926.

"Cubs to Drop, Alexander Opines." *Washington Post*, Aug. 25, 1927.

"Custom Dictates Long Warm-Ups for Pitchers." *Los Angeles Times*, May 10, 1957.

"The Customers Always Write." *New York Daily Mirror*, July 31, 1942.

"Cy Young Ruminates—Old Pete Pitches." *Los Angeles Times*, May 3, 1937.

"Daniel's Dope." *New York World-Telegram*, April 29, 1940.

Devaney, John, and Goldblatt, Burt. *The World Series: A Complete Pictorial History*. Chicago: Rand McNally, 1981.

Dickey, Glenn. *The History of National League Baseball Since 1876*. New York: Stein and Day, 1982.

"Doctor 'Fan' Treats Ol' Pete." *Los Angeles Times*, Nov. 1, 1949.

"Donkeys to Be Used by Mills, House of David." *Chicago Daily Tribune*, June 27, 1934.

"Duffy Florals and Mills Split Double

Header." *Chicago Daily Tribune,* May 10, 1937.

Durso, Joseph. *Casey: The Life and Legend of Charles Dillon Stengel.* Englewood Cliffs, N.J.: Prentice Hall, 1967.

Einstein, Charles. *The Fireside Book of Baseball.* New York: Simon and Schuster, 1956.

Evans, Christopher, and Herzog, William R. *The Faith of 50 Million: Baseball, Religion and American Culture.* Louisville: Westminister John Knox, 2002.

"Ex-Major Leaguers Meet in Tourney." *Washington Post,* Aug. 31, 1937.

"Fame Comes to Speaker, Lajoie and Cy Young." *Chicago Daily Tribune,* Jan. 20, 1937.

"Florals Beat House of David 4–3 Before 6,000." *Chicago Daily Tribune,* July 10, 1931.

"Fogel Barred Out of Baseball Councils." *New York Times,* Nov. 28, 1912.

"Fogel Will Be Given a Trial." *Washington Post,* Oct. 18, 1912.

"For the Record: Alex Didn't Have a Hangover." *New York Daily News,* Nov. 11, 1950.

"Forgotten Phil Buddy Gives Alexander a Job." *Chicago Daily Tribune,* May 15, 1940.

"Frankly Speaking: Alexander Pitching." *Christian Science Monitor,* April 28, 1950.

Frick, Ford C. *Games, Asterisks and People: Memoirs of a Lucky Fan.* New York: Crown, 1973.

Gallagher, Mark. *Day By Day in New York Yankees History.* New York: Leisure Press, 1983.

Gettelson, Leonard. *World Series Records.* St. Louis: The Sporting News, 1976.

"Giants are Beaten in 12th, 7–3. *New York Times,* Sept. 21, 1924.

"The Greatest Pitcher of All Time." *Bluebook Magazine,* July 1952.

Grimm, Charlie, and Prell, Edward. *Baseball, I Love You: Jolly Cholly's Story.* Chicago: Henry Regnery, 1968.

"Grover Alexander and His Bride." *New York Times,* June 17, 1918.

"Grover Alexander, 56, Set for Majors Again." *New York Daily Mirror,* Feb. 28, 1943.

"Grover Alexander Jailed." *New York Times,* Sept. 25, 1930.

"Grover Alexander Released by Phils." *New York Times,* June 4, 1930.

"Grover C. Alexander Collapses." *New York Times,* Oct. 31, 1949.

"Grover Cleveland Alexander." baseballlibrary.com

"Grover Cleveland Alexander is 'Smart Aleck,' Says Pegler." *Los Angeles Times,* Oct. 10, 1926.

Hawkins, Joel, and Bertolino, Terry. *The House of David Baseball Team.* Chicago: Arcadia, 2000.

"Heart-Break Life Story of Alex the Great Ends." *The Sporting News,* Nov. 15, 1950.

"He's Behind Eight Ball." *New York World-Telegram,* April 14, 1941.

"His Own Worst Enemy: The Rise and Fall of Grover Cleveland Alexander." *Nebraska History,* Spring 1990.

"Hitting Is Mixed with Other Lessons So Cubs Enjoy Toil." *Chicago Daily Tribune,* Feb. 23, 1932.

Honig, Donald R. *Baseball America.* New York: Macmillan, 1985.

"House of David Beats Sullivan and Mills, 4–3." *Chicago Daily Tribune,* May 22, 1933.

"House of David Cops Fray, 8–1." *Chicago Daily Tribune,* Sept. 14, 1933.

"House of David Faces Extinction With 'King' Missing." *New York Times,* April 8, 1923.

"House of David Faces Firemen, Duffy Florals." *Chicago Daily Tribune,* Aug. 21, 1932.

"House of David Held to 3 Hits; Mills Win, 9–0." *Chicago Daily Tribune,* June 28, 1934.

"House of David is Beaten 4–3 by Logan Squares." *Chicago Daily Tribune,* July 11, 1931.

"House of David Rift Causes State Threat of Intervention." *Los Angeles Times,* Aug. 9, 1928.

"House of David Signs Alexander to Contract." *Washington Post,* Jan. 17, 1932.

"House of David Team Boss in Bid to Alex, *Los Angeles Times,* July 30, 1930.

"How About Triple Crown for Hurlers?" *New York Times,* Nov. 18, 1978.

"How I Lost The World Series." *Baseball Magazine,* January 1916.

"In '26, Baseball Was Big and Redbirds Bigger." *St. Louis Post-Dispatch,* Jan. 4, 1976.

"Incredible Alex — The Mound Master." *The Sporting News,* June 14, 1969.

"Just Listening." *New York Times,* July 19, 1953.

Kavanaugh, Jack. *Ol' Pete: The Grover Cleveland Alexander Story.* South Bend, Ind.: Diamond Communications, 1996.

"King Baseball." *American Legion Magazine,* June 1938.

Leptich, John, and Baranowski, Dave. *This Date in St. Louis Cardinal History.* New York: Stein and Day, 1983.

Lieb, Frederick. *Baseball As I Have Known It.* Lincoln, Neb.: University of Nebraska, 1977.

_____. *The St. Louis Cardinals: The Story of a Great Baseball Club.* New York: Putnam's, 1947.

_____, and Baumgartner, Stan. *The Philadelphia Phillies.* New York: Putnam's, 1953.

"Lively Ball Homer Mania Doesn't Bother Ol' Alex." *Los Angeles Times,* April 22, 1928.

"Lost Chance Makes Tony Lazzeri Boil." *New York Times,* March 26, 1927.

"Low Ball is Best Asset of Old Alex." *Los Angeles Times,* Oct. 7, 1928.

Lyons, Jeffrey, and Lyons Douglas. *Out of Left Field.* New York: Random House, 1998.

"Manager of Dean Boys Cleaned Up." *Los Angeles Times,* Nov. 4, 1934.

Maranville, Walter. *Run, Rabbit, Run: The Hilarious and Mostly True Tales of Rabbit Maranville.* Cleveland: Society for American Baseball Research, 1991.

"Mighty Alexander Is Beaten By The Red Sox." *Los Angeles Times,* Oct. 12, 1915.

"Mighty Alexander Puts New York Team to Rout." *Los Angeles Times,* Oct. 4, 1926.

"Mighty Alexander Wins First Clash of Series." *Los Angeles Times,* Oct. 9, 1915.

"More on Alex." *New York Times,* Nov. 7, 1950.

"Mrs. Grover Cleveland Alexander Saved in River by Boy." *Washington Post,* June 16, 1929.

"Musing on a High Plane." *New York Times,* March 2, 1952.

"Neck Broken, Alexander Walks Out of Hospital." *New York Times,* May 14, 1948.

"No Passes in 51 Innings Is Record of Alexander." *New York Times,* May 14, 1953.

"O'Farrell's Memories Vivid of Redbirds' First Title." *St. Louis Post-Dispatch,* Jan. 25, 1926.

Okrent, Daniel, and Lewine, Harris. *The Ultimate Baseball Book.* Boston: Houghton Mifflin, 1991.

"Ol' Pete Found Seriously Injured." *Washington Post,* July 27, 1941.

"Ol' Pete Reminisces." *Los Angeles Mirror,* April 19, 1950.

"The Old Age of Alexander the Great." *New York Times,* Aug. 27, 1932.

"Old Alex at End of Road; Phils Release Him Outright." *Chicago Daily Tribune,* June 4, 1930.

"Old Alex to Blame For His Troubles— Not Baseball." *Boston Record,* May 12, 1941.

"'Old Pete' Alexander is Voted Place in Baseball's Hall of Fame by Writers." *New York Times,* Jan. 19, 1938.

"Old Pete Alexander, Mound Great, Dead." *Washington Post,* Nov. 5, 1950.

"Old Pete, at Series, Labels '26 Yankees Better Team." *The Sporting News,* Oct. 18, 1950.

"Old Pete Falls Down Stairs, Breaks Neck, Quits Hospital." *Washington Post,* May 14, 1948.

"Old Pete Informs World He's Alive and Still Pitching." *Washington Post,* Dec. 18, 1938.

"Old Pete: Intimate Details of Former Pitcher's Life Related by Alexander's Ex-Wife." *The Sporting News,* April 25, 1951.

"Old Pete Remains in Serious Plight." *Washington Post,* July 28, 1941.

"Old Pete Standee; Sic Transit Gloria." *New York Times,* Oct. 7, 1950.

"Ole Pete, Down on His Luck, Is Hired by a Former Rookie." *Washington Post,* May 15, 1940.

"On the Line With Considine." *Washington Post*, Dec. 12, 1939.
"On the Line With Considine." *Washington Post*, March 11, 1941.
"One Run in Each and He'll Win Every Game." *St. Louis Star Times*, Sept. 30, 1915.
"Pair for Alexander, One Being Shutout." *Washington Post*, Sept. 24, 1916.
"Pappy Warneke Has a Good Witness." *Chicago Daily Tribune*, Jan. 16, 1937.
"Pete Alexander." Society for American Baseball Research, 2003.
"Pete Alexander Taken by Death." *Los Angeles Times*, Nov. 5, 1950.
"Pete Was Game's Greatest Pitcher; Take Word of Killefer, Lobert, Rixey." *Philadelphia Evening Bulletin*, 1951.
"Phillies Win National League Pennant." *Los Angeles Times*, Sept. 30, 1915.
"Phils Release Alexander, Now 43." *Washington Post*, June 4, 1930.
Pietrusza, David. *Judge and Jury: The Life and Times of Judge Kenesaw Mountain Landis*. South Bend, Ind.: Diamond Communications, 1998.
"Pitching Skill Grows With Age, Records Reveal." *Chicago Daily Tribune*, Dec. 2, 1929.
"Red Sox Defeat Phillies Again, 2–1." *New York Times*, Oct. 15, 1915.
Ritter, Lawrence S. *The Glory of Their Times*. New York: W. Morrow, 1984.
"Robins Bow Twice to Alexander the Great." *New York Times*, Sept. 4, 1917.
"Rounding Third." *Los Angeles Times*, Feb. 11, 1926.
"St. Louis Folk Sit Brooding as Their Team Whips A's, 2–1." *Chicago Daily Tribune*, Aug. 21, 1929.
"St. Paul Prepares to Welcome Alex." *New York Times*, Oct. 12, 1926.
"Series Hero Older and Better." *Washington Post*, March 27, 1927.
"Setting the Pace." *New York Daily News*, Sept. 12, 1935.
"Sid Keener's Column." *St. Louis Post-Dispatch*, Dec. 23, 1936.
Simon, Tom. *Deadball Stars of the National League*. New York: Brassey's, 2004.
"65,000 See St. Louis Beat Yanks, 6–2; Alexander is Hero." *New York Times*, Oct. 4, 1926.
Skipper, James K. *Baseball Nicknames*. Jefferson, N.C.: McFarland, 1992.
Smith, Ron. *The Sporting News Chronicle of Baseball*. New York: BDD Illustrated Books, 1993.
"Sober When He Whiffed Lazzeri." *The Sporting News*, May 2, 1951.
"Spunky Aimee Still Loyal to Alexander the Great." *St. Louis Post-Dispatch*, Feb. 6, 1977.
"Star Twirler Put on Shelf." *Los Angeles Times*, March 4, 1926.
"Team Play Stressed by Alexander in Speech." *Washington Post*, Jan. 12, 1927.
"Terms Fail to Suit Alex Who Visits Phillies' President." *Washington Post*, Feb. 21, 1917.
"Then and Now," *The American Legion Monthly*, September 1927.
"Toledo Signs Alexander." *New York Times*, July 30, 1930.
"Tolerance of Drunks Sometimes Pays." *St. Louis Post Dispatch*, Oct. 21, 1972.
"Tragic Tale of Old Pete." *New York Daily News*, April 17, 1940.
"Tribute Paid Alex at 41." *Washington Post*, Feb. 27, 1928.
"Ty Cobb Is Voted No. 1 in Baseball's Hall of Fame." *Chicago Daily Tribune*, Feb. 3, 1936.
"A Very Smart Aleck." *New York Times*, Sept. 2, 1947.
"Veteran Aleck Again Signs to Toil as Cubs Moundsman." *Chicago Daily Tribune*, Jan. 23, 1926.
"Veteran Alex and Young Foe Go Full Route." *Chicago Herald and Examiner*, Oct. 8, 1925.
"Veteran Stars of Baseball Anxious; Alexander Now Trading Material." *Washington Post*, Nov. 1, 1928.
"Views of the Sport." *New York Herald Tribune*, Sept. 1, 1948.
"Wage Uphill Fight in Last Two Games." *New York Times*, Oct 14, 1926.
"Weeghman Obtains Alexander and Killefer for Cubs." *New York Times*, Dec. 12, 1917.
"The Winning Team Fouls Out on Facts." *St. Louis Post-Dispatch*, June 21, 1952.

"Yesterday." *Sports Illustrated*, Oct. 9, 1978.

"Young Players Who Are Making Good in the Major Leagues." *Chicago Daily Tribune*, July 30, 1911.

"Young Southpaw is Master of Alexander." *Washington Post*, Oct. 12, 1915.

Index

Adams, Bert 41
Aldridge, Vic 93, 95, 127, 132, 133
Alexander, Aimee 1, 72, 73, 74, 77, 91, 101, 102, 105, 106, 109, 113, 119, 124, 125, 127, 136, 137, 138, 142, 147, 149, 153, 155, 158, 159, 160, 161, 186, 187, 189, 193, 194, 195, 196
Alexander, Alva 10
Alexander, Charles 10
Alexander, George 10
Alexander, Grover Cleveland: career-threatening injury 14; death 8, 207; describing his drinking 126; election to Hall of Fame 178–181; first divorce 136–137, 142; first pro contract 12; joins House of David team 152; major league debut 25; marriage 72; 1915 World Series 50–55; 1926 World Series 112–123; at 1950 World Series 4–8, 199–200; released by Phillies 146; remarriage to Aimee 155; second divorce 189; strikeout of Tony Lazzeri 118–123; suspended by Cubs 103–105; traded to Cubs 68; traded to Phillies 143; at war 72–74
Alexander, Margaret "Martha" 9, 10, 125
Alexander, Mary 10, 37
Alexander, Nicholas 10
Alexander, Raymond 10
Alexander, Warren 10
Alexander, William 10, 11, 14, 172
American Association 14, 100, 149
American Legion 181, 195
Anson, Adrian "Cap" 90
Archer, Billy 64
Arrowsmith 110
Associated Press 186, 194, 195
Auerbach, Arnold "Red" 40
Ayers, Yancy "Doc" 83

Bailey, Abraham "Sweetbreads" 84
Baker, Frank "Home Run" 17
Baker, William F. 34, 35, 50, 53, 63, 64, 68, 69, 143
Baker Bowl 6, 22, 26, 35, 38, 44, 52, 58, 61, 62, 65, 66, 83, 98, 107, 140, 146
Bancroft, Dave 41, 50, 61, 64, 87
Bancroft, Frank 38, 56, 87, 93
"The Barber Shop" 172
Barnum, P.T. 153
Barnard Hospital 193
Barr, George 154
Barry, Jack 17
Bartlett, Tommy 5
Baseball Centennial Committee 184
Baseball Writers Association 177, 179
Baumgartner, Stan 44, 46, 88
Bebber, Chester 194
Bebee, Fred 22, 26
Bell, Herman 115
Bell, Les 105, 108, 115, 116, 117, 121, 122, 130, 131, 170
Bellevue Hospital 189
Bender, Charles Albert "Chief" 36, 59, 60, 156
Bennett, Floyd 110
Berliner, Emile 11
Berra, Lawrence "Yogi" 5, 96
Bescher, Bob 47, 59
Black Sox 69, 86, 159
Blades, Ray 105, 129, 131
Blake, Sheriff 132
Book-of-the-Month Club 110
Boston Beaneaters 40
Boston Braves 3, 25, 26, 27, 28, 31, 37, 38, 41, 44, 45, 46, 47, 48, 49, 50, 57, 58, 59, 60, 61, 62, 63, 65, 66, 75, 81, 82, 84, 88, 96, 139, 146
Boston Celtics 40
Boston Record 187

231

Index

Boston Red Sox 5, 8, 48, 49, 50, 51, 52, 53, 79, 112, 192, 195
Bottomley, Jim 105, 108, 112, 113, 115, 117, 130, 134, 170
Branham, William 184
Bransfield, Kitty 23
Braves Field 58, 81, 89, 146
Breadon, Sam 103, 105, 108, 109, 126, 128, 131, 137, 140, 141, 142, 143, 162, 163, 164, 170, 171, 172, 173, 188, 192, 193
Brecheen, Harry "The Cat" 192
Brennan, Ad 26, 31, 37
Bresnahan, Roger 20, 21, 27, 34
Broadview Hotel 192
Broeg, Bob 91, 122
Brooklyn Dodgers/Robins 26, 27, 33, 38, 45, 46, 47, 48, 49, 52, 54, 58, 59, 60, 61, 62, 63, 65, 66, 80, 81, 82, 84, 88, 89, 92, 94, 99, 105, 106, 107, 115, 122, 128, 129, 130, 131, 132, 139, 140, 145
Brown, Bobby 4, 8
Brown, Mordecai 28, 36
Brown, Warren 78
Bryan, William Jennings 11, 124
Buckner, Emery 110
Burkett, Jesse 79
Burns, Bill 27
Burns, Eddie 51
Burr, Alex 75
Bush, Guy 132
Butler, Artie 47
Byrd, Richard 110
Byrne, Bobby 41

Caldwell, Ray 83
Camnitz, Howie 32
Camp Funston 72, 73, 74
Camp Mills 72, 73
Camp Souge 73
Carey, Max 183
Carlton, Steve 57
Carmichael, John P. 119, 172, 186
Carr, Charlie 15
Carr, Harry 57
Carter, Paul 84
Case University 87
Chalmers, George 18, 26, 30, 31, 42, 44, 45, 46, 52
Chance, Frank 21, 40, 179
Chapman, Ray 85, 102
Chappell, Larry 75
Chicago Bears 40
Chicago Bulls 40
Chicago Cubs 17, 21, 23, 27, 29, 32, 33, 34, 40, 45, 46, 47, 49, 58, 60, 61, 62, 63, 64, 65, 66, 70, 71, 77, 78, 79, 80, 81, 88, 89, 93, 94, 96, 99, 100, 101, 105, 107, 108, 114, 115, 120, 127, 128, 129, 132, 136, 145, 149, 157, 181, 182, 196
Chicago Daily News 172
Chicago Tribune 69, 72, 79, 101, 105, 108, 146, 148, 157
Chicago Whales 68
Chicago White Sox 20, 25, 36, 75, 84, 86, 91, 93, 115, 147
Cincinnati Reds 3, 4, 15, 20, 22, 24, 26, 32, 33, 37, 38, 41, 45, 48, 49, 58, 59, 60, 61, 62, 63, 72, 80, 81, 84, 85, 88, 89, 90, 93, 94, 99, 102, 105, 106, 107, 108, 115, 127, 132, 133, 139, 146, 181
Civil War 10
Clark, George Rogers 136
Clark, Stephen 176
Clark, Potsy 72
Clarke, Fred 21
Cleland, Alexander 176
Cleveland, Grover 10, 11
Cleveland Indians 15, 25, 72, 75, 83, 85
Cleveland Spiders 88
Cobb, Ty 36, 88, 177, 178, 179, 184
Cochrane, Mickey 178
Coffee Pot Park 42
Cohan, George M. 182
Coleman, Jerry 5
Collins, Eddie 17, 87, 178, 179, 184
Collins, Jimmy 178, 179
Collins, Pat 108, 121
Collison, Jim 2
Columbia Broadcasting System 136
Combs, Earle 108, 114, 115 , 117, 119, 121, 134
Comiskey, Charles 36, 69
Conger, Pat 196
Conklin, L.B. 165
Considine, Bob 154, 185
Connor, Johnny 172, 182
Coombs, Jack 60
Cooney, Jimmy 103, 107, 112
Cooper, Wilbur 96, 99, 102
Cooperstown Social Club 176
Corum, Bill 180
Coveleski, Stan 83
Cravath Clifford "Gavy" 30, 41, 42, 44, 45, 47–48, 51, 52, 53, 58, 64, 85
Crawford, Pat 175
Criger, Lou 28
Cronin, Joe 133
Crosley Field 58, 90, 99, 102, 190
Cross, Harry 102
Cruise, Walter 89

Index

Crusinberry, James 69, 72, 105, 108
Cunningham, Billy 4, 6, 7, 187, 188
Curtis, Cliff 25
Custer, George 111
Cuyler, Hazen "KiKi" 130

Daimler, Gottlieb 10
Daley, Arthur 141, 194
Dallas Steers 147
Danish Independence Day 11
Davis, Virgil "Spud" 145
Dead ball era 23, 30, 35, 82, 86
Deal, Eddie 158
Dean, Jerome Hannah "Dizzy" 154, 162
Dean, Paul 154, 162
Deane, Bill 2
Declaration of Independence 110
Delahanty, Ed 179
Dell, Bill "Wheezer" 46, 58
Demaree, Al 41, 42, 44, 46, 52, 57, 58, 59, 60, 64, 66
Dempsey, Jack 110
Denver Post 158, 168
Detroit Racing Association 187
Detroit Tigers 15, 19, 75, 83
Dickey, Glenn 76
Didrickson, Mildred "Babe" 154, 157
Dillhoefer, Bill "Pickles" 68
Di Maggio, Joe 5
Ditka, Mike 40
Doak, Bill 83, 84
Doan, Ray 153, 154, 155, 156, 157, 158, 159, 160, 162, 163, 164, 165, 166, 167, 168, 169, 173
Dr. Strangeglove 45
Dodge, John 59
Dooin, Charles "Red" 17, 18, 19, 21, 27, 29, 30, 31, 37, 39, 41, 93
Doolan, Mickey 24, 37, 41
Donkey baseball 155
Dope Book 191
Doubleday, Abner 176, 177
Douglas, Phil "Shufflin' Phil" 78, 79, 80, 81, 82, 83, 86
Douthit, Taylor 114, 115, 134, 170
Drysdale, Don 63
Duffy's Florals 157
Dugan, Joe 108, 112, 114, 117, 121
Dugey, Oscar 41, 56
Dunn, Peter 189
Durham, Israel 16
Durocher, Leo 162

Eastern League 149
Ebbets Field 59, 81, 145

Ederle, Gertrude 110
Effrat, Louis 5, 6
Elias Sports Bureau 191
Evans, Billy 55
Evers, Johnny 23, 78, 87, 89, 96, 179

Faber, Urban "Red" 83
Federal League 15, 36, 39, 41, 65, 68
Feller, Bob 187
Felt, Dorr 11
Ferguson, Harry 145, 187, 188
Fillingin, Dana 83
Finch, Frank 91, 101, 119
Finneran, Bill 27, 34
Fischer, Bill 93
Fisher, Ray 83
Fitzgerald, J.V. 71
Fitzsimmons, Freddie 128
Fogel, Horace 16, 17, 18, 20, 21, 30, 31, 33, 36, 37, 49, 62
Forbes Field 27, 32, 58, 65, 90
Ford, Edwin "Whitey" 8
Ford, Henry 110
Foster, Rube 49, 51, 52
Foxx, Jimmy 133
Frederick, MaryAnn 2
Freigau, Howard 98
Friberg, Bernie 93, 99
Frick, Ford 159, 160, 162, 163, 164, 165, 166, 167, 169, 170, 171, 172, 174, 175, 176, 184, 187, 188, 192
Frisch, Frankie 21, 29, 87, 94, 108, 126, 129, 134, 162, 170
Fuhr, Bill 2
Fullerton, Hugh 50, 55, 85
Funkhouse, Frank 139

Gas House Gang 127, 162
Gehrig, Lou 106, 108, 111, 113, 116, 118, 133, 135, 185
Gettelson, Leonard 191
Gibson, Bob 114
Gibson, George 100, 103
"Give My Regards to Broadway" 182
Gleason, Bill "Kid" 23
The Glory of Their Times 124
Gonzalez, Mike 98
"Good field, no hit" 98
Goodman, Benny 110
Goodwin, Marv 83
Gould, Jim 126
Graham, Frank 166, 167
Grandon, Michael 2
Grant, Eddie 22, 75
Grantham, George 94, 95

Graumke, Bill 5
Graves, Abner 176
Green Bay Packers 40
Green Hotel 71
Griffith, Clark 22, 36, 69
Grimes, Burleigh 65, 83, 87, 89, 94, 106, 128, 133
Grimes, Ray 90
Grimm, Charlie 95–96, 99
Grove, Robert "Lefty" 112, 188

Hafey, Charles "Chick" 105, 109, 110, 115, 117, 130, 134, 170
Haines, Jess 89, 105, 109, 114, 115, 117, 118, 120, 121, 123, 128, 129, 131, 133, 135, 140, 167
Hall of Fame 21, 64, 89, 94, 96, 105, 112, 117, 175, 177, 180, 181, 183, 184, 188, 193
Hallahan, William "Wild Bill" 76, 113
Hamner, Granny 8
Harlem Globetrotters 153
Harper, George 134
Harridge, Will 176, 184
Harrison, James 120
Hart, Fred 81
Hartnett, Charles "Gabby" 89, 96, 172, 173, 183
Heckler, Leroy 182
Heckler, Leslie 182
Heckler, William 182
Heilmann, Harry 87
Heintzelman, Ken 4, 5, 8
Helms Hall of Fame 196
Hendrix, Claude 78, 79, 84, 85
Hendrix, Jack 94
Henry, Bill 105
Herzog, Buck 41
Hildebrand, George 120, 194
Hilltop Park 25
Hindenberg Line 74
Hogan, Shanty 133
Hollocher, Charlie 79
Hollywood Receiving Hospital 194
Honig, Donald 134, 177
Hooper, Harry 49, 52, 53, 112
Hoover, Herbert 136
Hornsby, Rogers 5, 72, 84, 87, 93, 94, 103, 105, 107, 108, 111, 112, 113, 116, 117, 118, 119, 121, 125, 126, 128, 135, 137, 154, 155, 167, 170, 178, 183, 196
Hotel Adelphia 103
Hotel Lincoln 136
Hotel St. Catherine 101
Houdini, Harry 110

House of David 150, 152, 153, 154, 155, 156, 157, 158, 164, 166, 168, 186
"How to Curve a Baseball" 54
Howard County Telephone Company 12
Hoyt, Waite 108, 115, 117, 120, 134, 135
Hubbell, Carl 133, 141, 146, 187
Huey, Robert 56
Huggins, Miller 117, 135
Huntingdon Street Grounds 35
Hurst, Don 124, 144, 145
Hussey, Mrs. E.H. 168, 182

Jackson, Phil 40
Jackson, Travis 94
James, Bill 38, 57
Jennings, Hugh 19
"John Barleycorn" 97
Johnson, Dick 2
Johnson, Hazel 38
Johnson, Walter 6, 28, 36, 38, 55, 57, 63, 68, 86, 88, 138, 141, 177, 184
Jones, Bobby 110
Jones, Randy 93
Joss, Addie 25
Jurgens, Arndt 185

Kachline, Cliff 2
Kansas City A's 93
Kavanaugh, Jack 16, 32, 97, 98
Keeler, Willie "Wee Willie" 178
Keeley, Leslie 101
Keeley Institute 101, 140
Keen, Vic 105
Keener, Sid 160, 162, 163, 164
Kelly, George 94, 196
Kiernan, John 154, 187, 188
Killefer, Bill 24, 27, 30, 31, 42, 45, 47, 51, 53, 56, 57, 58, 60, 63, 64, 65, 69, 70, 71, 78, 89, 91, 92, 93, 98, 99, 100, 103, 126, 158, 183
Kirksey, George 180
Klein, Chuck 144, 145
Kling, Johnny 40
Knabe, Otto 24, 37, 41
Knox College 12
Koenig, Marty 108, 115, 116, 117, 119, 121
Konstanty, Jim 3, 8
Koufax, Sandy 63
Koupal, Lou 145

Lajoie, Napoleon 178, 184
Lambeth, Otis 72
Landis, Kenesaw Mountain 80, 86, 159, 160, 161, 162, 163, 164, 169, 173, 176, 184
Lane, F.C. 16

Laney, Al 176, 182, 183
Lang, Al 42, 43, 44
Langley, Frank 181, 182
Lavender, Jimmy 60, 64, 65
Lazzeri, Tony 4, 5, 6, 11, 108, 111, 114, 116, 118, 119, 120, 121, 122, 123, 134, 135, 140, 155, 167, 172, 179, 180, 183, 193, 194, 195
Lee, Robert E. 111
Lehr, Clarence 187
Lehritz, Jim 117
Leonard, Hubert "Dutch" 49, 52
Lerian, Walt 143
Levis, Paul 172
Lewis, Duffy 49, 52, 53
Lewis, Sinclair 110
Lieb, Fred 4, 5, 6, 15–16, 17, 32, 115
Lifebuoy soap 35
Lincoln, Abraham 9
Lindbergh, Charles 128
Lindstrom, Fred 94
Link, Bob 2
Little Red Book of Baseball 191
"Live Wires" 17, 21, 34
Lobert, Hans 22, 29, 31, 32, 38, 41, 124
Locke, William H. 34, 35
Logan Squares 157
Lombardi, Vince 40
Look magazine 121
Lopat, Eddie 4
Los Angeles County General Hospital 195
Los Angeles Times 57, 71, 105, 146, 154, 175, 196
Lucas, Charles "Red" 102, 132, 139
Luderus, Fred 22, 26, 27, 29, 31, 42, 45, 51, 52, 61, 64
Lynch, Quentin 5
Lynch, Tom 27, 28, 34

Mack, Connie 17, 27, 36, 96, 112, 116, 184
MacPhail, Larry 17
Madon, Mary B. 143
Maddux, Greg 46
Magee, Lee 80, 84
Magee, Sherry 21, 23, 27, 28, 30, 31, 34, 37, 41, 80, 86
Maharg, Bill 147
Malone, Pat 139
Mann, Les 80
Maranville, Walter "Rabbit" 95, 96, 98, 99, 100, 103, 134, 181
Marquard, Rube 28, 32
Martin, Elwood "Speed" 84, 88
Martin, Johnny "Pepper" 162
Mason City Globe Gazette 2
Masonoff, Roy B. 143

Mathews, Wid 175
Mathewson, Christy 7, 25, 27, 28, 29, 32, 44, 46, 48, 63, 64, 66, 75, 88, 93, 107, 138, 140, 141, 177, 178, 179, 183, 191
May, Jakie 80
Mayer, Erskine 42, 44, 45, 51, 67
Mays, Carl 85, 102, 172
Mazeroski, Bill 117
McAleer, Jimmy 88
McCarthy, Joe 100, 101, 102, 103, 105, 106, 126, 137, 149, 182, 196
McCurdy, Harry 143
McGinnis, Stuffy 17, 87
McGraw, John 20, 21, 25, 27, 29, 31, 34, 44, 46, 58, 61, 62, 79, 80, 81, 82, 88, 132, 137, 140
McKechnie, Bill 58, 131, 134, 135, 137, 140, 141, 159
McKim, Donald K. 7, 177
McNichol, Jim 16
McQuillan George 22, 59
Meadows, Lee 60, 61, 65, 66, 72, 85, 86, 90, 94
Meany, Tom 183
Medwick, Joe 162
Merkle, Fred 47, 78
Meusel, Bob 108, 111, 113, 114, 116, 117, 120, 134
Middle West Division 73
Miller, Hack 93
Minneapolis Millers 30
"Miracle Braves" 96, 116
Mitchell, Clarence 72, 83, 131, 137
Mitchell, Fred 70, 71, 81, 85, 87, 103
Mokan, Johnny 112
Moore Earl 24, 25, 26, 31
Moran, Pat 17, 18, 20, 21, 27, 30, 31, 39, 40, 41, 42, 43, 44, 46, 48, 50, 52, 53, 54, 59, 62, 64, 66, 68, 76, 93, 183
Moren, Lew 22
Morris, E.E. 72
Morrison, Johnny 102
Mueller, Walter 90
Murderer's Row 118, 134
Murphy, Charles 34
Murray, Billy 21
Muscatine Journal 2
Muscatine Public Library 2
Museum of Modern Art 136
My Greatest Day in Baseball 119

National Baseball Hall of Fame 2, 5
National Broadcasting Company 110
National Football League 72
National League Park 35

Index

Nebraska Historical Society Museum 2
Negro Leagues 156, 158
Nevrivy, Ed 2
Nevrivy, Jo 196
New York Daily Mirror 189
New York Giants 7, 20, 21, 22, 25, 27, 29, 31, 32, 33, 34, 36, 44, 45, 46, 48, 49, 58, 60, 61, 62, 63, 64, 65, 66, 72, 78, 79, 80, 81, 82, 83, 88, 89, 90, 92, 93, 94, 95, 98, 102, 106, 108, 126, 128, 129, 130, 131, 132, 133, 139, 140, 145, 146, 196
New York Herald Tribune 182
New York Highlanders 25
New York State League 15, 18, 19
New York Stock Exchange 136
New York Times 5, 102, 114, 120, 141, 144, 151, 154, 157, 176, 183, 187, 194
New York Yankees 3, 4, 8, 75, 83, 85, 86, 94, 106, 108, 111, 112, 114, 115, 116, 117, 119, 120, 122, 125, 130, 133, 134, 135, 165, 179, 196
Niehaus, Al 95
Niehoff, Bert 41, 65
Notre Dame University 136
Noyes, Winnie 72

Oakes, Rebel 27
O'Connell, Dan 86
O'Doul, Francis "Lefty" 144, 145
Oeschger, Joe 44, 67, 82
O'Farrell, Bob 87, 89, 93, 98, 105, 109, 115, 116, 117, 120, 121, 122, 126, 127, 128, 129, 131, 134, 158, 170
Oklahoma Indians 12
Olympics 157
Omaha World-Herald 5, 136
One for the Book 191
O'Neill, Elma 9, 125
O'Rourke, Patsy 17, 18
Osborne, Earnest "Tiny" 92, 93
Ott, Mel 146
Oughton, John 101

Pacific Coast League 41
Paige, Satchel 156, 158
Paley, William S. 136
Parker, Dan 189, 190, 192
Paskert, George "Dode" 22, 25, 31, 41, 42, 45, 58, 59, 64, 66, 78, 86
Pass-a-Grill 44
Paul, H.J. 142
Peepland 182
Pegler, Westbrook 142, 143, 148
Pendergast, Mike 60, 68
Pennock, Herb 108, 112, 113, 115, 121, 134

"Pepper" 155
Pershing, John J. 74, 79
Pesky, Johnny 192
Pfeffer, Jeff 80
Philadelphia Athletics 17, 18, 19, 27, 36, 59, 60, 72, 96, 112, 116, 136, 142, 188
Philadelphia Phillies 3, 5, 6, 8, 15, 16, 17, 18, 21, 22, 24, 26, 27, 28, 29, 30, 31, 33, 34, 36, 37, 38, 40, 41, 42, 44, 45, 46, 48, 49, 50, 51, 52, 53, 54, 55, 56, 57, 58, 60, 61, 62, 64, 65, 66, 67, 68, 69, 71, 72, 74, 77, 81, 85, 88, 90, 91, 93, 94, 98, 99, 106, 108, 112, 123, 124, 128, 129, 131, 139, 140, 143, 144, 145, 146, 147, 148, 162, 187
Pickens, Bill 64
Pipgras, George 134
Pipp, Wally 106
Pittsburgh Pirates 21, 26, 29, 32, 33, 34, 41, 45, 47, 49, 58, 59, 60, 62, 65, 80, 81, 87, 90, 92, 94, 96, 98, 100, 102, 105, 106, 114, 127, 128, 130, 131, 133, 139, 140
Plank, Eddie 36
Polo Grounds 22, 25, 44, 47, 72, 82, 108, 141
Prohibition 38, 83
Pulitzer Prize 110
Purnell, Benjamin 152
Purnell, Mary 152

Quinn, Jack 83

Randall, Jim 23
Raschi, Vic 4
Ray, Bob 154
Reed, Milt 37
Reese, John D. "Bonesetter" 87, 107, 127
Reichler, Joe 191
Reinhart, Art 114
Retrosheet 2
Reulbach, Ed 27, 28, 29, 32, 40
Reynolds, Allie 4
Rhem, Flint 105, 107, 108, 115, 122, 128, 129, 131, 133
Rhodes, Dusty 117
Rice, Sam 87
Rickey, Branch 103, 131, 173, 175, 187, 188
Ring, Jimmy 126
Ringling, Charles 110
Ritter, Lawrence 38, 124
Rixey, Eppa 30, 37, 42, 43, 45, 52, 57, 59, 60, 61, 65, 66, 67, 84, 89, 90, 123, 132
Roaring '20s 91, 110, 136, 152
Roberts, Robin 3, 7, 8
Robertson, Dave 79, 86
Robinson, Wilbert 48, 58, 59, 62

Index

Rochester Redbirds 137
Rogers, Tom "Shotgun" 59
Root, Charlie 102, 106, 127, 129
Rose, Pete 177
"The Round-Up" 71
Rowan, Jack 22, 25, 26
Rudolph, Dick 48, 58, 83
Ruether, Walter "Dutch" 114
Ruth, George Herman "Babe" 5, 30, 48, 49, 51, 83, 94, 108, 111, 113, 114, 115, 116, 117, 119, 120, 121, 122, 127, 133, 134, 135, 154, 155, 177, 184, 185, 186, 196
Ryan, Quin 98

St. John's Hospital 140, 172
St. Louis Browns 111, 113, 142
St. Louis Cardinals 4, 18, 20, 21, 27, 29, 34, 45, 47, 48, 49, 58, 60, 61, 62, 65, 66, 72, 78, 81, 84, 86, 87, 88, 89, 92, 93, 98, 103, 105, 108, 110, 111, 113, 114, 115, 116, 117, 119, 120, 122, 125, 126, 127, 128, 130, 132, 133, 134, 139, 140, 142, 146, 147, 156, 162, 173, 179, 181, 187, 188, 192, 194
St. Louis Post-Dispatch 122, 171
St. Louis Star-Times 160
St. Mary's Hospital 192
St. Paul Phonograph 12, 14, 15, 196
St. Valentine's Day Massacre 136
San Diego Padres 93
Saperstein, Abe 153
Sauer, Kearney 194
Savas, Ted 2
Sawyer, Eddie 3
Schechter, Gabriel 2
Schulte, Frank 183
Schultz, Joseph 175
Scott, Everett 50
Seaton, Tom 30, 32, 36, 37, 65
Shawkey, Bob 86, 115, 116
Sheehan, Tom 91
Sherdel, Bill 105, 111–112, 113, 115, 116, 129, 133, 134, 135, 140
Sherman, W.J., Jr. 169
Shocker, Urban 108, 113
Shore, Ernie 49, 50, 51, 52, 53
Shotton, Burt 41, 145, 146, 147
Simmons, Al 133
Simmons, Curt 4
Sisler, George 87, 178, 184
Skipper, Sandi 2
Slaughter, Enos 192, 193
Smith, Oscar 150
Sneaky Pete 2
Snyder, Frank 58
Society for American Baseball Research 2

Sothern, Denny 145
Southern League 59
Southworth, Billy 105, 109, 114, 129, 137, 138, 140, 194
Spahn, Warren 30, 57
Speaker, Tris 36, 49, 178, 184
Spencer, Ed "Tubby" 31, 32
Spirit of St. Louis 128
Spitballs 31
Sporting News 4, 41, 91, 101, 186, 191, 193
Sporting News Complete Record Book 191
"Sports of the Times" 188
Sportsman's Park 93, 105, 112, 115, 128, 140, 141, 142, 146, 156, 171, 192
Stallings, George 48
Staples, Ed 173
Statz, Arnold "Jigger" 93, 99
Steinberg, Steve 2
Steinfeldt, Harry 183
Stengel, Charles Dillon "Casey" 58, 61, 149, 150
Stern, Bill 193
Stock, Milt 41, 42, 50, 61, 64, 66
Stockton, J. Roy 121
Street, Charles "Gabby" 28, 138, 141, 162
Sullivan, Billy 28
Sweetland, Les 145
Syracuse Journal 15
Syracuse Stars 15

Taft, Charles P. 17
Tarleton, Bob 147, 148
Tecklenburg, Jeff 2
Tenace, Gene 117
Tener, John 62
Terry, Bill 94
Texas League 133, 147, 149
Thevenow, Tommy 114, 115, 116, 117, 129, 131, 145
Thistle Down 187
Thomas, Miles 115
Thompson, Fresco 145
Thorpe, Jim 22
Tincup, Ben 44
Tinker, Joe 36, 61, 94
Titus, John 23, 27, 30
Toledo Mud Hens 149, 150
Toman, J.C. 165, 167, 168, 172
Toney, Fred 48
Toporcer, George "Specs" 87, 122, 124, 136, 170
"Town Ball" 176, 177
Traband, Harvey 165
Traynor, Harold "Pie" 130
Trick pitches 82–83

Index

Troy, Robert "Bun" 75
Tunney, Gene 110
Tyler George "Lefty" 78, 80

Union Pacific Railroad 10
United Press (International) 180, 187, 189, 193
University of Illinois 72

Valentino, Rudolph 110
Vance, Dazzy 92, 99, 132
Vander Meer, Johnny 190
Vaughan, Irving 101
Vaughn, Hippo 78, 79, 80, 84, 86, 88
Veeck, Bill 17, 153
Veeck, William, Sr. 79, 81, 85, 95, 98, 99, 100, 101
Vidmer, Richard 114

Wagner, Honus 49, 58, 177, 182, 183, 196
Wagner, Jap 12, 13
Waldorf Hotel 68
Walker, Harry 192
Walker, Jimmy 3, 110
Walsh, Ed 28
Walsh, Runt 37
Walters, William "Bucky" 123
Wambsganss 131
Waner, Lloyd 128
Waner, Paul 128
"War to end all wars" 1, 68, 75
Wares, Buzzy 180
Washington, George 9
Washington Monument 138
Washington Post 28, 33, 71, 146, 154, 168, 185
Washington Senators 6–7, 15, 22, 36, 57, 68, 84, 114, 138
Webster, J.F. 12

Weeghman, Charles 68, 69, 70, 71, 72, 73, 78
Weiss, George 126
"Welcome Travelers" 5
Wenzel, Dutch 72
West Point 176
WGN 98
Wheat, Zack 47, 183
"Whiskey Face" 40
White, Bill 186, 187
Whitney, Arthur "Pinky" 145
Whitted, George "Possum" 41, 42, 47, 65
Whiz Kids 3
Wicall, Harold 149
Williams, Cy 49, 83, 144
Wilson, Hack 94, 134, 145
Wilson, Jimmy 131
Wilson, Woodrow 51, 68
Wolf, Clarence 16
Wood, Joe 49
Woodward, Frank 82
World Series 3, 4, 5, 6, 7, 8, 11, 20, 40, 49, 50, 51, 53, 54, 56, 69, 79, 84, 86, 93, 96, 108, 111, 112, 116, 117, 120, 125, 126, 127, 128, 131, 133, 137, 140, 142, 147, 154, 156, 165, 167, 179, 180, 183, 192, 193, 195
World War I 91, 114, 124, 183, 194
Wright Aeronautical 191
Wrigley, William 71, 81, 87, 91, 93, 96, 100
Wrigley Field 59, 81, 84, 87, 88, 94, 98, 102, 127, 129

Yankee Stadium 3, 4, 7, 8, 112, 116, 119, 180
Young, Cy 6, 28, 88, 141, 175, 178, 184
Youngs, Ross 94

Zachary, Tom 134
Zimmerman, Heinie 47